# Praise for previous editions of *An Insider's Guide to the UN*

"*An Insider's Guide* is my UN bible. Linda Fasulo knows all the right questions and brings back all the answers readers need to know to navigate the UN."—**Olivia Ward**, *Toronto Star*

"This unique book combines a solid guide to the workings of the United Nations with illuminating insights from credible and serious experts."—**Barbara Crossette**, former *New York Times* bureau chief at the United Nations

"A short-order account of how the organization works in the glare of its public profile and in the shadow of its secret negotiations."—*Times* (London)

"It is an excellent introduction to the work of the U.N. and a valuable tool for anyone who wants to understand the complexities of the Organization in a clear and highly readable style."—**Heraldo Muñoz**, former Ambassador of Chile to the United Nations

"With fine journalistic clarity, the author leads readers through the complex organizational structure of the United Nations, shedding light on its mission, evolution, and controversies. . . . This concise, highly readable volume is an invaluable and essential source of information for general readers, report writers, and Model UN delegates."—**Christine C. Menefee**, *School Library Journal*

"On first glance, a generalist's hoped-for introduction; on second glance, a specialist's new and valued tool."—**Duncan McNiff**, Foreign Policy Association (Editor's Pick)

"Fasulo has produced a living primer for those interested in finding their way around the UN. It is an excellent book—full of solid fact and juicy opinion—just the kind of thing everyone wants to read."—**Shashi Tharoor**, former UN Under-Secretary-General for Public Information

"[A] wonderful insider's guide . . . packed with great information."—**John McLaughlin**, TV host, *The McLaughlin Group*

D0169837

AN INSIDER'S GUIDE TO THE UN

# AN INSIDER'S GUIDE

## TO THE UN

### THIRD EDITION

## LINDA FASULO

Yale UNIVERSITY PRESS

New Haven and London

Copyright © 2003, 2009, 2015 by Linda Fasulo.

First edition 2003. Second edition 2009. Third edition 2015.

Yale University Press books may be purchased in quantity
for educational, business, or promotional use. For information,
please e-mail sales.press@yale.edu (U.S. office) or
sales@yaleup.co.uk (U.K. office).

Set in Scala type by Integrated Publishing Solutions.

Printed in the United States of America.

*Library of Congress Cataloging-in-Publication Data*

Fasulo, Linda M.
   An insider's guide to the UN / Linda Fasulo. — Third
edition.
      pages cm
      Includes bibliographical references and index.
   ISBN 978-0-300-20365-3 (paperback)
   1. United Nations—Popular works.   I. Title.
   JZ4984.6.F37 2015
   341.23—dc23
            2014023099

A catalogue record for this book is available from the
British Library.

This paper meets the requirements of
ANSI/NISO Z39.48–1992 (Permanence of Paper).

10  9  8  7  6  5  4  3  2  1

# CONTENTS

**13**  The UN to the Rescue                               176

**14**  Sustainable Development in the New
        Millennium                                         188

**15**  Global Connections                                 208

**16**  Climate Change                                     220

**17**  Keeping Tabs on How Nations Vote                   229

**18**  The Call for Reform                                236

**19**  Paying for It All                                  244

**20**  Action in the Field with UNHCR: A Staffer's
        Challenging First Assignment                       254

Appendixes

  **A**  Diplomat for a Day: The Model UN                  259
  **B**  The Universal Declaration of Human Rights         267
  **C**  UN Member States                                  275

         List of Selected Abbreviations                    281

         Sources                                           283

         Index                                             287

Working as a news correspondent at the United Nations has given me a firsthand perspective on one of the world's most high-profile and important organizations. Nowhere else in the world can you watch an international group of diplomats, officials, and experts discuss the great challenges of our day and make decisions that can affect our lives for years to come. Addressing threats to international peace and security, promoting human rights, combating poverty and disease, and reducing the risks of international terrorism and the spread of weapons of mass destruction are among the big issues the UN can act on in a year.

Before the day's decisions have been voted on at the UN, the agenda has been set and the diplomats and their staff have prepared themselves. Most disagreements have played out in relative privacy, and the public sees a polished performance. Many onlookers will accept this performance at face value and never give it another thought. For those who want to know more, who ask how the decisions were negotiated and reached and what their chances are for making a lasting impact, I have written this book, relying on my personal observations as well as the experiences and insights of other insiders.

Flags of member nations at the UN headquarters in New York City.
UN Photo / Andrea Brizzi.

## A World of Change

As the world has continued to change, so has the UN, which is experiencing a surge of activity as crises proliferate. In many of the recent crises we have seen a divided Security Council, where the United States and its allies, on the one hand, and Russia and China, on the other, have disagreed on how best to proceed. A prime example is the multiyear civil war in Syria. By the same token, the big powers have often agreed on increasing the number of the UN's peacekeeping missions and on expanding their purview to include human rights issues. Human rights have attracted increasing attention from member states as important aspects of ensuring and protecting peace within nations and also of enhancing the UN's efforts at social and economic development. The UN is also being asked to provide humanitarian aid much more frequently than before, in response to armed conflicts and to natural disasters like tsunamis and famines. Threats like international terrorism and the proliferation of nuclear and chemical weapons weigh ever more heavily on minds around the world. The UN has taken a more active role against terrorists and in the process has itself become a victim of terrorist attacks. Other global issues, such as climate change, are also rising in public awareness and in the UN. As a result, the UN's general operations are experiencing a rapid budget escalation.

### Founding Date

The UN was officially established on October 24, 1945, when the UN Charter was ratified. October 24 is celebrated every year as UN Day. President Franklin D. Roosevelt and Prime Minister Winston Churchill coined the name "United Nations," first used in the "Declaration by United Nations" on January 1, 1942.

## A New Edition

I was pleased when Yale University Press gave me the opportunity to update the book in a third edition. Once I began revis-

ing and updating, however, I found that the degree of change both
inside and outside the UN has been so large in just the few years
since 2009 that I had to rethink many of the chapters and write new
ones—on the new international political landscape, humanitarian
assistance, sustainable social and economic development, and the
importance of the UN as a global coordinator and norm-setter. As
part of my research, I interviewed more UN insiders, each with his
or her own knowledge and experience with the world body. These
new voices, I hope, give the book a more complex flavor and greater
depth of information and insight.

Despite all the changes, the UN remains the world's main multilateral forum and coordinator of international efforts to address
common problems and issues. This book is arranged to provide the
reader with a topical overview of how the UN works: its organization, governing principles, and key functions. The book begins with
historical background and moves quickly to the UN's chief executive officer, the secretary-general, and then to an examination of the
new global political landscape. Succeeding chapters discuss the US
ambassador and then the UN's most prominent "principal organs,"
the Security Council, including its peacekeeping operations, and the
General Assembly. Next the book takes an informal trip through the
UN Village, that little corner of New York City populated by diplomats from all over the world. In the final chapters, the book explores
such global issues as international terrorism, nuclear proliferation,
human rights and the responsibility to protect (R2P), and climate
change. Other chapters look at the many agencies and programs
that carry out the UN's broad efforts in social and economic development, disaster relief, eradication of diseases, and reducing the
trade in addictive drugs. The book concludes with chapters on the
state of UN reform and finances and, in a final flourish, describes
the experiences of a UN insider during his early days at the world
body, as a staffer coping with the thousands of Vietnamese "boat
people" who fled their country after the takeover by the North Vietnamese forces during the 1970s.

In the face of rapid and wrenching change, we have to wonder
how an international organization created seven decades ago, in a

very different world, can maintain its relevance and effectiveness today, let alone in the future. That is the UN's greatest challenge—one that the insiders who run the UN and its associated agencies, the diplomats who represent its member nations, and the many experts who monitor and analyze the world body have also been asking. Most believe it can step up to the new challenges while reforming its own shortcomings, but that is by no means the unanimous view. I hope that this book will help readers make their own assessment of the UN's current status and future prospects.

## ACKNOWLEDGMENTS

This book and its third edition would not have been possible without the encouragement, advice, and support of many people. To all of the diplomats, UN officials, analysts, and experts whom I have interviewed, I express my sincere appreciation for their interest and participation as "insiders" in this book. They include UN Secretary-General Ban Ki-moon, UN Deputy Secretary-General Jan Eliasson, and High Representative for Disarmament Affairs Angela Kane. They also include former UN Deputy Secretary-General Lord Mark Malloch-Brown; former US Secretary of State Madeleine Albright; former US Assistant Secretary of State for International Organization Affairs Esther Brimmer; US Ambassadors John Bolton, John Danforth, Richard Holbrooke, Zalmay Khalilzad, Joseph Melrose, John Negroponte, and Nancy Soderberg; Ambassadors Munir Akram (Pakistan), Colin Keating (New Zealand), David Malone (Canada), and Danilo Türk (Slovenia); and officials at the UN and experts on the UN, including Sebastian von Einsiedel, Shepard Forman, Felice Gaer, Richard Gowan, Jeffrey Laurenti, Edward Luck, William Luers, Hillel Neuer, Stewart Patrick, Brian Urquhart, and Ruth Wedgwood, who all graciously shared their unique and invaluable personal insights and experiences.

It has been a consistent pleasure over the years to work with the wonderful professionals at Yale University Press, those in the editorial and executive divisions as well as the marketing, sales, and publicity departments. One could not ask for a better publishing experience. Thanks especially to my editor Bill Frucht, who proposed this new edition, and to assistant editor Jaya Chatterjee.

I also express my appreciation to my friends and colleagues at the UN, National Public Radio, and elsewhere who gave encouragement along the way. To my longtime friend and colleague Bill Zeisel, of QED Associates, I offer my appreciation for his continued and invaluable role in this project and his exceptionally discerning eye in the preparation of the manuscript for all three editions. I also appreciate the interview transcriptions done by Vanessa Rocha.

I thank my son, Alex, for his research assistance, my mother, Mary, for her help in transcribing recorded interviews, and my husband, Rob, for enthusiastic support. For their assistance and constant encouragement I am incredibly appreciative.

AN INSIDER'S GUIDE TO THE UN

## CHAPTER 1

# What Is the UN?

*I say to my colleagues that you have to start from the fact that the United Nations is a mirror, a reflection of the world as it is, whether we like it or not. There are dictatorships, there are violations of human rights, there's war and conflict, and yes, we must be realistic. But the United Nations is also a reflection of the world as it should be—the "We the peoples," the principles and purpose of the Charter.*
—Jan Eliasson, deputy secretary-general of the UN

The United Nations came into existence as a result of the most terrible war in history. During World War II, US president Franklin D. Roosevelt, British prime minister Winston Churchill, and the leaders of other Allied combatant nations agreed that it was necessary to create a world organization that would help ensure the peace in future years. Their ideas are enshrined in the Preamble to the UN Charter:

*We the peoples of the United Nations determined*
to save succeeding generations from the scourge of war, which twice in our lifetime has brought untold sorrow to mankind, and to reaffirm faith in fundamental human rights, in the dig-

nity and worth of the human person, in the equal rights of
men and women and of nations large and small, and
to establish conditions under which justice and respect for the
obligations arising from treaties and other sources of international law can be maintained, and
to promote social progress and better standards of life in larger
freedom,

*and for these ends*
to practice tolerance and live together in peace with one another
as good neighbors, and
to unite our strength to maintain international peace and security, and
to ensure, by the acceptance of principles and the institution of
methods, that armed force shall not be used, save in the common interest, and
to employ international machinery for the promotion of the economic and social advancement of all peoples,

*have resolved to combine our efforts to accomplish these aims*
Accordingly, our respective Governments, through representatives assembled in the city of San Francisco, who have exhibited their full powers found to be in good and due form, have
agreed to the present Charter of the United Nations and do
hereby establish an international organization to be known as
the United Nations.

When the war ended in 1945, the new organization began with
enormous goodwill, moral support from all sides, and strong US
leadership. The world waited to see if the UN could rectify the shortcomings of the League of Nations, its predecessor organization,
which dissolved in the late 1930s, victim of totalitarian regimes
and US indifference. Could the UN be the uniting force among
the victorious nations, whose ideologies and political interests
often seemed at odds? The Cold War soon replaced idealistic collaboration with power politics between the West and the East. Until
the breakup of the Soviet Union, confrontation between the blocs

We the peoples of the United Nations

We the peoples

**Determined**

to save succeeding generations from the scourge of war, which twice in our lifetime has brought untold sorrow to mankind, **and to** reaffirm faith in fundamental human rights, in the dignity and worth of the human person, in the equal rights of men and women and of nations large and small, **and to** establish conditions under which justice and respect for the obligations arising from treaties and other sources of international law can be maintained, **and to** promote social progress and better standards of life in larger freedom,

**And for these ends**

to practice tolerance and live together in peace with one another as good neighbours, **and to** unite our strength to maintain international peace and security, **and to** ensure, by the acceptance of principles and the institution of methods, that armed force shall not be used, save in the common interest, **and to** employ international machinery for the promotion of the economic and social advancement of all peoples,

**Have resolved to combine our efforts to accomplish these aims**

Accordingly, our respective Governments, through representatives assembled in the city of San Francisco, who have exhibited their full powers found to be in good and due form, have agreed to the present Charter of the United Nations and do hereby establish an international organization to be known as the United Nations.

*Preamble to the Charter of the United Nations Published by the United Nations Department of Public Information Photographs and Exhibit Section*

"We the peoples," from a poster about the UN Charter. UN Photo / Milton Grant.

defined most UN relationships, discussions, debates, programs, and activities.

Today, although Americans do not expect the UN to solve the world's problems, at the least they would like it to be a more effective agent in dealing with the forces that are transforming our world. Exactly what these forces are, and how they are changing our lives, is hotly debated and discussed. What we can say with certainty is that the forces of change will need to be addressed by living, breathing people, not computer software or mechanical robots. The UN is, above all, a place for people and a hotbed of the human factor. As one of my UN insiders says, people really do matter at the UN, and they act in a context full of illusion, opinion, perception, and emotion. But the UN is far from simple. It straddles the globe, operating in almost every nation on earth, and it has a bewildering variety of offices, programs, and personnel. Let's begin, then, with some basic points and language that will appear throughout the book.

## The UN System

The UN is made up of six principal organs, all based in New York City except the International Court of Justice, which is based in The Hague, Netherlands:

The Secretariat

The Security Council

The General Assembly

The International Court of Justice (ICJ)

The Trusteeship Council (no longer meets)

The Economic and Social Council (ECOSOC)

—Plus UN programs and funds focused on development, humanitarian assistance, and human rights. They include the UN Children's Fund (UNICEF), the UN Development Program (UNDP), and the Office of the United Nations High Commissioner for Refugees (UNHCR).

—Plus the UN specialized agencies, which coordinate their work with the UN but are separate organizations. These agencies, such as the International Monetary Fund (IMF), the World Health Organization (WHO), and the International Civil Aviation Organization (ICAO), focus on specific areas.

—Plus thousands of nongovernmental organizations (NGOs) that are independent citizens' organizations associated with the UN. They are concerned with many of the same issues as the UN, such as human rights, arms control, and the environment. NGOs are not part of the UN but have become important to its functioning in many key areas.

The UN's New York City headquarters is considered international territory.

## Exactly What Is the United Nations?

As the Preamble of the Charter declares, the world's peoples, acting through their representatives, seek to create a peaceful, just, and prosperous world through common action. But exactly what is the nature of this common effort? For one thing, it is not a form of "world government," as some may think. Although the UN's fundamental document, the Charter, begins with the words "We the peoples," the organization's members are sovereign nations, 193 of them, not individual people. It is these member states that appoint the executives who direct the organization, and it is the member states that pay most of the costs. Furthermore, the UN does not maintain a military establishment, it has no troops of its own, and it can impose its will on nations only in rare and unusual circumstances, when great powers like the United States are prepared to back up the UN's decisions with their own military and political might.

The UN's special character is not always well understood. The late US diplomat Richard Holbrooke used to tell a story about a speaking engagement in Odessa, Texas, when "some guy asked, 'What do you think about this world government thing?' I said there was no such thing, and he said, 'What about the UN, that's a world government, they are trying to take away our liberties.' And I said, 'Well, sir, that is just not true.' There are people out there who think the UN has that kind of power and insidious influence, and the truth is the exact opposite: the UN is too weak, not too strong. You start with a certain percentage of people completely misunderstanding the UN, criticizing it from the wrong point of view. 'Too strong' is their fear when in fact 'too weak' to be effective is the truth."

As we will see throughout the book, the UN has many parts, many facets, each of which can offer a particular feel of the world body. Nancy Soderberg, a US diplomat at the UN in the Clinton years, goes so far as to claim, "There is no such single thing as the UN." Rather, the UN "is 193 countries with different agendas and a whole collection of civil servants who work there, and it's all Jell-O. You can't say what the UN is because you touch one area and it comes out looking differently on the other side." John Bolton, former US ambassador to the UN under President George W. Bush, adds that people have a hard time understanding the organization because "they don't know what the different pieces do, and some of the humanitarian agencies, which do work well, get lost in the shuffle."

Nevertheless, the UN can be described in relatively few words. Jeffrey Laurenti, formerly at the Century Foundation, defines the organization as a "supra-political association incorporating all governments and drawing on their political authority. It is a weak mem-

brane in terms of decision making and implementation but is nonetheless a political expression of a global sense of purpose and shared
interests. The UN speaks to the aspirations of humankind. It com-
mands public attention in most of the world as a place where world
public opinion is developed and voiced and where global policy gets
hammered out."

## Scanning the UN Flowchart

To gain a better sense of this unique global entity, let's begin with
its organizational structure, which will introduce us to key elements
that will appear repeatedly in the following chapters.

The accompanying flowchart lays out the basic structures and entities. Along the left side are the six principal organs, some of which
are household names: the General Assembly (which consists of delegates from all member nations of the UN), the Security Council (in
which five permanent member states have the right to veto any resolution they don't like), the Economic and Social Council (ECOSOC),
the Secretariat (which is the UN's executive body), the International
Court of Justice (ICJ, better known as the World Court), and the
Trusteeship Council (which did its job so well it has lost its reason for
being). With the exception of ECOSOC and the Trusteeship Council,
these principal organs get considerable media coverage and are, in
some ways, the most significant movers and shakers within the UN.

When we move to the right on the chart, the scene gets more
complicated. Here we find a varied collection of entities and organizations, some of which are older than the UN itself and operate with
almost complete independence from it. Best known to the public
are the "Specialized Agencies," such as the United Nations Educational, Scientific, and Cultural Organization (UNESCO), the World
Health Organization (WHO), the World Bank, and the International
Monetary Fund (IMF). Another group, here called "Funds and Programmes," includes one very well known body, the United Nations
Children's Fund (UNICEF), and several others that appear frequently in the news, like the United Nations Environment Program
(UNEP, which monitors climate change and other environmental

issues) and the United Nations High Commissioner for Refugees (UNHCR). It also contains a new entity, UN Women, established by the General Assembly in 2010, which merges the resources and roles of four predecessor bodies, the Division for the Advancement of Women (DAW), the International Research and Training Institute for the Advancement of Women (INSTRAW), the Office of the Special Adviser on Gender Issues and the Advancement of Women (OSAGI), and the United Nations Development Fund for Women (UNIFEM). We will examine UN Women later in the book.

To the left of the funds and programs on the chart are the "Subsidiary Bodies," featuring one standout, the Human Rights Council, which meets in Geneva and receives heavy press coverage. An arrow shows that these bodies report to the General Assembly. Below these subsidiary bodies are additional ones, including the International Criminal Tribunal for Rwanda (ICTR). All of these report to the Security Council, as the arrow shows.

Moving directly to the far right, we find "Related Organizations," containing such high-profile entities as the International Atomic Energy Agency (IAEA) and the Organization for the Prohibition of Chemical Weapons (OPCW). They report to the General Assembly. Below them on the chart are the "Specialized Agencies," noted earlier, which report to ECOSOC. Some, like the International Telecommunication Union (ITU), remain little known despite their vital importance to the smooth functioning of our daily lives. Many run their own affairs with little interference and, as critics have complained, without much communication with the peer agencies, programs, or commissions with which they share interests.

Going to the chart's left side, not quite at the bottom, we find a grab bag of entities. The "Functional Commissions" include some that on first glance seem to poach on the ground of other entities. For example, the Commission on the Status of Women seems to overlap UN Women, listed under "Funds and Programmes." The overlap is more apparent than real, however, because the functional commissions concentrate on policy, while the funds and programs are oriented more toward implementation. "Regional Commissions," also listed here, are among the least known of UN bodies.

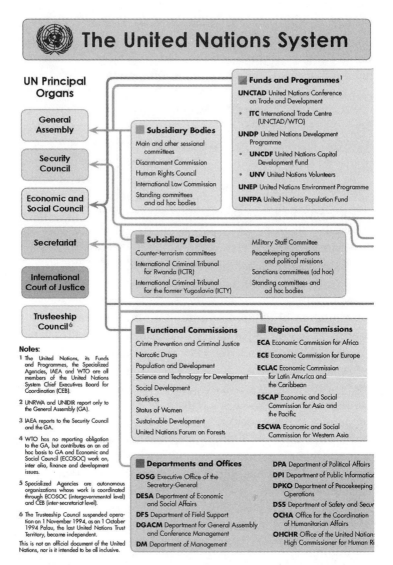

# The United Nations System

**UN Principal Organs**

- General Assembly
- Security Council
- Economic and Social Council
- Secretariat
- International Court of Justice
- Trusteeship Council[6]

**Funds and Programmes**[1]

**UNCTAD** United Nations Conference on Trade and Development
- **ITC** International Trade Centre (UNCTAD/WTO)

**UNDP** United Nations Development Programme
- **UNCDF** United Nations Capital Development Fund
- **UNV** United Nations Volunteers

**UNEP** United Nations Environment Programme

**UNFPA** United Nations Population Fund

**Subsidiary Bodies**

Main and other sessional committees
Disarmament Commission
Human Rights Council
International Law Commission
Standing committees and ad hoc bodies

**Subsidiary Bodies**

Counter-terrorism committees
International Criminal Tribunal for Rwanda (ICTR)
International Criminal Tribunal for the former Yugoslavia (ICTY)

Military Staff Committee
Peacekeeping operations and political missions
Sanctions committees (ad hoc)
Standing committees and ad hoc bodies

**Functional Commissions**

Crime Prevention and Criminal Justice
Narcotic Drugs
Population and Development
Science and Technology for Development
Social Development
Statistics
Status of Women
Sustainable Development
United Nations Forum on Forests

**Regional Commissions**

**ECA** Economic Commission for Africa
**ECE** Economic Commission for Europe
**ECLAC** Economic Commission for Latin America and the Caribbean
**ESCAP** Economic and Social Commission for Asia and the Pacific
**ESCWA** Economic and Social Commission for Western Asia

**Departments and Offices**

**EOSG** Executive Office of the Secretary-General
**DESA** Department of Economic and Social Affairs
**DFS** Department of Field Support
**DGACM** Department for General Assembly and Conference Management
**DM** Department of Management

**DPA** Department of Political Affairs
**DPI** Department of Public Information
**DPKO** Department of Peacekeeping Operations
**DSS** Department of Safety and Secur
**OCHA** Office for the Coordination of Humanitarian Affairs
**OHCHR** Office of the United Nation: High Commissioner for Human Ri

**Notes:**

1 The United Nations, its Funds and Programmes, the Specialized Agencies, IAEA and WTO are all members of the United Nations System Chief Executives Board for Coordination (CEB).

2 UNRWA and UNIDIR report only to the General Assembly (GA).

3 IAEA reports to the Security Council and the GA.

4 WTO has no reporting obligation to the GA, but contributes on an ad hoc basis to GA and Economic and Social Council (ECOSOC) work on, inter alia, finance and development issues.

5 Specialized Agencies are autonomous organizations whose work is coordinated through ECOSOC (intergovernmental level) and CEB (inter-secretariat level).

6 The Trusteeship Council suspended operation on 1 November 1994, as on 1 October 1994 Palau, the last United Nations Trust Territory, became independent.

This is not an official document of the United Nations, nor is it intended to be all inclusive.

The UN system. UN Department of Public Information, August 2013.

**UN-HABITAT** United Nations Human
Settlements Programme

**UNHCR** Office of the United Nations High Commissioner
for Refugees

**UNICEF** United Nations Children's Fund

**UNODC** United Nations Office on Drugs and Crime

**UNRWA**[2] United Nations Relief and Works Agency
for Palestine Refugees in the Near East

**UN-Women** United Nations Entity for Gender Equality
and the Empowerment of Women

**WFP** World Food Programme

### Research and Training Institutes

**UNICRI** United Nations Interregional Crime
and Justice Research Institute

**UNIDIR**[2] United Nations Institute
for Disarmament Research

**UNITAR** United Nations Institute for Training
and Research

**UNRISD** United Nations Research Institute
for Social Development

**UNSSC** United Nations System Staff College

**UNU** United Nations University

### Other Entities

**UNAIDS** Joint United Nations Programme on HIV/AIDS

**UNISDR** United Nations International Strategy
for Disaster Reduction

**UNOPS** United Nations Office for Project Services

### Related Organizations

**CTBTO Preparatory Commission** Preparatory
Commission for the Comprehensive Nuclear-Test-Ban
Treaty Organization

**IAEA**[1,3] International Atomic Energy Agency

**OPCW** Organisation for the Prohibition of Chemical
Weapons

**WTO**[1,4] World Trade Organization

### Advisory Subsidiary Body

Peacebuilding Commission

### Specialized Agencies[1,5]

**FAO** Food and Agriculture
Organization of the United Nations

**ICAO** International Civil Aviation
Organization

**IFAD** International Fund for
Agricultural Development

**ILO** International Labour Organization

**IMF** International Monetary Fund

**IMO** International Maritime
Organization

**ITU** International Telecommunication
Union

**UNESCO** United Nations
Educational, Scientific
and Cultural Organization

**UNIDO** United Nations Industrial
Development Organization

**UNWTO** World Tourism Organization

**UPU** Universal Postal Union

**WHO** World Health Organization

**WIPO** World Intellectual Property
Organization

**WMO** World Meteorological
Organization

**World Bank Group**

- **IBRD** International Bank for
Reconstruction and Development

- **ICSID** International Centre for
Settlement of Investment
Disputes

- **IDA** International Development
Association

- **IFC** International Finance
Corporation

- **MIGA** Multilateral Investment
Guarantee Agency

### Other Bodies

Committee for Development Policy

Committee of Experts on Public
Administration

Committee on Non-Governmental
Organizations

Permanent Forum on Indigenous Issues

United Nations Group of Experts
on Geographical Names

Other sessional and standing
committees and expert, ad hoc
and related bodies

**OIOS** Office of Internal Oversight Services

**OLA** Office of Legal Affairs

**OSAA** Office of the Special Adviser on Africa

**SRSG/CAAC** Office of the Special Representative
of the Secretary-General for Children
and Armed Conflict

**SRSG/SVC** Office of the Special Representative of the
Secretary-General on Sexual Violence in Conflict

**UNODA** Office for Disarmament Affairs

**UNOG** United Nations Office at Geneva

**UN-OHRLLS** Office of the High Representative
for the Least Developed Countries, Landlocked
Developing Countries and Small Island
Developing States

**UNON** United Nations Office at Nairobi

**UNOV** United Nations Office at Vienna

Published by the United Nations Department of Public Information   DPI/2470 rev.3—13-38229—August 2013

They address economic development in the regions of Africa, Europe, Latin America and the Caribbean, Asia and the Pacific, and Western Asia. The "Other Bodies" listed here deal mainly with issues of civil society, public administration, and other matters important to developing nations.

Running across the bottom of the chart is a list of "Departments and Offices," encompassing the departments of the UN Secretariat (which is overseen by the secretary-general, currently Mr. Ban Ki-moon).

## How It Works

We now have a good schematic picture of the UN's structure. But this is only a beginning. When we think about the organization in action, flowcharts aren't very helpful, because they don't show how the parts interact or how effective or efficient they are. They don't show, for example, that regional blocs control most of the votes in the main deliberative body, the General Assembly. The blocs are invisible yet powerful actors on the UN stage.

### Common Concerns

"Suffice it to say the United States and the United Nations share global concerns. If we didn't have a United Nations, we'd have to invent one. We're grateful for the leadership that is exhibited by the Secretary-General, and I am committed on behalf of President Obama to make certain that we strengthen our relationship with the UN even further in the years ahead."                                    —John Kerry, US secretary of state

The fact that the UN is overseen by 193 member states, often with varying agendas, can contribute to a degree of administrative waffling and diplomatic theatrics. Brian Urquhart, who participated in creating the UN, argues, however, that the shortcomings have to be balanced against the strengths. "There's quiet diplomacy, which goes on twenty-four hours a day," he says. "There's the secretary-general and the Secretariat, who, contrary to general belief, are rather effective and not, incidentally, a great bloated organization.

. . . The UN is not very efficient, I have to say, in some respects, because it's recruited from all over the world, and you have to work hard to get a common standard going, but it does work." He concludes, "The UN is like an insurance policy: you hate paying for it, but it's useful if something goes wrong."

Secretary-General Ban Ki-moon emphasizes the unique position of the UN as an honest broker. "At the United Nations we have great convening power to find global solutions to our global problems." And problems there surely are, from terrorism and nuclear proliferation to worldwide hunger and disease. These threats "cannot be approached as items on a list," says the secretary-general. "The trick is to see them as part of a broader whole. In truth, solutions to one are solutions to all. The key is to see the interconnections among all the problems that come to our door at the UN."

## What's in It for Us?

Putting aside international diplomacy, why should Americans care about the UN? Pressed to identify a specific UN-related item or service they have encountered recently, people might mention UNICEF trick-or-treat boxes and holiday cards. But is that all?

> ### What It Means to You
>
> "I know that the UN often frustrates Americans, and I am acutely aware of its shortcomings. But that is precisely why the United States must carry out sustained, concerted, and strategic multilateral diplomacy. Many countries invest heavily in deliberations on what they view as 'the world stage.' That in part explains why diplomacy at the UN can be slow, frustrating, complex, and imperfect. But that is also why effective American diplomacy at the United Nations remains so crucial."
> —Susan E. Rice, former US ambassador to the UN

The UN sets standards that affect us every day. "You may think that you have never benefited personally from the UN," says former US secretary of state Madeleine Albright, "but if you have ever traveled on an international airline or shipping line or placed a phone call overseas or received mail from outside the country or been thankful for an accurate weather report—then you have been served directly or indirectly by one part or another of the UN system." Zalmay Khalilzad, who was US ambassador to the UN under President George W. Bush, notes that for a global power like the United States, the world body is a very important instrument that should be made as effective as possible and "reformed as we go forward so that it can maintain the confidence of people and countries around the world."

## Managing the Unmanageable

"If you look at peace and security I don't think the UN does anything amazingly well. But that isn't why we turn to the UN. We turn to the UN because we want to find politically and operationally sustainable ways of managing crisis when we don't have a better idea. Vast tracts of the Democratic Republic of the Congo, huge areas of West Africa, Haiti, Kosovo, are in a more . . . decent state today than if the UN had not been there."
—Richard Gowan, New York University

The central role of the United States in creating and supporting the UN gives it a special place in UN affairs and has led many insiders to remark on the close and sometimes contentious relationship between the two entities. "The United Nations has no better friend than America," declares Secretary-General Ban Ki-moon. Arguing from national polls, he says that "most Americans want US foreign policy to be conducted in partnership with the UN. They understand that working together is in the best interest of the United States, the United Nations, and, most importantly, the peoples of the world."

An eminent diplomat who served under the Clinton administration as US ambassador to the UN from 1999 to 2001 offered a parallel analysis. "I need to underscore repeatedly that the UN is only as good as the US commitment," said Richard Holbrooke, who negotiated the Dayton Accords ending the war in Bosnia in 1995. "The UN cannot succeed if the US does not support it."

## Committed to the UN's Values

"We [the United States] are vigorous supporters of the indispensable work that the UN does in combating poverty and assisting development, fighting malaria, TB, and HIV/AIDS, promoting human rights, and advancing the status of women and a whole host of other areas. We are also strongly committed to the UN's core mission of preserving international stability and peace. It's precisely because of our hope and respect for the UN as an institution that we want this institution to operate as efficiently, effectively, and economically as possible."
—Samantha Power, US ambassador to the UN

Another UN insider, speaking from a very different background, agrees with Holbrooke's assessment. Mark Malloch-Brown spent many years running one of the UN's major agencies before becoming the deputy secretary-general during the last year of Kofi Annan's tenure as secretary-general. From this perch Malloch-Brown gained a deep appreciation of the importance of the United States in almost all aspects of the UN's work. "You can't have an effective UN without very strong American engagement in the organization," he says. "The US has to be there in a strong leadership role."

The US domestic political establishment includes experts and advisers who favor a more go-it-alone foreign policy, and for them the UN sometimes seems a greater hindrance than help. The dominant view, however, has been for the US government to cooperate with and enable the UN as much as possible, as long as it doesn't threaten fundamental American interests. Esther Brimmer, a former assistant secretary of state for international organization affairs who is now on the faculty of the George Washington University's Elliott School of International Affairs, emphasizes the value of the UN for conducting diplomacy and addressing pressing issues. "For the United States, the United Nations is an important foreign-policy tool. The UN's system has important mechanisms, institutions where you can actually get things done. And for certain issues, when you need to have global reach, you need to work with different parts of the UN system depending on what the topic is." She explains the concept of the diplomatic toolkit. "The toolkit is a phrase you'll hear used a lot because that's how many US policymakers think about what they're trying to do. What tools do I have to use to accomplish this objective? One of the important ones might be alliances, it might be other relationships, it might be public partnerships. Another one is working within the UN system."

President Barack Obama is on record as saying that "no country has a greater stake in a strong United Nations than the United States. The United States benefits from a global institution intended to advance the rule of law, the peaceful resolution of disputes, effective collective security, humanitarian relief, development, and respect for human rights."

## The UN and the Nobel Peace Prize

The Nobel Peace Prize has been awarded on eleven occasions to the UN, its specialized agencies, and its staff. The Office of the UN High Commissioner for Refugees has received the prize twice.

| Year | Recipient |
| --- | --- |
| 2013 | Organization for the Prohibition of Chemical Weapons |
| 2007 | Intergovernmental Panel on Climate Change and Al Gore Jr. |
| 2005 | International Atomic Energy Agency and Mohamed ElBaradei |
| 2001 | United Nations and Kofi Annan |
| 1988 | United Nations Peacekeeping Forces |
| 1981 | Office of the UN High Commissioner for Refugees |
| 1969 | International Labour Organization |
| 1965 | United Nations Children's Fund |
| 1961 | Dag Hammarskjöld |
| 1954 | Office of the UN High Commissioner for Refugees |
| 1950 | Ralph Bunche |

Madeleine Albright argues that the United States does not have the choice of acting "only through the UN or only alone." Rather, she says, "we want—and need—both options. So in diplomacy, an instrument like the UN will be useful in some situations, useless in others, and extremely valuable in getting the whole job done." The UN can help make the world a better place, she continues, and this is to our advantage because we know that "desperation is a parent to violence, that democratic principles are often among the victims of poverty, and that lawlessness is a contagious disease." Albright concluded: "We cannot be the world's policemen, though we're very good at it."

## CHAPTER 2

# Founding Documents

*[The UN is] immensely important because it represents legitimacy and international law, without which we'll all eventually go into the ditch. It represents a place where in emergencies you can actually do something . . . that will be accepted even by people . . . who would not accept an intervention by the US or any other single country.*
—Brian Urquhart, former aide and adviser
to UN secretaries-general

Two documents provide the framework for the UN's purpose, organization, and values. The first is the Charter, ratified in 1945, which functions as the Constitution does for the United States and, like the Constitution, has been amended over time to reflect changing needs. The second is the Universal Declaration of Human Rights, a manifesto of human dignity and value that remains as fresh and radical as it was when adopted in 1948.

## The Charter

The Charter was signed on June 26, 1945, by fifty nations and entered into force several months later, on October 24. The chap-

An Egyptian representative signs the UN Charter at the San Francisco conference, June 26, 1945. UN Photo / Yould.

ters and articles constitute a treaty and are legally binding on the signatories. Article 103 of the Charter stipulates that if a member state finds that its obligations under the Charter conflict with duties under "any other international agreement," the state must place its Charter obligations first.

Nineteen chapters lay out the major components of the organization, including its director (the secretary-general), its lines of authority, and the responsibilities and rights of its members—that is, of the governments that constitute the UN membership. Chapter I describes the purpose of the UN, emphasizing international peace and security, and Chapter II lists the qualifications for membership.

Most of the information about the elements of the new organization, including its six principal organs, appears in Chapters III through XV. Chapter IV describes the role and responsibilities of the General Assembly and its constituent member states, including the one-nation, one-vote principle and the obligation of each nation to contribute to the financial needs of the UN. According to Article 19, a member state that falls two years behind in paying its dues may lose its vote in the General Assembly, unless the failure to pay "is due to conditions beyond the control of the Member." Chapter V deals with the Security Council, specifying its five permanent members—China, France, the Soviet Union (now Russia), the United Kingdom, and the United States—and stipulating the periodic election of ten "non-permanent" members. Article 27 of the chapter also mentions the famous "veto" that the five permanent members (P5) can deploy if they want to prevent the council from taking a specific decision, but it does so indirectly, without ever using the word "veto," by stating that decisions of the Security Council "shall be made by an affirmative vote of nine members including the concurring votes of the permanent members."

Like the US Constitution, the Charter can be amended (Chapter XVIII), a process requiring the approval of two-thirds of the member states, including all five of the permanent members of the Security Council. And as in the United States, amendments come rarely. One change, in 1965, enlarged the Security Council from eleven to fifteen members; two other changes concerned enlarging the Economic and Social Council (ECOSOC).

## The Charter and National Sovereignty

"Sovereign entities have created a supra-association in which they have invested a small measure of sovereignty, at least for the purpose of preventing war. The UN Charter represents very small concessions of sovereignty to the global entity, the UN, but it was primarily to prevent a return to war."                    —Jeffrey Laurenti, international affairs analyst

The Charter clearly envisions the members as sovereign and independent states (Chapter I, Article 2) and requires that they resolve their disputes with one another without endangering international peace and security (Article 3). Member states are also asked to avoid threatening other nations with the use of force (Article 4) and to assist the UN with any actions it may take (Article 5). The final article of Chapter I attempts to balance the internal affairs of each member state with its international actions and responsibilities. It states that the UN is not authorized to intervene in domestic affairs of a member state, but it also says that this restriction does not limit the right of the UN under Chapter VII. That chapter gives the Security Council the authority to resolve international disputes through negotiation, economic, military, and other sanctions, and even the use of force.

President Franklin Roosevelt, one of America's most skilled political leaders, worried that the new United Nations might fail to gain approval in Congress, which is what happened to its predecessor, the League of Nations. That would have been a fatal blow to the fledgling organization. The president therefore carefully chose the US delegates to the meetings that created the UN, including important leaders in Congress and in American society. When he died in April 1945, he left behind an able team to carry out the final acts of creation and presentation to Congress.

The sole female delegate to the San Francisco conference, which met in April 1945, was Virginia Gildersleeve, an eminent educator from New York City, who was responsible for dreaming up the opening to the Charter's preamble—"We the peoples of the United Nations"—which is based on the opening of the preamble to the US Constitution: "We the people of the United States." She persuaded her fellow delegates that this would be a compelling way to introduce the new organization to the world, and history has borne out her insight.

After the UN was established and the United States and other nations had ratified the Charter, much work remained to be done, including addressing the question of the basic rights that humans should expect to enjoy. This time it was another Roosevelt, Franklin's widow, Eleanor, who contributed significantly.

Eleanor Roosevelt had gained a reputation as a champion of the poor and disenfranchised. President Harry Truman now appointed her to the distinguished list of delegates to the first meeting of the General Assembly in London in 1945. There she served as the sole female member of Committee III, slated to address humanitarian, social, and cultural matters. She also became closely involved in creating the UN's other founding document, the Universal Declaration of Human Rights.

## The Universal Declaration of Human Rights

After Eleanor Roosevelt's impressive performance in London, the White House and the State Department asked her to represent the government on the nascent UN Human Rights Commission and to help draft what became the Universal Declaration of Human Rights. Some experts at the time believed that the League of Nations had been fatally flawed because its charter lacked a strong statement in favor of human rights. Many supporters of the UN had originally hoped to launch the new organization with both a charter and a declaration of human rights. "I felt extremely strongly that human rights were something which simply had to be developed into an international rule," recalls Brian Urquhart, who participated in the commission's proceedings. "It simply wasn't good enough to try to rely on people to behave reasonably well: they don't. The Nazis were an extreme, but they are not unique."

The new Human Rights Commission, with Eleanor Roosevelt as its chair, began meeting to write the declaration in April 1946. It kept meeting for the next two and a half years, in New York City and then Geneva, Switzerland, until it hammered out a consensus document. Many difficulties arose as the eighteen delegates, who represented a wide spectrum of political, social, cultural, and religious views, discussed and debated the nature of rights—indeed, the meaning of being a human being—and the proper relation between the individual and the state.

An unexpected debate arose over the use of the noun "man" to stand for "humankind" in the first article of the draft. The original text read, "All men are created equal." An Indian woman, Hansa Mehta, complained that the word could be misunderstood to ex-

Eleanor Roosevelt with the Universal Declaration of Human Rights (Spanish version), November 1, 1949. UN Photo.

clude women. The UN's Commission on the Status of Women voted unanimously to ask the Commission on Human Rights to substitute "all people" for "all men." Eleanor Roosevelt was divided on the issue because she had never felt excluded by the use of "man" in the Declaration of Independence. But she relented, and the phrase "all human beings" became the definitive term in the draft.

When the Universal Declaration was finished, it was sent to the General Assembly, which debated it anew. Finally, at 3:00 am on December 10, 1948, the General Assembly voted to adopt the draft. (The full text is printed in appendix B.)

Resting on Enlightenment ideals of human dignity, the Universal Declaration is unique both in its breadth and in its success as an international standard by which to identify the basic rights that every person should enjoy. Most human rights laws, and many national constitutions, reflect its provisions. It is an inspiration to people seeking freedom and to organizations advancing the cause of freedom and justice. Brian Urquhart praises the Universal Declaration "as one of the most important actions in the twentieth century because it changed the perception of human society from being a society where governments were dominant to a society where individual rights were the thing that everybody, including governments, had to worry about."

Unlike the Charter, the Universal Declaration is not a treaty, and its provisions therefore are not law, but the declaration has been largely incorporated into two international treaties that came into effect in 1976 and that have been accepted by most member states: the International Covenant on Economic, Social, and Cultural Rights and the International Covenant on Civil and Political Rights. The UN refers to these covenants and the Universal Declaration as the International Bill of Human Rights.

CHAPTER 3

# The Secretary-General and the Secretariat

*I believe in the power of relationships. For years I have carried in my wallet . . . a well-worn scrap of paper inscribed with Chinese characters pertaining to one's age and phase in life. At 30, you are in your prime of life. At 50, you are said to know your destiny. At 60, you possess the wisdom of the "soft ear."*
— Ban Ki-moon, secretary-general of the UN

"Equal parts diplomat and advocate, civil servant and CEO, the Secretary-General is a symbol of United Nations ideals and a spokesman for the interests of the world's peoples, in particular the poor and vulnerable among them." This official UN description captures the sweeping responsibilities assigned to the world body's chief executive officer and suggests the great challenges they bring. Choosing a new secretary-general is a major event, not only for the UN system but for its 193 member states and all the world's peoples.

On October 13, 2006, the UN General Assembly selected a sixty-one-year-old South Korean, Ban Ki-moon, as the eighth secretary-general, to succeed Kofi Annan, whose two five-year terms had set precedents for international activism and public visibility. The new

Secretary-General Ban Ki-moon speaks at a press conference on the earthquake and tsunami in Japan, March 11, 2011. UN Photo / Evan Schneider.

man attracted wide media attention. The secretary-general has sometimes been referred to as the world's secular pope and carries heavy responsibilities in such vital and sensitive areas as peacemaking, human rights, and UN reform. Yet outside the diplomatic community, few had heard of Ban Ki-moon. No wonder people around the globe were asking, Who is this fellow?

Ban Ki-moon was born in a South Korean farming village in 1944 and grew up while his country was defending itself against aggression from the north—a war fought under US leadership with the official sanction of the UN. The young man's life took a decisive turn in high school when he met his wife and won an essay contest sponsored by the Red Cross that led to a visit to the United States. He credits a brief meeting with President John F. Kennedy in Washington, DC, with helping him decide to pursue a career in diplomacy. Back in South Korea, Ban joined the Ministry of Foreign Affairs in 1970 and gradually moved up the career ladder, earning respect for his intense work ethic and his diplomatic skills. In 1974 he was posted to New York City as first secretary of the South Korean Permanent Observer Mission to the UN, and in 1991 he became director of the foreign ministry's United Nations Division. Meanwhile, in 1980, he became director of Korea's International Organizations and Treaties Bureau in Seoul. After two postings to the Korean embassy in Washington, DC, and more assignments in Korea and Austria, he became his country's foreign minister in 2004. By then he had also earned a master's degree in public administration at Harvard University's prestigious Kennedy School of Government.

## Choosing the Secretary-General

Ban Ki-moon declared his candidacy for secretary-general of the UN in February 2006 and launched a vigorous campaign for the position with strong support from his home government. Candidates for the top post at the UN have to work hard and strategically if they expect to win. Ban's efforts got a huge boost when it became known that both China and the United States favored his candidacy. His chances were also aided by the unwritten agreement that the post of secretary-general should rotate among regions of the world. Accordingly, Javier Pérez de Cuéllar, from Peru, served two terms (1982–91) and was followed by Boutros Boutros-Ghali, of Egypt, who served one term (1992–97), and Kofi Annan, a Ghanaian, who served two terms (1997–2006). Because Africa had contributed two consecutive secretaries-general, and Europe had produced several secretaries-general, ending with Kurt Waldheim (1972–81) of Austria, the post was expected to go next to Asia (which, in the UN system, includes the Arab states of the Middle East). Ban Ki-moon was therefore well positioned, but he faced competition from another Asian, Shashi Tharoor of India, an experienced UN staffer closely associated with Kofi Annan.

## Secretaries-General

| | |
|---|---|
| Trygve Lie (Norway) | 1945–52 |
| Dag Hammarskjöld (Sweden) | 1953–61 |
| U Thant (Burma) | 1961–71 |
| Kurt Waldheim (Austria) | 1972–81 |
| Javier Pérez de Cuéllar (Peru) | 1982–91 |
| Boutros Boutros-Ghali (Egypt) | 1992–97 |
| Kofi Annan (Ghana) | 1997–2006 |
| Ban Ki-moon (South Korea) | 2007–present |

Once Ban and Tharoor had declared, the UN began the formal process of deciding on a winner. The procedure involves two UN bodies: the Security Council, which recommends a candidate, and the General Assembly, which ratifies the choice. The Security Council decides on the nomination at "private" meetings for which there is no public record except for brief communiqués from its president. In 2006, the fifteen members of the council held a series of straw polls that made Ban Ki-moon the favorite, with Tharoor second. Observers did note a surprisingly strong showing by Vaira Vike-Freiberga of Latvia, the only woman and the only non-Asian among the candidates, whose name was placed in two straw votes. When the final poll showed Ban Ki-moon as the nominee, the council passed his name to the General Assembly, and in the ensuing vote Ban was elected the eighth secretary-general. And five years later he was elected to a second term.

## The Secretariat

*From the UN Charter, Chapter XV*

ARTICLE 97

The Secretariat shall comprise a Secretary-General and such staff as the Organization may require. The Secretary-General shall be appointed by the General Assembly upon the recommendation of the Security Council. He shall be the chief administrative officer of the Organization.

## An Evolving Job Description

The position of the secretary-general is only briefly described in the UN Charter and has evolved over time. "In the Charter of the UN," observed Richard Holbrooke, "the role of secretary-general is only described with a single phrase, that the UN will have a chief administrative officer. It doesn't describe the authority of the secretary-general as the Constitution describes the powers for the president and Congress. It's all been done, like the British constitution, by precedent and strong secretaries-general, of whom we've had two, Dag Hammarskjöld and Kofi Annan."

Mark Malloch-Brown adds that the Charter "doesn't envisage significant powers for the secretary-general in international relations." Rather, he says, the internationally active secretaries-general have succeeded by "convincing genuinely important individuals, heads of government and so on, that they can be helpful." Michael Sheehan, a former assistant secretary-general for peacekeeping, says that one of the secretary-general's roles is to "tell the Security Council what it has to know, not what it wants to hear. So the Secretariat is not just a puppet on a string of the member states; it has a role, and there's

Secretary-General Dag Hammarskjöld in Katanga, Republic of the
Congo, August 14, 1960. UN Photo / HP.


a dialogue between the Secretariat and the member states." In this
dialogue the secretary-general often deploys his status as an impartial and well-intentioned leader, lending his good offices to address
international conflicts and issues. In other words, he has a bully
pulpit, and he is expected to use it.

The many responsibilities of the secretary-general make the post
one of the most demanding imaginable. It requires intelligence and
experience, certainly, but also drive, vision, and infinite tact and pa-
tience. The secretary-general must be able to communicate with the
entire UN family as well as with all the nations of the world while
overseeing a global array of programs and agencies. His daily activities range from attending sessions of the Security Council, General
Assembly, and other UN bodies, to meetings with world leaders and
government officials, to frequent travel around the globe. He greets
world leaders when they arrive at the UN's New York headquarters
for the September opening of the General Assembly, and he hosts

Secretary-General Ban Ki-moon meets with former secretary-general
Kofi Annan in Geneva, March 4, 2008. UN Photo / Mark Garten.

them at a special luncheon. He also chairs the UN System Chief
Executives Board, routinely referred to as the CEB, which consists
of the directors of all the world body's funds, programs, and specialized agencies, who meet twice annually to coordinate their various
activities throughout the UN system.

## The Secretariat

Alongside all the specific and general duties, charges, and responsibilities, the secretary-general is responsible for overseeing the Secretariat, which is the UN's chief executive arm. The Secretariat is headquartered in New York City, in the sleek modern building that rises
dramatically beside the East River, but it also has offices in Addis Ababa,
Bangkok, Beirut, Geneva, Nairobi, Rome, Santiago, and Vienna.

All told, the Secretariat has about forty-three thousand staff. In

What Is. What Should Be.

"Our job is to diminish the gap between the world as it is and the world as it should be, and that's a long haul. In this phase, seeing the world as it should be, you bring in the elements of improving the situation—peace, security and development, human rights—and then you also get a sense of what our job is all about. Forget that you can't change the world in a day, but you have to know that this is the world as it is, and don't forget the way the world should be. If I do, then I'm not doing my job. This is what drives me."        —Jan Eliasson, deputy secretary-general of the UN

keeping with the letter and spirit of the Charter, which aimed to create an international civil service, member states agree not to exert improper influence on the Secretariat's staff, and the staff, in turn, take an oath that they will be responsible solely to the United Nations and will not seek or take direction from any other authority. Chapter XV, Article 100, of the Charter states very clearly that "each Member of the United Nations undertakes to respect the exclusively international character of the responsibilities of the Secretary-General and the staff and not to seek to influence them in the discharge of their responsibilities." Article 101 mandates that "the paramount consideration in the employment of the staff and in the determination of the conditions of service shall be the necessity of securing the highest standards of efficiency, competence, and integrity. Due regard shall be paid to the importance of recruiting the staff on as wide a geographical basis as possible."

Kofi Annan is credited with advancing a series of administrative reforms in the Secretariat begun by his predecessor, Boutros Boutros-Ghali (the reforms are discussed in chapter 18). Annan encouraged development of a corporate culture aimed at making results, not efforts, the test of effectiveness. Ban Ki-moon is credited with continuing the reform efforts. His deputy, Jan Eliasson, observes that while the Secretariat's staff quality may vary by individual, "there are extremely inspiring and great minds and true internationalists . . .

it's very high quality." He notes that to be a good member of the staff, "you have to be both very realistic about the world as it is, you can't live in the clouds, you have to know what is the situation and be very realistic about that. But you must never forget that we are unique in serving this organization."

Former Canadian ambassador David Malone estimates that "40 percent of the Secretariat staff are movers and shakers and carry the full burden of action. About 30 percent do no harm and do no good, and about 30 percent spend their time making trouble. Which means that the 40 percent who get work done are fairly heroic, and they exist at all levels of the system."

How to manage this far-flung staff has become an issue as the number of member states has grown, UN activities have increased, and local and regional crises have proliferated. A later chapter will address the broad issue of UN reform, which focuses heavily on improving administrative efficiency and accountability within the UN system. Here our main point is to see how the secretary-general can discharge his duty to oversee the Secretariat's staff and ensure that they are carrying out his policies and the expressed wishes of the Security Council, General Assembly, and other UN bodies. Clearly, the secretary-general's oversight implies a focus on coordination to ensure that the various offices and key personnel are pulling together, not in separate directions. He does this through his Team, which consists of the deputy secretary-general, the Senior Management Group, and special personal representatives, envoys, and advisers, with occasional assistance from volunteers known as Messengers of Peace and Goodwill Ambassadors.

## The Deputy Secretary-General

Until recently the secretary-general was pretty much a one-man band. Then Kofi Annan decided that he needed to delegate more of his duties as secretary-general. His solution was to persuade the General Assembly in 1997 to create a new post, deputy secretary-general.

The deputy is in effect the UN's chief operating officer, assisting

the secretary-general in the management of his staff and the Secretariat, representing the UN at conferences and official functions,
and chairing the Steering Committee on Reform and Management
Policy. The deputy secretary-general is also charged with "elevating
the profile and leadership of the United Nations in the economic
and social spheres," areas attracting increasing UN attention and
resources.

Annan named a Canadian diplomat, Louise Fréchette, to the new
position in 1998. She was succeeded in 2006 by Mark Malloch-
Brown of the United Kingdom, former head of the UN Development Program (UNDP). In 2007, Ban Ki-moon selected Asha-Rose
Migiro, a lawyer and a former foreign minister of Tanzania to the
post. Jan Eliasson became deputy secretary-general in 2012. He is
a former Swedish diplomat and foreign minister and an experienced member of the UN family. Eliasson was the first UN under-
secretary-general for humanitarian affairs (1992–94), a post that
involved him deeply in social and economic development and gave
him field experience in many troubled places, such as Somalia and
Sudan.

"The secretary-general asked me to help out, to alleviate his
burden because he has so much on his plate," says Eliasson, who
relishes his work and routinely works long hours. "The leadership
team meet every day when they are in town, they are in constant
contact. On weekdays, evenings, and almost every weekend we have
video conferences." Eliasson's special concerns are the political
section, which contains peacekeeping and political issues, human
rights, and development. "These are my areas. I am not operational
from the point of view that I micro-manage the department, but
I am overseeing it and I try to live up to the formula that I myself
had the honor of formulating: that there's no peace without development and no development without peace. Today I would say there
is no lasting peace without respect for human rights and the rule of
law. In other words, these areas are connected, and we need to work
for them at the same time." His special position in the UN system
enables him to "bring people around the table, put the issues in
the center, and see them from the political and security aspect, the

Secretary-General Ban Ki-moon at a seminar with his special representatives, personal representatives, and envoys in Mont Pèlerin, Switzerland, March 2, 2014. UN Photo / Eskinder Debebe.

developmental aspect, and the human rights and rule of law aspect. That has proven very useful for me and I hope for my colleagues."

## The Senior Management Group

The deputy secretary-general is a member of the Senior Management Group (SMG), described as "a high-level body, chaired by the Secretary-General, which brings together leaders of United Nations departments, offices, funds, and programmes." In January 2014 the SMG had forty-one members plus the secretary-general. Skimming the membership list alphabetically by personal name, we see Valerie Amos, Humanitarian Affairs and Emergency Relief Coordinator; Jeffrey Feltman, Department of Political Affairs; Tegegnework Gettu, General Assembly Affairs and Conference Management; Angela Kane, Disarmament; Hervé Ladsous, Peacekeeping Operations; Wu Hongbo, Economic and Social Affairs; and Leila Zerrougui, Children and Armed Conflict. We could just as well have cited the Special Adviser on Africa, the Special Representative on Sexual Violence in Conflict, the UN High Commissioner for Refugees, the Special Adviser on Change Implementation, or the Secretary-General of the UN Conference on Trade and Development—and still we would not have covered the entire SMG. Even this quick scan shows, however, that these directors, managers, and senior advisers address an extraordinarily wide range of issues, covering all parts of the globe. It also shows, through the variety of personal names, that this is truly an international staff.

## Personal Representatives, Envoys, and Advisers

Like any high-powered CEO, the secretary-general has to deal with all kinds of issues, even those with which he may have little direct experience or expertise. And so the secretary-general does what you might expect: he finds people he trusts who can act as his eyes, ears, and representative for the region, issue, or conflict at hand. In January 2014, for Africa alone, Ban Ki-moon had designated some twenty-one men and women as his representatives. The number of representatives and their names change continually to accommodate the ever-changing shape of the world, but a brief list will give a flavor of the mix: in early 2014 they included the Special Representative of the Secretary-General to the African Union; the Special Representative of the Secretary-General for Côte d'Ivoire and Head of UNOCI (UN Operations in Côte d'Ivoire); the Special Adviser to the Secretary-General and Mediator in the Border Dispute between Equatorial Guinea and Gabon; the Special Representative of the Secretary-General and Head of UNSMIL (UN Support Mission in Libya); and the Special Envoy of the Secretary-General for the Sahel. These various appointees often have rather open-ended briefs, in keeping with the fluid nature of the situations in which they operate.

## Messengers of Peace and Goodwill Ambassadors

Unlike the personal representatives of the secretary-general and the members of the SMG, the UN's Messengers of Peace have names with broad recognition. Is there anyone who hasn't heard the name Yo-Yo Ma, even if they have never heard him play the Dvořák cello concerto or another classic musical work? Then there is human rights advocate and Nobel Prize winner Elie Wiesel, actor George Clooney, and pop musician Stevie Wonder. The practice of appointing distinguished and famous artists, thinkers, and advocates as Messengers of Peace began in 1998 and is intended to "help focus worldwide attention on the work of the United Nations." As volunteers, these messengers travel to venues around the world and appear in the media as representatives of the secretary-general and the UN system.

Yet another kind of representative, the Goodwill Ambassador, has become popular among the UN bodies. A Goodwill Ambassador is a notable person who advocates on behalf of a specific UN fund, program, or agency. The Goodwill Ambassadors of UNICEF, for example, include an American tennis star and an Irish-born actor. The UN Environment Program (UNEP) features a Brazilian supermodel, a French photographer and journalist, and an American actor, while the UN High Commissioner for Refugees has signed up a Chinese actress, a Turkish singer, a Kazakh singer and composer, and a British supermodel, among others.

## A New Agenda

When Ban Ki-moon became secretary-general, he was little known to the Western media, who speculated that he would probably maintain a lower public profile than his predecessor, Kofi Annan, an activist secretary-general who stretched his office to pursue an expanded vision of international diplomacy and action.

Ban Ki-moon has developed his own official style, which begins with long working days and extends to visits to every corner of the world and frequent public statements about global problems, dangers, and crises. Early in his tenure, for example, Ban went to Sudan to visit Darfur, where internal violence was rampant. "I went to listen to the candid views of its people—Sudanese officials, villagers displaced by fighting, humanitarian aid workers, the leaders

## Deeds More than Words

Secretary-General Ban Ki-moon has "modesty of pretense and modesty of promises" but not "modesty of ambition and delivery." Rather, he is "proving to be a blue-collar Secretary-General, rolling up his sleeves and being devoted and resilient but not making headlines and doing bad things."    —Edward Luck, former assistant secretary-general of the UN

of neighboring countries," Ban reported upon his return. "I came away with a clear understanding. There can be no single solution to this crisis. Darfur is a case study in complexity. If peace is to come, it must take into account all the elements that gave rise to the conflict." An optimist by nature, Ban declared that while "complexity makes our work more challenging and difficult . . . it is the only path to a lasting solution."

Former US ambassador John Bolton observes that Ban takes a more measured approach than Annan, whose "ambitions were too sweeping." Bolton sees broad agreement among observers that Ban's "low-key style of management is widely approved by all different parts of the world." Former US diplomat William Luers rates Ban "a better talker than orator. He likes one-on-one and conversational exchanges. He sets priorities and doesn't try to do too much. He is an extremely hard worker and very focused on core problems."

What are these core problems? Ban Ki-moon stated his agenda when he assumed office. It began with protecting the global climate, because otherwise we are all threatened. It asserted the human duty to intervene when nations or regions fall into chaos and destruction, and it demanded an end to nuclear proliferation, because that could lead, among other evils, to terrorist groups gaining possession of weapons of mass destruction. The agenda highlighted the need to fulfill the eight Millennium Development Goals, or MDGs (discussed in chapter 14), which are intended to raise the poorest nations to an acceptable level of social and economic development. And it included reform of the UN's fiscal and management structure to make the organization more efficient and give it the means

Secretary-General Ban Ki-moon and his wife, Yoo Soon-taek, visit a primary school in Ouagadougou, Burkina Faso, April 23, 2008. UN Photo / Eskinder Debebe.

to address an escalating series of needs and demands from the world community.

At the beginning of his second term, in 2012, Ban laid out a five-year "action agenda" that restated much of his previous view and elaborated on the main points. He spoke of the need to define a post-MDG development framework that would also address issues of energy, food, clean water, and the health of the oceans and their living resources. Prevention received extended treatment, including prevention of violent conflict and human rights violations, as well as the "responsibility to protect," often referred to as R2P, which will be discussed in chapter 11. Among the final agenda items Ban placed "supporting nations in transition," meaning member states that seek to become more democratic, transparent, and prosperous, and "working with and for women and young people," referring to violence against women, women's political and social and economic participation, and improved efforts to "address the needs of the largest generation of young people the world has ever known."

## Walking the Line

Two years later, at a news conference in December 2013, Ban restated his determination to advance the agenda, but with some surprisingly sobering words. "I am just amazed that there are still so many challenges unresolved," he replied when asked about the lessons he had learned as secretary-general. "The number of crises now seems to be increasing [more] than during my first term. At the beginning of my first term, the situation in Darfur was the key, most serious issue." Now, he said, there were "so many issues," such as the civil war in Syria and murderous conflict in the Central African Republic and Mali: "You name all these issues." The secretary-general also pointed a finger at the member states. "Another lesson is that I have seen some weakening political will. Sometimes, national interest prevails over some global problems. We first try to address all global threats, global crises. Good global initiatives and solutions will help domestic solutions, too."

Whatever the secretary-general presents as his agenda, he must pursue it with the support, or at least without the opposition, of the UN member states, especially those that have the most international clout. Most observers assess Ban's working relationship with the US government as correct and generally good. Stewart Patrick of the US Council on Foreign Relations argues that Ban is "pretty much in sync with US goals and he doesn't get out ahead of them." Richard Gowan of New York University says the United States is happy with Ban "most of the time" and views the secretary-general as "a solid, good soldier."

Ban's ability to work collaboratively with China and the United States has produced results. For example, he conducted difficult negotiations on climate change (then opposed by both China and the United States) and intervention in Darfur (opposed by China). He has also been willing to speak out even when his comments might seem out of sync with the interests of powerful member states. During the conflict in Syria, in 2013, Ban urged nations to refrain from supplying arms to the combatants while the Russian government was providing arms to the Assad regime and the US government and other governments were mulling a possible arms transfer to some of the rebel groups. Ban Ki-moon's position is perhaps more nuanced than one might expect.

Ban's agenda is his guide for his second and last term as secretary-general. Then someone else will assume the post and define the priorities and action plans. Who will that be? Speculation on a successor begins soon after the incumbent has entered the final term, and it mounts as the term nears its end. Regional factors suggest that Ban's successor will not come from Asia or Africa, which have given us the last three secretaries-general, nor from Latin America, home of Secretary-General Javier Pérez de Cuéllar (1982–91). That leaves Europe. But since Western Europe has provided several secretaries-general and Eastern Europe none, it may now be Eastern Europe's turn. Aside from geographical factors, the other key determinant will be the preferences of a few major powers. What kind of secretary-general might the United States want? Richard Gowan doubts that Washington wants another high-profile activist like Kofi Annan, but, he notes, a lower-profile candidate might not seem exactly right either.

Only as the candidates walk on the stage will we be able to assess the field and speculate on which of them is most likely to gain US backing—and that of other key governments. The sitting US administration, when it evaluates the candidates, will have to consider not only the personal qualities and values of each but the nature of the rapidly changing world in which the secretary-general will operate.

## CHAPTER 4

# A New Global Landscape

*We need support from many regional and subregional organizations. We need support from business communities, we need support from religious communities and local communities and even philanthropic organizations, first of all, to solidify our political will. Second, to mobilize our resources, which are used as tools—if we do not have effective tools, how can we do it?*

—Ban Ki-moon, secretary-general of the UN

The UN was created in a war-torn world in 1945. Soon it found itself operating in a very different kind of conflict, the Cold War, which saw many nations align themselves with one of the two major powers, the United States or the Soviet Union. Along the way, massive transformations altered nations, cultures, and worldviews. European colonies were besieged by anticolonial movements, leading to the creation of more than a hundred new nations since the 1950s. Additional global changes came with the unraveling of the Soviet bloc starting in 1989, and more than two decades later we are experiencing the fallout, as the formerly bipolar world becomes tripolar. China's rising wealth and assertiveness, alongside a Russian Federation eager to retain its great-power status and a United States that is still regarded as the world's dominant economic, political, and military power, has greatly complicated, and some would say impeded, the functioning of the UN Security Council, an issue we will explore later. Next to the top-tier powers is an array of second-tier powers, including Japan, Germany, France, and the United Kingdom. Certain nations in Asia (e.g., South Korea, India), Africa (South Africa), and Latin America (Mexico, Brazil) with growing weight and visibility have also made the global political landscape more diverse and less concentrated. Regional or common-interest organizations like the Association of Southeast Asian Nations (ASEAN) and the BRICS (Brazil, Russia, India, China, South Africa) have given voice to the agendas and aspirations of nations in the emerging political and economic landscape. An observer of the UN in 1945, time-warped to today, would find a truly transformed world.

## Dispersed Power

The emphasis on multiple actors has attracted notice among experts and policymakers, who have noted the proliferation of "centers" around the world. The Group of Twenty Finance Ministers and Central Bank Governors, also known as the G20, is a group of finance ministers and central bank governors from nineteen countries with large economies plus the European Union. Representatives of the G20 have held summits regularly since 2008 and speak for the countries with most of the world's economic output and trade and two-thirds of its population. Stewart Patrick of the US Council on Foreign Relations argues that the G20 has "given a little bit of competition to the United Nations framework." He doubts that it will ever replace the Security Council, "but there are concerns within the United Nations broader general membership that the G20 over time may become some sort of global director that will infringe upon the Security Council's prerogative." That seems unlikely, Patrick thinks, "because of course the same differences that apply within the Security Council would apply even more so given the diversity of the G20."

New Thinking

"We cannot afford to be burdened with labels such as 'rich' or 'poor,' 'developed' or 'developing,' 'North' or 'South,' or 'the Non-Aligned Movement.' In the twenty-first century these false divisions rarely serve anyone's interests. In facing challenges of the scale that lie before us, all peoples and nations should focus on what we have in common: our shared desire to live freely and securely, in health, with hope and with opportunity. Those are the interests and aspirations of the American people, and they are shared by billions around the world."
—Susan E. Rice, former US ambassador to the UN

Other, newer factors have come into play, such as the digital revolution and its associated information explosion and the rise of social media. Joseph S. Nye Jr., described by Madeleine Albright as "America's foremost expert" on power, sees the information revolution as transforming global politics by providing political access to everyone, including both well-intentioned mainstream individuals and groups and those with dissenting or even destructive agendas. "The problem for all states in today's global information age," he writes, "is that more things are happening outside the control of even the most powerful states." Nye has commented on the rise of alternative centers of policy and action. "One of the dilemmas of multilateral diplomacy is how to get everyone into the act and still get action. The answer is likely to lie in what the Europeans have dubbed 'variable geometry.' There will be many multilateralisms that will vary with the distribution of power resources in different issues."

These alternative "minilateral" frameworks of cooperation express multilateral relations on a limited scale and don't necessarily require or even invite UN participation. Patrick includes among them the Shanghai Cooperation Organization (a Eurasian political, economic, and military association), as well as the G7 (a conference of the finance ministers of the seven largest developed nations: Canada, France, Germany, Italy, Japan, the United Kingdom, and the United States), the G8 (the G7+Russia), and the many security summits and ad hoc groups that form to address specific problems. "You're also getting greater reliance on regional organizations, and they're increasingly giving the UN a run for the money," he remarks.

In traditional multilateral relations, explains Esther Brimmer of George Washington University, "particularly in a global body, you focus on member states as a whole trying to work toward an issue. Now the minilateral approach in effect says you try to take a small core of states to work on an issue, to hammer out the terms of the issue, bringing together maybe stakeholders who are relevant for the issue or who are credible voices in other regions, and you build out from that, having come up with a deal, with a frame, with a smaller group. Or it says you have a group that participates in some-thing voluntarily and creates a framework and agreement, and then others opt into it and it builds out by other states self-selecting to be part of the group."

Minilateral relations are happening like this in international trade, she says, but also in other areas, such as counterterrorism. "The idea is you have maybe thirty-odd countries that self-select to work on greater cooperation among their counterterrorism experts. Then they launch and link it to the UN, and then you have other countries that self-select to be part of it and want to build up from there." She calls it a "vanguard approach" that "builds out to the oth-ers." Her question, though, is "Will these minilateral mechanisms contribute to global norms because, as the vanguard, they are able to work out the tough issues and then bring them to others, or do they constitute an alternative?" If an alternative, it would seem that they might circumvent the UN.

The question may be on the mind of Deputy Secretary-General Jan Eliasson when he says, "I would want to see these regional or common-interest groups relate their programs, their plans, their objectives to the global reality. In today's world I can see that like-minded countries come together, but if they do so in contrast to global cooperation, then I think we will have a negative develop-ment." Secretary-General Ban Ki-moon has urged the UN to think more collaboratively, not just to accomplish its goals more effec-tively but to ensure its place in the global discussion. "That is a very important lesson which I learned, and that is why I have been appealing and reaching out to Member States: please, let us work together."

## Looking for a Response

Whether the member states are listening is another matter. Eliasson worries that habits of mind and action are preventing the UN from responding quickly enough. "The agenda for international organizations was mainly composed during the 1960s to the 90s and the beginning of this century," he notes, but a lot has changed since then. He asks rhetorically, "To what degree do we have serious discussions in the United Nations on the new global trends?" Not enough, he concludes, not nearly enough. "I don't think we have drawn the conclusions for [creating] a good international system to deal with this new global landscape."

### Working Together

"U.S. leadership will remain crucial in the period ahead. At a time when families and governments everywhere are feeling severe financial strains, the benefits of working with the United Nations are clear: burden sharing, wise use of the global taxpayers' money, and international solutions in the national interest. I look forward to strengthening the U.S.-UN partnership and working closely with Secretary of State Kerry towards our shared goals of peace, development, and human rights."
—Ban Ki-moon, secretary-general of the United Nations

Some insiders see an opportunity for the UN in this new landscape. According to Mark Malloch-Brown, who was deputy secretary-general under Kofi Annan, the influence of leading nations like the United States and Russia is diminished, but the importance of the United Nations is actually enhanced "because where else can you seek answers in the situation of power dispersal?"

But the same forces that make the UN more essential may also circumscribe its work by pushing it to act cooperatively or in liaison with other actors, whether they are national governments, regional organizations, global institutions like the World Bank, or grassroots organizations representing specific ethnic or religious groups. Secretary-General Ban Ki-moon has made it clear that in the new global landscape the UN must partner more with other organizations, recognizing that "nobody—no organization, no country, however powerful, however resourceful one may be—can do this alone."

## CHAPTER 5

# The American Ambassador

*Permanent representatives [of the United States] have to spend a lot of
time in Washington, and that's what's distinctive. Part of their influence
and power at the UN is directly linked to people's perceptions of their
clout in Washington. So when the permanent rep can't make a meeting
because he or she has to be in Washington, that is seen as a sign of clout.*
— Jeffrey Laurenti, international affairs analyst

Each of the 193 member nations maintains a UN mission in New
York City, directed by a head, known as the permanent representative, or perm rep, who carries the title of ambassador. The term of
the permanent representative varies by nation, usually extending
over several years. So the word "permanent" shouldn't be taken too
literally, but it conveniently denotes the key person in a delegation
of representatives. The United States maintains the largest delegation, located at 799 United Nations Plaza (on the corner of East
Forty-fifth and First Avenue), across the street from UN headquarters. A staff of more than a hundred, including advisers, handles
the political, economic and social, legal, military, public-diplomacy,

and management interests of the United States at the United Nations. Five ambassadors—the permanent representative, the deputy permanent representative, the alternative representative for special political affairs, the representative on the UN Economic and Social Council (ECOSOC), and the representative for management and reform—are the point persons for this large and active mission.

Even more personnel come to the US mission during September–December to help cope with the hundreds of heads of state, diplomats, and their staff from around the world who attend the opening session and working meetings of the General Assembly (GA). For example, Joseph Melrose, who has served as the acting US representative for management and reform at the United Nations, notes that "during the GA we bring in six mostly retired ambassadors or senior officers to make sure we talk to everyone because we know that the US perm representative can't." It makes sense to take advantage of the great experience and contacts of these senior people. "I always thought that it was a logical approach to bring back these diplomats to deal with the regions they have experience in," he observes, and to "go out to talk to every country in a region and solicit their thoughts and views, explain your position, and show a little respect, that you're not ignoring them because they are small in population." A country "like a Bhutan or the Maldives that isn't high on our strategy list here, we can't just blow them off, because at the GA they have a vote."

The large size of the US mission is related to the need for enough staff for the many positions and situations that a high-powered presence requires. "The US is always there," remarks Melrose. "It never has a vacant chair [in a committee or other venue] unless we're making a political statement." Small countries are in a very different position, he notes. "You think of a country like Bhutan that at one point was interested in serving on the Security Council, and you wonder, How are they going to staff it when they have only five people? . . . They have to have someone of senior rank available all the time, and there's a cost to that in terms of manpower and salaries, all those things. "

Secretary-General Ban Ki-moon (right) confers with former US ambassador to the UN Richard Holbrooke. UN Photo / Eskinder Debebe.

## The Perm Rep

The US permanent representative has a high-visibility job and
one of the most complicated owing to US geopolitical eminence and
the nature of US policymaking. "The job of an American ambassador at the UN is particularly tough," says former Canadian ambassador David Malone. "Most ambassadors at the UN get one set of
instructions that are channeled through the foreign minister, and
occasionally they will hear from their head of government or head
of state." In the US system, the ambassador's influence may depend
on whether the president gives the post cabinet rank, as Clinton and
Obama did, or places it under the direct authority of the secretary of
state, as George W. Bush did.

Consummate diplomatic skill is required to manage such a complicated chain of command while still accomplishing desired goals
at the UN. "To influence developments, you have to work with the
secretary-general and the Secretariat," comments former UN am-

## US Permanent Representatives to the UN, 1946–2014

Edward R. Stettinius Jr. (March 1946–June 1946)

Herschel V. Johnson (acting) (June 1946–January 1947)

Warren R. Austin (January 1947–January 1953)

Henry Cabot Lodge Jr. (January 1953–September 1960)

James J. Wadsworth (September 1960–January 1961)

Adlai E. Stevenson (January 1961–July 1965)

Arthur J. Goldberg (July 1965–June 1968)

George W. Ball (June 1968–September 1968)

James Russell Wiggins (October 1968–January 1969)

Charles W. Yost (January 1969–February 1971)

George H. W. Bush (February 1971–January 1973)

John P. Scali (February 1973–June 1975)

Daniel P. Moynihan (June 1975–February 1976)

William W. Scranton (March 1976–January 1977)

Andrew Young (January 1977–April 1979)

Donald McHenry (April 1979–January 1981)

Jeane J. Kirkpatrick (February 1981–April 1985)

Vernon A. Walters (May 1985–January 1989)

Thomas R. Pickering (March 1989–May 1992)

Edward J. Perkins (May 1992–January 1993)

Madeleine K. Albright (February 1993–January 1997)

Bill Richardson (February 1997–September 1998)

Peter Burleigh, Chargé d'Affaires (September 1998–August 1999)

Richard C. Holbrooke (August 1999–January 2001)

John D. Negroponte (September 2001–June 2004)

John C. Danforth (June 2004–January 2005)

John R. Bolton (August 2005–December 2006)

Zalmay M. Khalilzad (April 2007–January 2009)

Susan E. Rice (January 2009–July 2013)

Samantha Power (August 2013–present)

bassador Zalmay Khalilzad about his approach to diplomacy, "but you also need to convince sufficient UN members to have decisions made." Compared with Afghanistan and Iraq, which were his previous ambassadorial postings, "it's a very divergent assignment" because "you are not coming to a sovereign entity, and the secretary-general is not a president or a prime minister." Khalilzad was also mindful of his base in the US government. He saw himself as the "bridge between the administration and the UN headquarters," explaining "both the opportunities and the challenges that the UN presents to people in Washington."

David Malone suggests that US Ambassador Richard Holbrooke felt sufficient support in Washington to define a "Holbrooke policy" at the UN and to expect others to follow it. Amazingly, says Malone, they generally did. "Nobody really spoke back to him. He had the ear of the president. The vice president liked and respected him. . . . He essentially made policy on every subject that he discussed at the UN, and he then advised Washington on what their policy was henceforth to be. That said, it's clear he often took the pulse of Washington and chose his key issues carefully. It was a very interesting performance."

### Three-Ring Circus

On being an ambassador to the UN: "You don't have complete control over your schedule; things come up all of a sudden. It's a bit like a three-ring circus. You've got the General Assembly, the Security Council, the six [General Assembly] committees. Things can come up in those committees that need your attention."
—John Negroponte, former US ambassador to the UN

Few permanent representatives have assumed office under more difficult conditions than John Negroponte, appointed by President George W. Bush and sworn in as US representative to the UN on September 18, 2001, only one week after the 9/11 terrorist attacks on

SS

ADOR

AN AMBASSADOR

teenth of September," he noted in an interview given shortly after
his appointment, "and my experience has been very much shaped
by the events of September 11 and our response to that."

Negroponte needed all his diplomatic skills as US permanent
representative, although he used them very differently than in his
previous posts. In some of his former diplomatic assignments,
when he was ambassador to Mexico and to the Philippines, for example, he had time to become an expert on the nation and its culture, but at the UN he had to deal with an endless variety of people
and issues. "To be a representative here, you have to know a little
bit about a lot of issues. And managing your own time so you make
sure you know what you need to know in order to be effective is a
challenge because some days on your agenda there are three or four
various conflicts that come up."

After Negroponte left the UN to become ambassador to Iraq in
2004, John C. Danforth became permanent representative. A lawyer and former politician with foreign affairs experience, Danforth
spent eighteen years as a Republican senator from Missouri before
retiring—he thought—from full-time public life. After Danforth's
departure in early 2005, the White House made a controversial appointment in John R. Bolton, under secretary of state for arms control and international security, who was perceived by some in and
out of Congress as unfriendly to the UN. Indeed, Congress refused
to approve Bolton's appointment, and the new permanent representative served in what was effectively an interim position before
resigning at the end of 2006. During his tenure Bolton helped secure Security Council sanctions against North Korea for its nuclear
program.

John Bolton was succeeded by Zalmay Khalilzad, an experienced
diplomat whose more traditional diplomatic style offered a sharp
contrast to Bolton's lawyerly approach. Longtime UN insider Mark
Malloch-Brown recalls having coffee with Khalilzad in September
2007 in the General Assembly's delegates lounge, where "even the
coffeemaker considered himself Zal Khalilzad's best friend."

## Pointed Messages

We commonly think of diplomats as writers and speakers, persons accustomed to communicating in words. But nonverbal communication finds a place, too. Madeleine Albright, who served as US permanent representative to the UN (1993–97) and later US secretary of state, became known for wearing jewelry that was intended to send a message. As she writes in her book, *Read My Pins: Stories from a Diplomat's Jewel Box*, communication by jewelry began by accident, when Albright was negotiating with representatives of Saddam Hussein's regime, after its forces had been ejected from Kuwait by a US-led coalition acting with the UN's blessing. The terms that ended the Gulf War required that the Hussein regime accept UN inspections to ferret out any weapons of mass destruction. The dictator's refusal to honor the agreement brought criticism from Ambassador Albright, which in turn led the government-controlled Iraqi media to publish an unflattering poem entitled "To Madeleine Albright, Without Greetings."

Not long after, when Albright met with Iraqi officials, she mulled over what jewelry she should wear. She selected a pin, bought years before, in the image of a serpent. "I didn't consider the gesture a big deal and doubted that the Iraqis even made the connection," she wrote. When leaving the meeting, however, she met a member of the UN press corps, who asked why she had worn that particular pin. "As the television cameras zoomed in on the brooch I smiled and said that it was just my way of sending a message."

## The Obama Administration

When Barack Obama was elected president in 2008, he promptly nominated a close adviser, Susan E. Rice, as the new UN ambassador. Educated at Stanford University and later Oxford, Rice quickly gained a reputation for toughness. "If I were to characterize her," remarked her friend Madeleine Albright, "whether it's playing basketball or anything else, she's fearless." Rice served as UN specialist on the Clinton National Security Council staff and then became an assistant secretary of state for Africa. During those years she

Samantha Power, US ambassador to the UN, addresses a Security Council emergency meeting on Ukraine, March 1, 2014. UN Photo / Mark Garten.

witnessed the aftermath of the Rwanda genocide, including fields strewn with mutilated corpses, and resolved that the world must not allow such acts to occur again. Rice cited among her accomplishments as perm rep the Security Council's vote to authorize NATO strikes in Libya and additional sanctions against North Korea for its nuclear weapons program and against Iran for its aggressive uranium enrichment program.

When Rice moved on to become the president's national security adviser, in Obama's second term, she was replaced at the UN by Samantha Power, an Irish-born academic and journalist who wrote an award-winning book on genocide and became a foreign policy adviser to candidate and later president Obama. Like one of her predecessors, John Bolton, Power had to make a quick and sharp transition, from a world where people called a spade a spade to one where they usually preferred the term "manufactured digging instrument." Like Bolton, she can talk about the UN bluntly. When she accepted her new post in a speech at the White House, she remarked that in her journalist assignments she had seen UN aid workers "enduring shellfire to deliver food to the people of Sudan. Yet I've also seen U.N. peacekeepers fail to protect the people of Bosnia" and raised the pressing question "of what the United Nations can accomplish for the world and for the United States."

Whatever the office's rank, many of the US permanent representatives have cited its high-profile nature as giving it a quality all its own. John Danforth remarked that the difference came home to him, quite literally, only a few days after he assumed his post in New York, when he opened the morning newspaper and saw a front-page story presenting his comments at the UN the previous day with the opening "the US says." Turning to his wife, he quipped, "That's me. I am the United States when I speak." He found it "a very sobering moment."

CHAPTER 6

# The Security Council

*In order to ensure prompt and effective action by the United Nations, its Members confer on the Security Council primary responsibility for the maintenance of international peace and security, and agree that in carrying out its duties under this responsibility the Security Council acts on their behalf.*

—UN Charter

The Security Council is the United Nations' enforcer, charged with making the world a safer, more stable place by preventing or stopping armed conflict among and even within nations. It has the authority to examine any conflict or dispute that might have international repercussions and to decide matters affecting the fate of governments, establish peacekeeping missions, create tribunals to try persons accused of war crimes, apply economic sanctions to misbehaving governments, and in extreme cases declare a nation to be fair game for corrective action by other member states. It is the only UN principal organ whose resolutions are binding on member states, which means that governments do not have the option of choosing which of the council's decisions they will or will not accept and help implement.

The council's preeminent authority has made it increasingly popular as the prime center of activity whenever a major international crisis erupts. After the Cold War, when East-West relations began to thaw, the council became much more active and more willing to extend its reach. The number of its formal meetings and informal consultations has fluctuated over the years, from 117 in 1988 to 532 in 2002 and to 373 in 2012.

## A Hands-On Council

Since 1988 the Security Council has evolved—a point stressed by Edward Luck, who for several years was an assistant secretary-general and special adviser to Secretary-General Ban Ki-moon. An expert about the council, he remarks that "people forget how the council has changed over the years. Some say it is archaic, created in 1945, but if you look at its working methods since the mid-1990s, it has changed. It's more open." The council is much more likely, nowadays, to invite nonmembers to speak before it and to ask advice from UN officials and agencies. Council members sometimes make on-site visits to peacekeeping missions or other UN operations. "It is an interactive council," claims Luck. "It doesn't just sit on Mount Olympus."

Stewart Patrick sees the Security Council, and the UN generally, as "really indispensable," a place "where we can go explain ourselves and where we can get legitimacy for US purposes if we explain them and the intention is right. We don't always win, but we couldn't turn our back on the United Nations without extreme damage to our reputation and our national interest." When the United States and its allies decided to invade Iraq in 2003 and topple the Saddam Hussein regime, the Bush administration tried unsuccessfully to gain the council's backing for invasion. After the war, the US government worked hard to mend its fences with the UN and encouraged the world body to become more closely involved in the shattered country's reconstruction and reconciliation. According to Edward Luck, "people throughout much of the world" have come to accept that the council's authorization is "either mandatory or highly preferable prior to the use of force." Luck sees that as a significant development. "Hardheaded realists should take note, for something is changing in terms of international norms and public perceptions regarding the rules of warfare, the use of force, and sources of legitimacy."

## Subsidiary Bodies

The council's need to stay abreast of a wide array of global issues has led it to establish subsidiary bodies, committees that monitor specific places or issues of concern. A recent list of such bodies includes some forty entries, ranging from Afghanistan to Counterterrorism to Children in Armed Conflict, although most concern the implementation of UN sanctions (discussed below). The "penholders" for situation-specific agenda items usually take the lead in drafting council resolutions. Subsidiary bodies can also provide the organizational basis for many of the fact-finding activities that the council undertakes. For example, US Ambassador Susan Rice participated in Security Council missions to Haiti, to assess the security situation and the work of the UN Stabilization Mission in Haiti (MINUSTAH), and to West Africa.

## P5 and E10

The Security Council consists of fifteen members. China, France, the Russian Federation, the United Kingdom, and the United States, known as the Permanent Five, or P5, hold their seats by authority of the Charter. The other ten, the E10, are elected by the General Assembly to two-year terms. The council is presided over by the president, whose office rotates monthly according to the English alphabetical listing of council member states.

The Permanent Five carry special weight in the council, in part because of their permanent status and their historical importance as powerful nations and in part because each holds a trump card in the form of a veto. When a P5 member votes no on a resolution, that kills it, even if the other fourteen council members vote yes. The veto was more common when the world was divided into communist and noncommunist blocs, but it remains a potent fac-

Members of the Security Council arrive in Juba, South Sudan, August 12, 2014. UN Photo/JC McIlwaine.

Table 1. Security Council meetings, resolutions, and vetoes, 1998–2012

| Year | Meetings | Resolutions Considered | Resolutions Adopted | US Vetoes | Chinese Vetoes | Russian Vetoes |
|---|---|---|---|---|---|---|
| 2012 | 199 | 55 | 53 | 0 | 2 | 2 |
| 2011 | 235 | 68 | 66 | 1 | 1 | 1 |
| 2010 | 210 | 59 | 59 | 0 | 0 | 0 |
| 2009 | 194 | 49 | 48 | 0 | 0 | 1 |
| 2008 | 244 | 66 | 65 | 0 | 1 | 1 |
| 2007 | 202 | 57 | 56 | 0 | 1 | 1 |
| 2006 | 272 | 89 | 87 | 2 | 0 | 0 |
| 2005 | 235 | 71 | 71 | 0 | 0 | 0 |
| 2004 | 216 | 62 | 59 | 2 | 0 | 1 |
| 2003 | 208 | 69 | 67 | 2 | 0 | 0 |
| 2002 | 238 | 70 | 68 | 2 | 0 | 0 |
| 2001 | 192 | 54 | 52 | 2 | 0 | 0 |
| 2000 | 167 | 52 | 50 | 0 | 0 | 0 |
| 1999 | 124 | 67 | 65 | 0 | 1 | 0 |
| 1998 | 116 | 73 | 73 | 0 | 0 | 0 |

*Source:* Adapted from US Department of State, Voting Practices in the United Nations, 2012: "Security Council Resolutions," http://www.state.gov/p/io/rls/rpt/c57662.htm; and Global Policy Forum, "Changing Patterns in the Use of the Veto in the Security Council," www.globalpolicy.org/security/data/vetotab.htm.

tor in Security Council deliberations. Both Russia and China used the veto in 2011, 2012, and 2014 to kill resolutions about the Syrian civil war, which US ambassador Samantha Power characterized as "the most catastrophic humanitarian crisis any of us has seen in a generation." The threat of a veto has not kept council members from proposing resolutions on Syria, but it has reduced their chance of gaining approval. In 2014 negotiations did lead to approval of a council resolution (2139) that called upon the Syrian government and its opponents to give humanitarian workers access to those in need of aid. However, the resolution did not speak of intervention, which would likely have prompted a Russian or Chinese veto (table 1).

One result of the council's prestige is that being elected to it is highly coveted by the UN's member states, which campaign for the honor vigorously and sometimes years in advance. Each E10 member serves a two-year term, and candidacies are apportioned through a quota system that the General Assembly has devised based on region: three seats for Africa, two for Latin America and the Caribbean, one for Asia, one for Arab nations, one for Eastern Europe, and two for Western Europe. Sometimes a seat is uncontested because the regional member states have agreed on who should hold it. The African Group, for example, seldom has contested races for the Security Council. Instead, the group rotates candidates based on subregions—Southern Africa, Central Africa, East Africa, North Africa, and West Africa—so that eventually every African nation will have the opportunity to serve for a two-year term.

## Security Council Composition

Permanent Five (P5) members: China, France, Russia, United Kingdom, and United States

Elected members (E10): three African nations, two Latin American and Caribbean nations, one Arab nation, one Asian nation, one Eastern European nation, and two Western European nations

The other regional groups, by contrast, have no fixed rotation on nominations, so nations, like Japan, that covet and pursue the honor are more likely to win a seat than those that are less interested or less influential. Japan did not become a UN member until 1956, yet it has held a Security Council seat ten times since then. At the other extreme is Saudi Arabia, a UN member since 1945, which finally won a Security Council seat in 2013 and then became the first member state ever to decline the honor, citing as its reason the inability of the Security Council to solve the Palestinian issue or to act decisively in the Syrian civil war.

## The P5 Club

Acting as a sort of club, the Permanent Five usually play a leading role in deliberations. Although the Security Council has a small membership compared with the General Assembly and tries to operate by consensus, it works most efficiently and effectively when one of the P5 exercises leadership. According to Jeffrey Laurenti, "The US is such a big power that it has enormous clout in the Security Council as its de facto 'majority, leader,' putting together the votes and resources to make things happen. The issues that arise there are generally those that most people and most governments acknowledge should be dealt with to some degree, and the United States is in a position to do things about them more than most members of the council." Given its clout, the United States can take a leading role in framing the council's agenda, especially when it sees advantages for its own international interests and policies. As Madeleine Albright notes, the UN's ability to intervene in certain emergencies often reduces the job of the United States. "This serves our interest because when the United States intervenes alone, we pay all of the costs and run all of the risks. When the UN acts, we pay a quarter of the costs, and others provide the vast majority of troops."

### Source of Legitimacy

The Security Council is "the most important international body in the world. Countries give it legitimacy because it can authorize the use of force for peacemaking or even a war, as in Korea, Kuwait, and Afghanistan."
—Richard Holbrooke, former US ambassador to the UN

The United Kingdom and France also play leading roles in the council. David Malone says they "work much harder than any of the other permanent members to come up with initiatives in areas far and wide. They send people of extraordinary skill to the council.

. . . They have hit the ground running faster than anyone else. The British are notorious for always having a draft in their back pocket. For these countries, their permanent membership really matters to their international identity precisely because their role in the world has shrunk. They're working very hard to stay permanent members of the Security Council."

The Russian Federation and China have emerged as important actors in the Security Council. Immediately after the breakup of the Soviet Union and the end of the Cold War, both nations tended to follow the US lead on the council, but in recent years they have staked out independent positions on certain key issues. "Russia sees its permanent seat as a very important piece of evidence that it's still a great power in the world," says former UN ambassador John Bolton. China has also become more assertive in the council. Says Bolton, "It's more active than I remember it was during the [George H. W.] Bush administration, when they had a largely passive role." Bolton sees China as more reserved than the other members of the P5, "but it's definitely changing and becoming more active, and there is every reason to think that tendency will continue."

The Russians and the Chinese are sensitive to UN resolutions that they believe interfere excessively in a nation's internal affairs. That was their justification for casting vetoes in 2008 against a US-sponsored resolution to impose sanctions on Zimbabwe's president and key personnel because of flawed national elections. As noted above, the Russians and the Chinese cast vetoes in 2011, 2012, and 2014 over proposed resolutions about the Syrian civil war, and in 2014 the Russians vetoed a resolution concerning a major conflict between themselves and Ukraine.

## The Sixth Veto

The E10 also have leverage in the Security Council, not through veto power but through their voting majority. Since it takes nine votes to pass a resolution, it is possible for the E10 to block passage if they vote as a bloc. This voting leverage is sometimes referred to as the "sixth veto."

Casting a veto, March 15, 2014. Vitaly I. Churkin, ambassador of the Russian Federation to the UN, vetoes a draft resolution on independence for Ukraine's Crimea region. The resolution, drafted by the US delegation, received thirteen votes in favor, one against (Russia), and one abstention (China). UN Photo / Eskinder Debebe.

Mark Malloch-Brown cites the UN intervention in Libya as a decisive moment, when the United States and its European allies chose a path of action that unsettled the Russians and the Chinese. When the Libyan government under Muammar Gaddafi ordered its tanks to Benghazi, evidently with the intent of suppressing the uprising there, the Security Council responded, with China and Russia abstaining, by authorizing NATO to conduct airstrikes to protect civilians. The NATO airstrikes succeeded, but they did not cease. Instead, NATO planes helped the rebels counterattack the government forces and eventually take control of the country. That was the problem, according to Malloch-Brown, who argues that the NATO

Tarek Mitri, special representative of the secretary-general and head of the UN Support Mission in Libya, briefs the Security Council, March 10, 2014. UN Photo / Evan Schneider.

strikes went considerably beyond the scope of the Security Council resolution. "There was a feeling that NATO used the resolution to go much further than the Russians and Chinese anticipated," he says. "The resolution to authorize airstrikes turned into a much broader regime-change exercise. It fulfilled the worst fear of those who thought that 'you can never give these guys an unlimited mandate for intervention to rescue civilians from imminent threat without them turning it into a broader mandate to serve their own geopolitical objectives.' It reopened the scars of the Iraq intervention."

His reference to Iraq touches on the Bush administration's decision in 2003 to invade the country and topple the Saddam Hussein regime without having been able to persuade the Security Council that the Iraqi government posed a significant international threat. The Iraqi and Libyan affairs combined, says Malloch-Brown, suggested to the Chinese and the Russians that "any humanitarian resolution is a slippery slope to intervention." Their concern that such resolutions might have hidden agendas has reduced trust among the P5, in his view.

Despite tensions arising from the UN's Libyan intervention, the civil war in Syria, and the conflict in Ukraine, the P5 have continued to find common ground on many important issues, even those in the turbulent Middle East. China, Russia, and the United States had no problem reaching a consensus position, for example, in the summer of 2014 when an especially aggressive group of fighters began taking over parts of Syria and Iraq and establishing what they called the Islamic State in Syria (ISIS). The group's remarkably and intentionally brutal methods against civilians, including the beheading of captives, brought condemnation from the world community and swift action in the Security Council. On August 15, 2014, the council unanimously passed Resolution 2170, placing sanctions on six key individuals associated with ISIS and another extremist group, Al-Nusra Front. It also demanded that these groups leave Syria and Iraq, condemned the recruitment of foreign fighters, and also condemned direct or indirect trade with the two groups. The quick response of the P5 calls to mind a remark by former US ambassador John Negroponte: "It's axiomatic that the solid achievements of the Security Council have tended to be when the P5 can act in harmony or consensus. If there is either strong disagreement or reluctance by one or more of the P5 members, that's when you start getting into difficulties."

## UN Sanctions

Among the Security Council's most frequently used tools to influence a country's or armed group's behavior is the sanction, a mechanism aimed at limiting or preventing interaction with the outside world in certain ways, such as engaging in trade or acquiring arms. Travel bans, the freezing of personal assets held in foreign countries, and diplomatic restrictions are also types of sanction. According to Secretary-General Ban Ki-moon, sanctions work best as a means of persuasion, not punishment.

## More Is Fewer

"The reality is that the more important the decision in the Security Council, the fewer the states that are involved in it. When you get to a really crucial moment like the Syrian chemical weapons crisis, that's not even the P5 making the decisions, that's the US and Russians. After the 2013 [North Korean] nuclear test the council actually came up with a pretty tough resolution, but that was negotiated bilaterally by the US and Chinese. Then the other P5 countries got it and then the rest of the council just waved it through."                —Richard Gowan, New York University

## Sweeping Iraq Sanctions

Sanctions have a long history at the UN but did not become common until the 1990s, when they seemed to offer an efficient and inexpensive way of pressuring nations and groups that threaten international peace and security. Soon it became evident, however, that sanctions might unintentionally harm civilians, too. Sometimes the poorest or most vulnerable members of society are most harmed when their nation is placed under a sanction, especially one affecting trade and commerce. Consider the case of Saddam Hussein's authoritarian regime in Iraq after the Gulf War.

When Iraq invaded Kuwait in 1990, the UN imposed sweeping sanctions intended to bar the aggressor from all foreign trade and financial dealings, except those with humanitarian purposes. After the United States and its allies, with the UN's blessing, routed the Iraqi armed forces and arranged a ceasefire (which the UN monitored) in 1991, the UN left the sanctions in place while stipulating that Iraq divest itself of weapons of mass destruction. Because the Iraqi government was not fully cooperating with inspections, the UN continued the sanctions through the years of the Saddam Hussein regime.

The Iraqi government was able to evade some of the sanctions, for the benefit of regime members, while complaining noisily and hypocritically that its citizens were being deprived of access to vital medicines, food, and other necessities. This campaign influenced the Security Council to create the Oil-for-Food Program, which gave the Iraqi government the option of exporting specified amounts of crude oil, under UN scrutiny, to pay for "humanitarian goods." Terms of the program were liberalized in 1998 and 1999 and again in 2002 to give Iraq access to most civilian goods. The last liberalization was done through a Security Council resolution offered by the United States in May 2002. The idea behind the resolution was to enable Iraqi citizens to get necessities more easily while making it harder for Saddam Hussein's regime to use trade to obtain arms and other forbidden items. Implementation of the program, however, was associated with accusations of financial corruption that touched even the UN, to the embarrassment of Secretary-General Kofi Annan. On May 22, 2003, two months after the US-led invasion of Iraq, the Security Council lifted the sanctions except for the sale of weapons and related matériel.

## Use of Force

*From the UN Charter, Chapter VII*

ARTICLE 42

Should the Security Council consider that measures provided for in Article 41 [which excludes the use of armed force] would be inadequate or have proved to be inadequate, it may take such action by air, sea, or land forces as may be necessary to maintain or restore international peace and security. Such action may include demonstrations, blockades, and other operations by air, sea, or land forces of Members of the United Nations.

## Targeted Sanctions

The unsatisfactory dealings with the Saddam Hussein regime led the Security Council to refine its ideas about sanctions and give them more bite with less harm to innocent parties. To give the concept of targeted sanctions some specificity, consider the elements of Security Council Resolution 1718, passed only days after North Korea tested a nuclear device on October 9, 2006. The test violated terms of the Nuclear Test Ban Treaty, which the North Korean government had signed, and was done against the expressed wishes of the council. Members of the council were especially alarmed because North Korea had also been testing medium-range missiles capable of transporting nuclear warheads—which raised a nightmare scenario of nuclear proliferation, of placing powerful weapons in the hands of an unpredictable rogue regime.

## Fleeting Alliances

"There are many points of view in the Security Council, and no permanent alliances on anything. There are a series of key positions that need to be accommodated, and this is getting more scary for countries that don't have a clear sense of where they stand internationally or where their next aid check is coming from."
—Colin Keating, former New Zealand ambassador to the UN

Resolution 1718 passed unanimously. It mandated that the Democratic People's Republic of Korea (North Korea) should "suspend all activity related to its ballistic missile program, abandon all nuclear weapons and programs, and abandon all weapons of mass destruction in a complete, verifiable, and irreversible manner." Representatives of various governments addressed the council after the vote, and almost all of them pointedly noted that the sanctions were not an end in themselves but a means to persuade North Korea to change its behavior, in which case the sanctions would be lifted. Speakers also emphasized that the sanctions were meant to put pressure on North Korea's leaders, not its citizens. As the British ambassador said, the resolution was "targeted at stopping the weapons of mass destruction and missile programmes and changing the behavior of those in authority in Pyongyang. It is not aimed at the people of North Korea, who are already suffering greatly."

Sanctions

*From the UN Charter, Chapter VII*

ARTICLE 41

The Security Council may decide what measures not involving the use of armed force are to be employed to give effect to its decisions, and it may call upon the Members of the United Nations to apply such measures. These may include complete or partial interruption of economic relations and of rail, sea, air, postal, telegraphic, radio and other means of communication, and the severance of diplomatic relations.

The nature of the sanction's targeting becomes apparent from the list of prohibited materials and actions. The list begins, predictably, with a section called "Arms Embargo," which requires UN member states to prevent the North Korean government from obtaining nuclear technology and such military equipment as combat aircraft, missile systems, and warships.

In the next section, luxury items are listed as a prohibited category, as if fancy chocolates and fine whiskey represented a threat to world peace. What was the Security Council thinking? After the sanctions vote and the ensuing speeches, many ambassadors and staffers were trading quips about how the ban on luxury goods would hit the Pyongyang government officials "where it hurt": in their collective sweet tooth. North Korea's leader, Kim Jong-il, and his cronies were notorious for coveting expensive imported delicacies and goods, exactly the kinds of products that ordinary Koreans could not afford to buy even if they had access to them. In that sense, the ban on luxury goods was as finely targeted as the ban on combat aircraft.

After luxury goods, the sanctions list the freezing of certain financial assets and then move on to another targeted item, personal travel. Kim Jong-il enjoyed getting out of Pyongyang and taking trips to visit his neighbors in China, where he could stretch his legs and pose for the press. The sanctions made that more difficult.

John R. Bolton, US permanent representative to the UN, addresses the Security Council about a nuclear weapons test by North Korea, October 14, 2006. UN Photo / Eskinder Debebe.

His son and successor, Kim Jong-un, must also live in the shadow of the sanctions, which were expanded and refined by the Security Council in 2013, in a vote significant for its strong support from the Chinese government, long considered North Korea's main ally.

The council has imposed similar sanctions on another would-be nuclear power, Iran, for failing to stop a uranium enrichment program despite passage of a Security Council resolution in 2006 demanding its cessation. Like North Korea, Iran has tested medium-range missiles that could carry atomic warheads, and it is possible that at some future date Iran will enter the club of nuclear powers, contrary to the provisions of the Nuclear Test Ban Treaty, which the Tehran government has signed. The Security Council passed another package of sanctions, Resolution 1929, in 2010, aimed at certain of Iran's businesses and shipping companies.

One of the strongest supporters of the Iran sanctions is the US government, which has consistently favored them as "an important

Deputy Secretary-General Mark Malloch-Brown and US Secretary of State Condoleezza Rice confer during a Security Council meeting on the Middle East, August 2006. UN Photo / Evan Schneider.

tool to prompt change of behavior of regimes that threaten international peace and security," to quote a State Department report. In keeping with this policy, the US government has pushed hard for additional UN sanctions against Iran, especially in the energy and financial sectors. There is speculation that the economic pinch of sanctions may have been a factor in the June 2013 presidential election, which put a less confrontational speaker at the head of Iran's government.

## Other Ways of Thinking about Security

Traditionally, the Security Council has viewed security as an issue of freedom from physical assault. The Universal Declaration of Human Rights, however, lists an array of securities, among them freedom from hunger, the right to adequate housing and decent employment, and the right to adequate health care, among others (see appendix B). Does the Security Council also oversee these forms of security? Historically the answer has been no. Rather, the council has left these matters to other parts of the UN system, especially the General Assembly and various agencies, programs, and commissions established to address issues like food supply, disaster relief, and health care.

This has its logic, because the Security Council imagines itself not so much an administrative system as an executive body for dealing with crises. However, the council did formally address a health-related issue for the first time, in January 2000, on the grounds that vital security interests were at stake. US ambassador Richard Holbrooke set a precedent by persuading the Security Council to discuss the impact of the AIDS crisis in Africa at a meeting chaired by US vice president Al Gore. A State Department report notes that although the discussion was "controversial at the time," it set the stage for later council meetings and a resolution about AIDS and caused language about HIV/AIDS to be included in peacekeeping resolutions.

The council took up another emerging area of threat in April 2007, when it debated climate change, specifically global warming. The daylong meeting was called by the United Kingdom to examine the relationship among energy needs, security, and climate. More than fifty delegates spoke, and although they generally agreed on the need for action about climate change, they disagreed on whether the Security Council was the right venue for discussing the issue. The representative from China made the point that even though climate change might have security implications, it was essentially an issue of sustainable economic development. He proposed that further discussions about the topic be conducted in the appropriate international forums, using such established frameworks as the Kyoto Protocol (which we discuss in a later chapter). The Egyptian representative declared that the issue of climate change actually lay within the mandate of other UN bodies, specifically the General Assembly and the Economic and Social Council.

Several other representatives made a similar point, and in doing so, they were alluding to a growing point of disagreement among member states. The expanded concept of security has been greeted as a welcome change by several major powers, especially the United States, which regard the council as the most effective place to address many of the world's most pressing problems. Among developing nations, however, the attitude is often very different. Pakistan's former permanent representative, Munir Akram, criticizes the council for encroaching on territory that he claims the Charter reserves to the General Assembly, which is dominated by the voting power of the less developed nations. During the past decade, he asserts, the Security Council has "begun to assume many functions that were originally intended for the General Assembly."

Council resolutions now address such issues as terrorism, nuclear nonproliferation, civilians in armed conflict, and violence against women and children. In October 2006, for example, the council held its first debate on the role of women in the consolidation of peace. The United States gave examples of how women have contributed to peace processes throughout the world, including Sierra Leone, the Democratic Republic of the Congo, and Nepal. The council also urged that peacekeeping operations take better account of gender issues and encouraged member states to place more women in peacekeeping operations. Violence against women during times of conflict has also drawn attention in the council. A debate in June 2013 addressed accountability for crimes of sexual violence on the national level and ways the UN can help countries bring perpetrators to account. As a signal of its determination to prevent sexual violence, the Security Council then passed Resolution 2106, which, among other things, urged UN sanctions committees to apply targeted sanctions against parties committing sexual violence during armed conflict.

The council's debate on gender related directly to peacemaking and peacekeeping, which are historic concerns of the UN. Munir Akram argues, however, that "these issues belong to the General Assembly. They are not part of the mandate of the Security Council, which is very tightly described in the Charter, which says the Secu-

At break during a Security Council meeting on energy, security, and climate, on April 17, 2007, Ján Kubis, foreign minister of Slovakia, speaks with Margaret Beckett, secretary of state for foreign and commonwealth affairs of the United Kingdom, as Bert Koenders (second from the right), minister for development cooperation of the Netherlands, and Emry Jones Parry (far right), permanent representative of the United Kingdom, look on. UN Photo / Evan Schneider.

rity Council is the primary organ, not the sole organ, responsible for the maintenance of international peace and security and to respond to threats to international peace and security." Strictly speaking, says Akram, the council should not be addressing "sector issues," such as terrorism or proliferation, "where there is no imminent threat to peace." So, for example, he has no problem with Security Council Resolution 1267 against al-Qaeda and the Taliban, "but beyond that, to deal with the systemic issue of terrorism as a phenomenon, that is something that rightly should be addressed by the entire membership."

Ambassador Akram's critique is part of the growing North-South tension within the UN that fuels much of the dynamic between the council and the General Assembly. The preference of Akram and his colleagues to describe the dynamic as one between the wealthy nations, on one hand, and the less affluent or poor nations, on the other, gives the discussion a remarkably social- and economic-class flavor, but applied to the entire globe. We will return to it in the next chapter.

## Restructuring the Security Council

Many UN member states have been urging a change in the Security Council to make it more reflective of today's international realities. Since the council was created in 1945, more than a hundred nations have come into existence, and a number of developing nations have recently become economic and trade dynamos. Recognizing the need to bring more member states into the council, the UN amended the charter in 1965 to increase Security Council membership from eleven to fifteen, which it is today, half a century later. There is a wide agreement among the member states that another expansion of the council is needed, and Secretary-General Ban Ki-moon has described the restructuring of the council as an "urgently needed reform."

Urgency has not led to action, however. To begin with, no restructuring can occur without the approval of the P5. That immediately removes from discussion any thought of eliminating or modifying the veto. The P5 are unlikely to agree to any change that would diminish their unique position in the UN system, and certainly not the veto, which each nation sees as its protection against Security Council resolutions that it might find objectionable.

Even if the United States and other P5 members were to embrace a restructuring, that would not resolve the sharp differences of opinion among other member states about which of them should be admitted to an enlarged council. "The problem, of course, is that the community remains quite divided," observes Stewart Patrick. Member states figuring most often as possible candidates are Brazil, India, Japan, Nigeria, Pakistan, and South Africa, but others are also mentioned. Members of major regional groupings, such as Africa and Asia, have been unable to agree on which of them should be selected for a permanent council seat. "The biggest impediment is the African bloc," says Patrick, "which has an unrealistic and quite maximal stance," referring to the effort to include no fewer than three African nations (with vetoes) on the council. Some states feel strongly that certain of their neighbors should definitely not become permanent members, particularly with veto power. Many insiders believe, for example, that China is unlikely to agree to having either Japan or India as a permanent, veto-holding member. In the absence of robust follow-up from Washington, notes Patrick, "the Chinese and Russians are quite happy to sit back and allow US silence to speak volumes, and so it doesn't put any pressure on them."

## Too Big to Work?

On restructuring the Security Council: "Any expansion risks making the council unworkable because it would become so big. If you expand it, you will just have more side groups to work out things. You can't have an efficient body and negotiate with twenty-six people on it."
—Nancy Soderberg, former US diplomat at the UN

Despite the obvious barriers to action, member states and their backers continue to devise plans for restructuring. Most of them address one or more of several key issues, such as the council's size, whether there should be a veto and, if so, who should have it, and fair representation of the world's major regions (Africa, Asia, Latin America, etc.). Because the General Assembly is the UN organ that would ultimately vote on a plan, that is where much of the discussion occurs.

The restructuring schemes are typically presented by informal groups within the UN membership, and these alignments can change over time. The African Group, consisting of the fifty-four member states from Africa, is coordinated by the Committee of Ten, or C10, made up of Algeria, the Democratic Republic of the Congo, Equatorial Guinea, Kenya, Libya, Namibia, Senegal, Sierra Leone, Uganda, and Zambia. It has favored new permanent seats with veto rights. However, South Africa and Nigeria are thought to be flexible on veto rights. The Group of Four, or G4, consisting of Brazil, Germany, India, and Japan, has preferred to add permanent seats but is flexible on veto rights. In 2012 it gathered almost eighty supporters for a draft resolution on adding permanent members, but the resolution did not mention veto rights. India, Brazil, and approximately forty other member states, many of them small island nations, constitute the L69 group, which favors new permanent seats with veto rights. Uniting for Consensus, or UfC, whose core members are Argentina, Canada, Colombia, Costa Rica, Italy, Malta, Mexico, Pakistan, the Republic of Korea, San Marino, Spain, and Turkey, has opposed new permanent seats and proposed a compromise model with longer-term and renewable seats. In a statement by the Italian ambassador Sebastiano Cardi, it has claimed that there is broad support among UN members for increasing the size of the council to at least twenty-five seats, a 60 percent enlargement.

One aspirant nation is Pakistan, whose former permanent representative, Munir Akram, analyzes the reform push as relying on several factors, beginning with the desire of "certain countries who think that they have now graduated to become great powers, to get a seat at the high table." Another factor is "the determination of those who have the power now, sitting at the high table, not to broaden the table too much except for their closest friends." The rest of the UN membership, consisting mainly of poor countries, "is worried that the oligarchy of power is going to be extended, at their expense, and that they will remain the proletariat while this extended oligarchy will continue to rule." These "proletarians" have no major national interest in rooting for one side or the other, although "the high-ranking powers are able to influence some small countries to support them."

Stewart Patrick acknowledges the reluctance of the P5 to share their authority, but he raises an interesting point. The incoming Obama administration studied the restructuring issue as part of its effort to engage with the United Nations in a broader, more multilateral way, says Patrick. During the course of the study several of the aspirant member states were elected members of the Security Council, and their behavior there, he argues, gave the administration pause. He is referring to the fact that Brazil and India abstained from voting on a US-backed Security Council resolution to approve NATO intervention in the civil war in Libya. Patrick attributes the inaction of the aspirant states to their different perspective on international affairs. Many developing nations, he notes, even democracies, "don't see the world in the same way [as the US]." They "have their own aspirations. They either have postcolonial mindsets or developing-country solidarity. Some are members of the Nonaligned Movement; some like Brazil are members of the G-77, a large a coalition of developing countries. They have rather more traditional interpretations of national sovereignty. They don't like sanctions, much less the use of force."

Informal discussions aside, the General Assembly has a committee devoted solely to a restructuring of the council. It bears the catchy name of Open-Ended Working Group on the Question of Equitable Representation on and Increase in the Membership of the Security Council. UN insiders often refer to it as the Never-Ending Open-Ended Working Group on the Question of Equitable Representation on and Increase in the Membership of the Security Council, because it has met for two decades without reaching a consensus on a "framework resolution" for consideration by the full assembly. "I'm not making any predictions about the future, but your kids will be grown up by the time we all wrap this up," declared John Ashe, president of the General Assembly, at a news conference in 2013, where he complained about a lack of political will to address council reform.

Brian Urquhart is not surprised. A UN insider since the organization's earliest days, he is convinced that Security Council reform is not easy, and for a single, simple reason: because "national prestige makes it extremely difficult to arrange." Many insiders would agree with his assessment, but the question of when and how the council might be changed seems to fascinate Americans nonetheless. Whenever I speak before groups of students or other members of the public, I am invariably asked for an opinion on this thorny issue, one that the Never-Ending Open-Ended Working Group is still pondering.

## CHAPTER 7

# The General Assembly

*The General Assembly shall consist of all the Members of the United Nations.*
—UN Charter

The General Assembly is a principal organ of the United Nations, its main deliberative body. Since the UN's founding in 1945 the assembly's membership has grown fourfold, from 51 original members to 99 in 1960, to 159 in 1990, up to its current total of 193 when South Sudan joined the UN in 2011. It typically deals with a varied and large number of agenda items during its annual three-month session, held from September to December. For many, the General Assembly is synonymous with the parade of world leaders who travel to New York each fall to address the UN body to offer their perspective on important issues of the day. Its real role, of course, is much more complicated than that.

## More and Less than Meets the Eye

Both more and less than it appears, the General Assembly was modeled on national parliaments, yet it has a global purview and visibility that no national legislature can match. It is a place where

Secretary-General Ban Ki-moon (shown on screens) presents his annual report to the General Assembly at the opening of the general
debate of its sixty-sixth session, September 21, 2011. UN Photo / Mark
Garten.

the UN's 193 member states, each having one vote, can address
almost anything imaginable. The UN Charter assigns the General Assembly authority to consider all matters relating to any international issue and any UN body or agency. The assembly commissions studies about international law, human rights, and all
forms of international social, economic, cultural, and educational
cooperation.

Despite the assembly's global representation, its resolutions are
recommendations and are legally binding only when they apply to
UN internal matters. Those domains where it has binding authority
are fundamental to the UN's operations. The assembly approves budgets and decides how much each member state should contribute. It
also elects the rotating members of three principal organs, the Security Council, the Economic and Social Council, and the Trusteeship
Council. In collaboration with the Security Council it elects the judges
of the International Court of Justice and appoints the secretary-general.

Under some conditions the Security Council may ask the General Assembly to meet in special session, and such sessions can also be requested by a majority of member states. Issues deemed more pressing may warrant an emergency special session of the assembly, convened on twenty-four hours' notice at the request of the Security Council or a majority of member states.

## The General Assembly

*From the UN Charter, Chapter IV*

ARTICLE 11

1. The General Assembly may consider the general principles of cooperation in the maintenance of international peace and security, including the principles governing disarmament and the regulation of armaments, and may make recommendations with regard to such principles to the Members or to the Security Council or to both.

2. The General Assembly may discuss any questions relating to the maintenance of international peace and security brought before it by any Member of the United Nations, or by the Security Council, or by a state which is not a Member of the United Nations in accordance with Article 35, paragraph 2, and, except as provided in Article 12, may make recommendations with regard to any such questions to the state or states concerned or to the Security Council or to both. Any such question on which action is necessary shall be referred to the Security Council by the General Assembly either before or after discussion. . . .

ARTICLE 13

1. The General Assembly shall initiate studies and make recommendations for the purpose of:
   a. promoting international co-operation in the political field and encouraging the progressive development of international law and its codification;
   b. promoting international co-operation in the economic, social, cultural, educational, and health fields, and assisting in the realization of human rights and fundamental freedoms for all without distinction as to race, sex, language, or religion. . . .

ARTICLE 17

1. The General Assembly shall consider and approve the budget of the Organization.
2. The expenses of the Organization shall be borne by the Members as apportioned by the General Assembly.
3. The General Assembly shall consider and approve any financial and budgetary arrangements with specialized agencies referred to in Article 57 and shall examine the administrative budgets of such specialized agencies with a view to making recommendations to the agencies concerned.

## Ceremonies and Procedures

The General Assembly starts its official year with opening sessions, usually on the third Tuesday of each September. A week later, at the general debate, which typically lasts about two weeks, world leaders address the assembly on issues they consider important.

### Power Lunch

The secretary-general hosts a luncheon for all the world leaders attending the general debate. Ban Ki-moon took the opportunity at the 2013 luncheon to remark on the singular character of the gathering. "Look around," he urged his listeners. "This is one of the most extraordinary meals anytime of the year . . . anywhere in the world. You cannot have all these Heads of State and Government in one place anywhere [else] in the world. Leaders from all the world's nations are sitting together around a common table."

It is impressive to see the gathering of nearly two hundred heads of state and high dignitaries, some wearing national garb. (For a list of member states see appendix C.) Nowhere else can so many of the world's leaders meet and exchange views, both publicly and privately. Before and after the speeches the air is thick with talk, as presidents, kings, and prime ministers use this rare opportunity to talk with scores of their peers on the sidelines of the assembly.

Then the dignitaries leave and the members get down to substantive work, which lasts until mid-December. For the 68th session, which began in September 2013, the agenda ran to 173 items, arrayed under nine broad categories, from (A) "Promotion of sustained economic growth and sustainable growth" to (I) "Organizational, administrative and other matters." The last category includes finances and runs from item 111 to item 173. Category H, "Drug control, crime prevention and combating international terrorism in all its forms and manifestations," is surprisingly brief (items 108–110), but G, "Disarmament," is extensive, running from items 88 to 107, with some items having many subsections. Under "Maintenance of international peace and security," we find some very general items, like "Situation in the Middle East" and "Question of Palestine," which offer possibilities for endless debate, interspersed with items that come out of another era, like "Consequences of the Iraqi occupation of and aggression against Kuwait" and "Implementation of the Declaration on the Granting of Independence to Colonial Countries and Peoples." Of particular interest to American readers may be the item "Necessity of ending the economic, commercial

## Symbolic Logic

"The General Assembly unfortunately has become a fairly useless body. At the symbolic level, it represents universality at the UN. All countries of the world, virtually, are members of it. But the way it works has meant that it rarely takes meaningful decisions, and it takes so many unmeaningful decisions that it has been largely written off by the media.

"There's one significant function of the General Assembly. It serves as the umbrella for treaty negotiations on everything from the International Criminal Court to treaties on climate change, biodiversity, you name it. The treaties matter tremendously in the conduct of international relations. The assembly has also become more active in human rights."
—David Malone, former Canadian ambassador to the UN

and financial embargo imposed by the United States of America against Cuba," which appears regularly on the agenda. These are only a few of the many topics, major and minor, new and outdated, relevant and irrelevant, political and apolitical, that define the GA's work after the general debate. There are some pressing topics here, but you need to sift through the pile to find them.

General Assembly affairs are marked by a consuming passion for giving every member state some part of the action. There is a strong feeling that everyone should participate in as many decisions, committees, and issues as possible. As a longtime UN insider, Jeffrey Laurenti, observes, "The UN is not a place where the notion of the small getting out of the way of the bigger has much traction. There is a high premium on schmoozing small and mid-level states." The parliamentary and administrative structure of the assembly reflects and embodies this need. At the beginning of each new General Assembly session, the members elect a president, twenty-one vice presidents (yes, twenty-one), and the heads of the six Main Committees that largely run the assembly.

Regional and national rivalries affect the politically charged voting for these positions. Formal and informal mechanisms ensure that the prerogatives and rewards of office are spread around. The presidency, for example, is rotated annually according to geographical region. If a member state from the Latin American and Caribbean region has the presidency one year, a member state from another region must have it the next year. This produces a certain inefficiency that is tolerated because of its perceived greater good.

## Committees

The speeches and debates of the full General Assembly often make good media events and excellent political theater, but they are not necessarily effective means of examining issues in depth and arriving at solutions. For that, the assembly relies heavily on a clutch of committees: a General Committee, a Credentials Committee, and six Main Committees. Committees are common in legislatures worldwide because they enable many issues to be examined simultaneously. In the US Congress, committees consider legislation in the form of "bills," which become "laws" when passed by the House and the Senate and signed by the president. General Assembly committees call their bills "resolutions." Each committee deliberates during the assembly session, votes on issues by simple majority, and sends its draft resolutions to the full assembly for a final vote. General Assembly resolutions, even when passed by vote, are recommendations, not laws, and are not binding.

The General Committee consists of the president, the twenty-one vice presidents, and the heads of the other committees. The Credentials Committee is responsible for determining the accredited General Assembly representatives of each member state. This is usually a pro forma matter except when a nation is divided by civil war and two delegations claim the same seat. Then this normally unobtrusive committee becomes the locus of intense politicking and high emotion. An example involved Afghanistan, where the sitting delegation was challenged by the Taliban regime when it seized power. The Credentials Committee listened to presentations by both sides and then "deferred consideration," effectively confirming the old delegation without explicitly rejecting the claim of the other one. Such sidestepping, or action through inaction, is a classic political ploy.

Each of the six Main Committees has both a number and a name, and either may be used to describe it, but insiders usually use only the number. First Committee (Disarmament and International Security) considers resolutions about global security and weapons of mass destruction, as well as more conventional weapons. Second Committee (Economic and Financial) is responsible for examining economic and social development and international trade, including the reduction of barriers that prevent developing nations from reaching their full export potential. Third Committee (Social, Humanitarian, and Cultural) is concerned with a hodgepodge of issues ranging from disaster relief to human rights. It also deals with international crime, including drugs, human trafficking, and money laundering, as well as government and business corruption. Fourth Committee (Special Political and Decolonization), despite its name, no longer addresses decolonization because there are no more colonies. Instead, it has made peacekeeping its primary mission. The committee also oversees the United Nations Relief and Works Agency for Palestine Refugees in the Near East (UNRWA). Fifth Committee (Administrative and Budgetary) oversees the UN's fiscal affairs and drafts the resolutions for the general budget that the General Assembly votes on. Sixth Committee (Legal) oversees important legal issues, such as human cloning, international terrorism, and war crimes.

### Six Main Committees of the General Assembly

First Committee, Disarmament and National Security
Second Committee, Economic and Financial
Third Committee, Social, Humanitarian, and Cultural
Fourth Committee, Special Political and Decolonization
Fifth Committee, Administrative and Budgetary
Sixth Committee, Legal

## Umbrella for Global Treaties

One of the General Assembly's most significant functions is to serve as a starting point for the many UN treaties (also called "conventions"). As David Malone notes, "The treaties matter tremendously in the conduct of international relations." They matter because most nations take them seriously and because they cover such a broad range of issues, from the welfare of children to protection of the natural environment. The Convention on the Rights of the Child, for example, signed by member states in 1989, recognizes the human rights of persons under age eighteen. Another treaty is the Convention against Torture and Other Cruel, Inhuman or Degrading Treatment or Punishment, whose purpose is pretty obvious; it was adopted by the General Assembly in 1984. The Convention to Combat Desertification in Those Countries Experiencing Serious Drought and/or Desertification, Particularly in Africa has an environmental and economic focus. Its aim is to mobilize governments and resources to protect livable lands from becoming arid. Adopted in Paris in 1994 by an intergovernmental negotiating committee, it was signed by most UN member states within a few years. Yet another treaty is the Convention on the Rights of Persons with Disabilities, adopted by the General Assembly in 2006 and available for signing by member states in March 2007. It acknowledges the right of all persons to participate fully in modern society, no matter their mental or physical limitations.

Any UN body can provide the impetus and organizational structure for a treaty. The World Health Organization (WHO), for example, entered the treaty arena in 2005 when it became the main actor in passage of the WHO Framework Convention on Tobacco Control (WHO FCTC). Adopted by the World Health Assembly on May 21, 2003, and entering into force on February 27, 2005, it was developed to address the globalization of the "tobacco epidemic" by recommending measures to reduce the consumer demand for tobacco products, such as setting higher prices, imposing taxes, and promoting public education about the dangers of tobacco use. WHO has used the convention to formulate a series of measures designed to reduce global tobacco use and thereby protect public health.

A member state becomes a party to a treaty by formally "consenting to be bound" by its terms, usually through the ratification of the treaty, if the treaty is still in the process of being approved by member states, or by "accession" to it if it is already in force. A treaty or convention comes into force once it has been ratified by a sufficient number of UN member states. The Convention on the Rights of the Child, to cite one instance, entered into force on September 2, 1990, a month after the twentieth member state ratified it. For those twenty states, the convention then became a fact of law, and as more states ratified or acceded to the treaty, they too became bound by its terms.

Typically a treaty has an oversight committee, called the convention secretariat, which monitors implementation. Among the duties of the fifteen-member WHO FCTC Convention Secretariat, for example, is to collect regular reports from signatories of the convention, which it makes public. All of this activity occurs under the general oversight of the General Assembly.

## Voting Blocs

One of the more contentious aspects of the General Assembly has been the presence of large voting blocs consisting mainly of developing member states. The UN Charter lays out a two-tier system of voting: important matters like budgets and admission of new members require a two-thirds majority vote to pass, whereas others need only a simple majority. That seems straightforward, except when it collides with the assembly's preference for resolving issues through consensus. Consensus happens about 85 percent of the time, but the process can be slow when nearly two hundred delegates are involved, and according to many UN insiders, the voting blocs only make the process slower.

Nancy Soderberg complains that "it's very difficult to be in the General Assembly because everything is done by consensus." Any decision represents "the lowest common denominator of 193 divergent countries, which is a pretty low standard." This means that the assembly effectively cedes decisive action to the Security Council. As Soderberg says, "Everyone pretends that they don't want to be run by the Security Council, but the key agenda is run by the council. The assembly can put out resolutions on laudatory, amorphous goals, but if you're really going to have an impact and do things, do it through the Security Council."

Insiders like Soderberg, accustomed to the relative speed and decisiveness of the Security Council, chafe at the inefficient and polarized approach in the General Assembly, which they attribute to two large voting blocs, the Nonaligned Movement (NAM), established in 1961, and the Group of 77 (G-77), established in 1964.

The Nonaligned Movement emerged during the Cold War, when the United States and the Soviet Union competed for influence in the world that was emerging through decolonization. Several nations, including India and Yugoslavia, sought to define a middle path that was not aligned with either great power. In those days most NAM

## The Trusteeship Council

Of the six principal organs of the UN, the Trusteeship Council is the least well known, and for good reason. On November 1, 1994, it suspended operations and ceased to exist except on paper. The demise of the council is the result of the UN's important role in decolonization, the process by which some eighty nations have come into existence since 1945. When decolonization began, most of Africa was controlled by a few Western nations, while the Netherlands, the United Kingdom, and France ruled large parts of Asia. Japan had ruled Korea for half a century. Scattered around the world, alongside the colonies, were territories, like Papua, New Guinea, and the Mariana Islands in the Pacific, that had been wards of the League of Nations and were now administered by Australia, the United States, and other nations. Article 75 of the Charter states that "the United Nations shall establish under its authority an international trusteeship system for the administration and supervision of such territories as may be placed thereunder by subsequent individual agreements. These territories are hereinafter referred to as trust territories." The UN wanted to ensure that trustee nations would truly look after the best interests of their charges and help them secure self-government, either on their own or as parts of larger entities. Palau, an island group in the Pacific, was the last trust territory. It became a UN member on December 15, 1994.

members were more closely associated with the Soviet Union than with the United States, recalls Pakistan's former permanent representative Munir Akram, but now "the NAM is more nonaligned than formerly." One member, India, regards itself as a major world power, whereas China, which certainly sees itself as a major power, is not a member of the Nonaligned Movement but works closely with it.

The Group of 77 was established "to coordinate the position of developing countries on trade and development issues," explains Akram. It gradually acquired a sense of identity. "There is diversity in this group," he says, "but there is a sense that on systemic issues of international economic relations their interests are not identical, but convergent, in the sense that all of them have an interest to change the present system of trade, finance, and technology control, because they feel that it is weighted against them or structured in ways that place them at a disadvantage."

The G-77 has a more institutionalized structure than the NAM and is situated within the UN framework. It describes itself as "the largest intergovernmental organization of developing countries in the United Nations," with the goal of enabling "the countries of the South to articulate and promote their collective economic interests and enhance their joint negotiating capacity on all major international economic issues within the United Nations system, and promote South-South cooperation for development."

The G-77 and the NAM exercise power through numbers. In 2013 the NAM had 114 members and 17 observers, and the Group of 77 had 133 members. Add up the numbers and you get 247 members, whereas the UN has only 193, so obviously there is much overlap between the two organizations. The point is that these two bodies can control votes in the General Assembly when they choose to.

Soderberg accuses the blocs of being out of step with current realities. "Look at the Nonaligned Movement," she says. "What are they nonaligned against now? There is no alignment, which means that they are really trying to oppose the United States more often than not, which makes no sense." Richard Holbrooke shared her exasperation. The Nonaligned Movement and the G-77 do tremendous damage because they "just don't serve the interests of most of their members. They are two groups that are pulled by old-school politics."

Akram has a very divergent take on this. A former head of the G-77, he complains that the Security Council is marginalizing the General Assembly through its continual accumulation of power. While admitting some of the criticisms leveled at the assembly— "their resolutions are too long, there are too many reports, there are too many items, that's all true"—he responds that "the same could be said of the Security Council," which "repeats many things that are in previous resolutions." Akram further argues that the Nonaligned Movement and the Group of 77 are potentially vehicles for positive change. The G-77 "can often coordinate its position and take common positions," and it benefits also from a new sense of confidence among the developing countries, in part because a number of them have had successful economic growth and a number are so-called emerging economies. From Akram's perspective, the NAM and the G-77 can potentially contribute to the UN's evolution, as well as to global social and economic development.

Just as clearly, John Bolton says, the regional bloc system "is a contributing factor to the ineffectiveness of the UN because it helps reinforce the status quo and becomes a way for countries to protect and get part of the benefits that accrue from the UN programs. It leads to a scratch-my-back-and-I'll-scratch-yours philosophy. That makes it unlikely you're going to have very effective change or reform."

## Decolonization and the Birth of Nations

Ironically, most of the nations that constitute the G-77 came into existence because of a global movement that the United States strongly supported. The word "decolonization" was on everyone's lips from the 1950s through the 1970s, when some eighty new nations emerged from the ruins of the empires of Belgium, France, the Netherlands, the United Kingdom, and others. After World War II, nationalist uprisings and resistance movements challenged the colonial world order and forced out the ruling nations or persuaded them to relinquish authority. The United States encouraged the UN to be a key player in ending colonization. In fact, one of the most important UN staff members working on anticolonialism was an African American diplomat, Ralph Bunche, who had joined the State Department in 1945 and worked in the San Francisco conference that helped organize the UN that spring.

Insider Brian Urquhart, who knew Bunche well, describes him as the "dynamo" of the decolonization movement "because he knew more about it than anybody else did, including most European colonial experts." Secretary-General Trygve Lie assigned him to the Middle East, where the UN was brokering Britain's withdrawal from its League of Nations mandate in Palestine while the resident Jewish

Heads of state and global leaders at Rio+20, the UN Conference on Sustainable Development, Rio de Janeiro, June 20, 2012. UN Photo / Mark Garten.

population was laying foundations for the new state of Israel. For his central role in negotiating a general settlement among the Israelis, British, Egyptians, and other interested powers, Ralph Bunche was awarded the Nobel Peace Prize in 1950.

The end of colonialism changed the world, and much faster than anyone expected. Decolonization also transformed the UN. The original UN had some fifty member states and operated like a small club. During the decades after 1945, the addition of so many new nations helped produce the Nonaligned Movement and the Group of 77.

## The World's Conference Host

The General Assembly sponsors and hosts conferences, many of which have played a key role in guiding the work of the UN. Since 1994, the UN has held more than a hundred conferences around the world on a variety of issues. High-profile meetings on development issues have put problems like poverty and environmental degradation atop the global agenda. In an effort to make the meetings into global forums that will shape the future of major issues, the UN has encouraged participation of thousands of nongovernmental organizations (NGOs), experts, and others not formally associated with the UN.

A landmark conference that continues to redefine the UN's mission was the Millennium Summit in September 2000, convened as part of the fifty-fifth session of the General Assembly designated the Millennium Assembly (September 12–December 23, 2000); follow-up conferences were held in 2005, 2010, and 2015. The lofty Millennium Development Goals (MDGs), which all member states agreed to meet by 2015, are discussed in chapter 14. To cite only two of many other examples, in 1992, the UN convened a conference on sustainable development known as the Earth Summit, with a major follow-up conference known as Rio+20 in 2012.

## More than a Flow Chart

Like all parts of the UN, the General Assembly is not separate unto itself. It functions as one very significant element in a much bigger entity, in collaboration (and sometimes competition) with the Security Council and the Secretariat, to advance an agenda that is set forth annually and is ultimately defined by the overarching mission of the world body. If life were as simple as an organizational chart, we might now imagine a straightforward, if complicated, schematic of the UN, like the one in chapter 1, and declare that we have solved the puzzle of what the UN is. Except that we must also consider that odd bit of real estate called the UN Village.

## CHAPTER 8

# Rubbing Elbows and Egos in the UN Village

*The amount of psychology in diplomacy is remarkable. States behave very much as human beings. It is very ego driven, I would say. We want to be there, we want to be where decisions are taken.*
—Danilo Türk, former Slovenian ambassador to the UN and assistant secretary-general for political affairs

The United Nations is known for operating in ways that may seem complicated and convoluted. The Secretariat's administrators can have their intricate procedures and protocols, and they follow their proper, not always straight and narrow, channels. The same is true in the General Assembly, where red tape decorates resolutions, studies, reports, and memoranda. In the many UN-related bodies, agencies, and commissions, a passion for creating and filing paper does occasionally obscure the central point of the organization.

When trying to understand the UN, however, it's important not to confuse administrative problems with issues of governance and decision-making. As talk turns into plan and action, the procedures diverge from what bureaucrats are accustomed to, and often the differences are the reason things get done. Then the UN becomes as simple and straightforward a place as can be imagined, because, as David Malone notes, "people really matter at the UN." Furthermore, "anything that happens at the UN happens because of certain individuals." Malone calculates that "at any given time, out of 193 ambassadors, about thirty-five control the game. Within the Security Council four or five ambassadors at any given time are dominant, perhaps a few more, counting the nonpermanent ones. This is also true in each of the General Assembly committees." So, if you know and work well with relevant figures among those thirty-five dominant people, you can do anything. And if you don't, forget it.

## The Village

Think of a small town where decisions are made by groups of key people who know one another and often socialize while standing at street corners or sipping coffee at a café. In fact, this is exactly how Richard Holbrooke described his experience as US permanent representative under President Clinton. Looking back on those sixteen months in New York, he remembered a place he called the UN Village. The village worked through small groups, formal or informal, endless meetings, caucuses, speeches, and meals.

### Where to Find It

Located on the Upper East Side, the UN Village has "its own language and time zone, where 'demand' means 'ask,' 'strong' means 'not so strong,' and 'severe' means 'not so severe,' and 'urges' means 'begs.' All a different lingo. Thousands of people live here who have very little interaction with the rest of the city."
—Richard Holbrooke, former US ambassador to the UN

Former US permanent representative John Negroponte also walked the streets of the UN Village. "I've called on 114 delegates," he remarked when asked about his first few months at the UN. "The diplomatic practice is that if you arrived after another delegate, then you go and call on them. If they've arrived after you have, then they go and see you. The new kid on the block comes around to see you." Negroponte tried even harder to meet with regional groups, where a lot of the business of the UN is done. He visited with the European Union "once every six or eight weeks" and with the South African Development Group, the Economic Council of West African States, and others. "Meeting with" can often mean drinks or dinner, sometimes at the elegant Waldorf Astoria.

There is another side to being a diplomat, however. Governance and decision-making frequently involve levels of persuasion, guile, gall, and secrecy that we would expect to find in a novel or movie about Wall Street. "Years ago, I wanted to talk to a top UN official," recalls former US ambassador Joseph Melrose. "I called her press attaché to arrange the lunch and asked if the official had a particular restaurant that she liked. 'If I were you, I wouldn't have lunch around here,' was the reply. 'I'd go to a restaurant farther removed from the UN, where no one will see the two of you having lunch.' And we did. So I basically started doing that. I would go not to the Japanese restaurant or the ONE UN hotel across the street. I'd take them to a place where we would be less likely to be recognized."

## Diplomatically Speaking

"We're diplomats, so whatever feelings people may have, they're going to be muted, guarded, and careful. I think most diplomats feel that you can disagree without being disagreeable. I think that's part of our work ethic, because otherwise you could live in quite unbearable circumstances."
—John Negroponte, former US ambassador to the UN

But confidentiality goes only so far. In a village where everyone knows everyone else, there are not likely to be many really big secrets, and the quirks and sensitivities of the residents are well known. Residents understand that for any given member state you don't touch certain issues or topics of discussion unless you're prepared for a strong reaction. When socializing with the Chinese

delegates, for example, you might choose not to discuss Tibet. The
Russian delegates may not appreciate being quizzed about their relations with Ukraine, just as the US delegates may not give you lots
of smiles if you ask when Washington expects to lift its economic
sanctions on Cuba.

Within the UN Village are "neighborhoods," some of them pretty
exclusive. Negroponte lived in one of the toniest, the Security Council. As he stated during his tenure, "Most of my dealings are in the
Security Council, which is a fairly small and tight-knit group, and
we meet each other one way or another every day. We get to know
each other pretty well. And so there is a certain camaraderie in the
Security Council." He also had to spend some time in that other
part of town, the General Assembly, where crowds of ordinary nations mill about, shouting and waving their hands. "I think where
the nerves sometimes get a little frayed around the edges as in some
of these big General Assembly special sessions, particularly when
you have to reach consensus on a document. Nerves can get frayed
and you have these marathon meetings that go on until eight in

## A Diplomat Rates the Media

"The professionalism among the reporters at the UN is one of my big dis-
coveries at the Security Council. They knew the background, knew what
to quote, and they also knew how to formulate an opinion. It was always
very clear what is quotation, what is opinion, so I could rely on the reports
from the local press. Sometimes things got tricky, on Iraq, on Kosovo. We
had questions: What do you mean? Did you say that? And sometimes
the one who comes to you with an accusation or interpretation can be
trumped by the original report. So I took the reports from the newspaper
or the press agency and said, 'Look, that is what was reported, that is
absolutely correct. It is your understanding or your explanation which creates a problem.' My respect for reporters grew exponentially as a result of
such experiences. People who work here are very knowledgeable and are
good reporters, so it's something that has to be respected."
—Danilo Türk, former ambassador of Slovenia to the UN

Diplomats confer prior to a Security Council meeting on Libya, April 4, 2011. From left: Vitaly I. Churkin of the Russian Federation, Li Baodong of the People's Republic of China, and Néstor Osorio of Colombia, who was president of the Security Council for April. UN Photo / JC McIlwaine.

the morning, and you have NGOs in the bleachers that are pushing single-minded positions. But even there, particularly if you can succeed in achieving consensus, if you can reach consensus on a document, I think there's always a huge sense of relief even among those who were opposed to positions we had. They can say to themselves, at least we produced something at the end of this."

Like all villages, this one has its cliques and factions. For one thing, the population is heavily male, although that has begun to change. In 2014 women accounted for no fewer than five of the fifteen ambassadors on the Security Council. The women who crash the party have described the experience in various ways. Madeleine Albright, who was US permanent representative, remembers the thrill of being not just a woman in that environment but "the woman who represents the United States," the dominant power.

John R. Bolton, US permanent representative to the UN, confers with the Guatemalan delegation at a General Assembly session to elect five nonpermanent members of the Security Council, October 16, 2006. UN Photo / Marco Castro.

Other women representatives may not feel the power rush, yet they recall the special quality of life at a men's club. Nancy Soderberg remembers old-fashioned gallantry. "One of the things that I just loved, being a young woman on the council, is that chivalry really does live there. They are so gentlemanly and just wonderful. At times they come up and kiss your hand and everyone stands up for you." Try that in the US Senate!

## Security Council Politics

The Security Council meets in its own "neighborhood," the Security Council Chamber, a room defined by its focal point, a horseshoe-

> ## Between Acts
>
> "You see another side of these guys when you get them out of the formal setting. Wang is very interesting. He's very quiet, but if you get him alone, he's very curious and down-to-earth and more open than other Chinese reps I've seen. You can actually have an argument with him about Tibet."
> —Nancy Soderberg, former US diplomat at the UN

shaped table that invariably features in media coverage of council activities. The delegates sit in chairs arrayed around the table, and in the center space are the transcribers who keep a record of proceedings. During renovation of the UN's complex of buildings, as they moved past their half-century of life, the Secretariat and the Security Council spaces were closed (2009–12). The Security Council's relocation, to a large basement conference room, involved re-creating the look and feel of the original chamber as much as possible, even to disassembling the horseshoe table and reassembling it in the temporary space.

Most member states regard participation on the Security Council as advantageous, but not everyone sees it that way. John Negroponte recalls that it took a while for Mexico to seek a council seat because of concerns that it would be a no-win situation. Some of his Mexican colleagues were thinking, "If we agree with the United States, then that will be taken for granted, and if we disagree with the United States, that will hurt us in our bilateral relationship with the United States." The Mexican president and others took the opposite tack, however, maintaining that Mexico needed to be more visible on the world stage and not worry about how the audience would react. Negroponte's Mexican counterparts asked him, "Will you hold it against Mexico if we take positions against the United States or at odds with the United States?" Negroponte replied with diplomatic aplomb, "Everything we do is going to be in the context of an excellent bilateral relationship. . . . We may have our differences, but it's a crucial relationship to us, and it's going to remain that, and we're going to deal with Mexico accordingly." History has borne out

Secretary-General Kofi Annan (center) in discussions with John Negroponte (right), US permanent representative to the UN, in the Security Council chamber, June 30, 2002. UN Photo / Eskinder Debebe.

Negroponte's advice: Mexico served on the council in 2002–3 and
2009–10 without suffering apparent injury to its relations with the
United States.

Concern over relations with the United States was definitely not
part of the mix when the Saudi Arabian government declined to
serve on the council after it was elected to the position in 2013. Citing frustration over the council's inability to resolve the long-run-
ning Palestinian issue and the more recent civil war in Syria, the
Saudis simply said no, in a unique rebuff to the council and the UN.

Much more private were the discussions that led to Security Council participation by one of the newly minted nations that emerged

Reality Check

"The Spokesperson's Office was for me the most exciting place to be. You work with journalists, and that means working harder and faster, always following the news and being ready to jump when they ask you a question. Journalists are a good reality check. Most people in the Secretariat talk to each other all day and, maybe if they're lucky, to a diplomat. Nothing could be more different than talking to journalists, and I did so all day long. They keep you on your toes. They keep you honest."
—Frederic (Fred) Eckhard, press secretary for Secretary-General Kofi Annan

from the dissolution of Yugoslavia in the 1990s. When the Slovenian government took stock of its diplomatic situation, one of the first matters considered was a possible candidacy for the Security Council. Danilo Türk was Slovenia's ambassador to the UN during the 1990s and Security Council president in August 1998. (Later he was elected president of Slovenia.) "I thought Slovenia would make a good show in the Security Council," he says, but that was not the universal opinion either in the UN or in Slovenia. "There was a debate" about whether or not it was needed, because membership in the Security Council "brings exposure" and having "to deal with issues that are very politically contested. It was not an easy decision, and I presented pluses and minuses." One of the pluses was that membership would strengthen the new nation's profile in the world community.

When Slovenia finally decided to throw its hat in the ring for the elections scheduled in 1997, the government had to decide which voting bloc it would run in. As always in the UN, a quota system ensures that each world region will have representation. In any given year, a certain number of places will open up for the Western Europe and Others Group or for the Latin American and Caribbean Group, for example, and countries in those regions will compete with one another for a seat. Sometimes the countries of a region will agree who should be elected to the open slots. At other times the countries will engage in a genuine political campaign involving arm-twisting, alliances, and occasional backstabbing.

Delegates sit and confer in a second-floor lounge near General Assembly Hall, January 1, 1993. UN Photo / Andrea Brizzi.

Danilo Türk did not face quite such high-powered politics when he guided Slovenia through its Security Council candidacy, but he did have to decide whether to campaign for the slot of Western Europe and Others or the slot of Eastern Europe. "Initially we didn't want to be a member of the Eastern European Group. We said we are geographically west of Vienna, we didn't think automatically that there should be any linkage between the former Yugoslavia membership in the Eastern European Group and Slovenian membership in the same group." The Slovenians later changed their minds "because we thought, it is important to get elected." They decided in 1996 to join the Eastern European Group, "where it is easier to get elected than in the Western because the competition is not as tough." Valuable time had passed, however, and there were two other candidates for the seat, Belarus and Macedonia. "Usually member states announce their candidature five years in advance, in some cases, ten or fifteen years in advance, and they campaign gradually. The last two years they campaign very intensely. Of course, if the seat is not contested, there is no campaign, but even then they have to talk to other members because they have to get two-thirds of the entire membership. We came very late and there were two other candidates, but I had to do it. Because if I didn't, I would be asked, 'Where were you, what were you doing?' Belarus withdrew at the last minute, a couple of days before elections, because they had no chance. We defeated the remaining candidate. So that's how Slovenia became a member of the Security Council."

And it was worth it, says Türk, if only for the international publicity. "We discovered that half of what was important internationally about Slovenia related to the Security Council in those two years [1998–99]. For a small country, this is an incredible exposure."

---

### Reciprocity and Good Manners

"One of the glories of the UN is that it is a system of multilateralism, which makes the reps of countries deal intimately with each other. This is retail global politics up close on the East River, so, as in a parliamentary system, niceness and conviviality count for a lot."
—Mark Malloch-Brown, former deputy secretary-general of the UN

---

Türk makes a broader point when he observes that smaller nations may not be as bound by rigid policies and positions as larger ones, giving them the opportunity to orchestrate some creative diplomacy where otherwise there might be conflict or confrontation.

"If a country like Slovenia fails, it is no problem, but if a big country fails with a proposal, that usually has political repercussions. So small countries, nonpermanent members, can be constructive and genuinely helpful members of the Security Council. They can afford some imagination and experimentation. I always believed that. I never thought that only permanent members count." Jeffrey Laurenti largely agrees. "Smaller country reps are freer agents and operate like parliamentarians in the European parliament."

## Working Efficiently

"Particularly when you're trying to rally a global response, the UN system can be helpful because it provides reach to many countries and more accessibility than if you were trying to do it country by country. When you're dealing with an issue that has global reach, global import, working with the UN system can actually be more efficient than trying to build some sort of group of countries outside. It's the multipliers: in an hour you can talk to twenty countries instead of two. It's building responses, building groups to go do things and take care of a crisis. The UN can be part of that."                    —Esther Brimmer, George Washington University

## Formally Informal or Informally Formal?

Once a member state becomes a player in a clique or faction, it needs to know the rules and procedures. One basic principle is that the most important business is done ostensibly in the open but actually in private. There's a reason why so many decisions, not just at the UN but in organizations the world over, are made by a few people in a back room. Chances are that if the terms of the agreement were discussed in public, with all the constraints of touchy issues, no one would agree to anything significant. So a common arrangement at the UN is to begin a debate or discussion in a large public setting such as the Security Council chamber and then, as the individual points become defined, to break up into smaller, less public groups. Finally, a few people sitting at a table resolve the most

Hillary Rodham Clinton, US secretary of state, and Sergey V. Lavrov, foreign minister of the Russian Federation, confer during a Security Council meeting on the Arab Spring, March 12, 2012. UN Photo / Eskinder Debebe.

contentious points, with no media presence and sometimes with no one taking notes.

In the Security Council, the opening discussions are referred to as the formals and the subsequent, less public talks as the informals. Nancy Soderberg came to regard the formal meetings as "just a staged show." In fact, "there is just nothing that happens in them." Rather, the serious negotiations happen at the informals, "because you can't negotiate in a formal setting, you can't talk to people." Occasionally the formal setting is good for sending signals to another member, but, "for the most part, you go in, there's a briefing that nobody pays attention to, and everyone reads prepared statements and nothing happens."

Sometimes, though, even the informals are too formal for serious talk. "The informals are not so informal," says Soderberg. "It still is pretty formal because you have a chair who does everyone in order. It's really hard to have negotiations when you have to wait your turn." The actual decision may already have been made anyway. But where? "In a back room," says Soderberg.

## Food for Thought and Action

"Food is probably the thing that holds the UN together," noted former US diplomat Richard Holbrooke. "Boy, do those guys like to eat!" The diplomatic scene overflows with large public receptions and smaller private gatherings at the nearly 200 UN missions and residences, invariably garnished with abundant, and sometimes delicious, food and drink. Staff at restaurants near UN headquarters serve international diplomats, some of them household names, with a nonchalance suggesting that it is just part of a day's work, which it is.

Often the UN Villagers do their eating right on the premises, in the Delegates' Dining Room or in the cafeteria, large rooms with floor-to-ceiling windows overlooking the East River. An informal seating hierarchy rules the Delegates' Dining Room, where the bigwigs usually sit on the left side while the commoners stay to the right. Periodically the buffet will feature the cuisine of a given member state. The dining room is open to the public and offers a chance to spy out some of the world's leading diplomats, though you may need a working knowledge of a few dozen languages for your eavesdropping. In the more casual cafeteria, which is not open to the public, people sit wherever they can find a quiet table, if chat is their focus. And chat usually is, because so much business is done over coffee and sandwiches or a salad.

### Club Rules

"It's a club, and at the UN you treat people with respect. You recognize that you may not have the same political viewpoint, but you don't insult them in public. That's the way business gets done. Generally speaking, people are polite to each other."
—Joseph Melrose, former US ambassador to the UN

Members of the Security Council on an annual retreat with the secretary-general and senior staff of the UN Secretariat in Manhasset,
New York. Secretary-General Ban Ki-moon (seated, center) and his
wife, Yoo Soon-taek (center left), pose with participants and their
spouses, April 23, 2013. UN Photo / Eskinder Debebe.

## Where's the Secretary-General?

Missing in this discussion is the secretary-general, whose official
residence is on Sutton Place, uptown from the UN headquarters and
geographically part of the village. The secretary-general has a different kind of social calendar than do the UN delegates and staff. The
need to travel frequently to all parts of the world takes the secretary-
general out of the village for much of the year. There is also a personality issue to consider. Some secretaries-general have been social
animals, like Kofi Annan, while others, like his predecessor, Boutros
Boutros-Ghali, and his successor, Ban Ki-moon, have chosen a more
private lifestyle while off duty (to the extent that a secretary-general
can ever be considered "off duty").

Every secretary-general, socially minded or not, expects to spend
time in the village, attending local dinners, affairs, cocktail hours,
and receptions. What is unusual is for a secretary-general to step outside the village and socialize with native New Yorkers. Kofi Annan

did much of his New York hobnobbing outside the village—and
not by accident. His longtime press spokesperson, Fred Eckhard,
relates that when Annan became secretary-general, he was advised
by a New Yorker to "get out of town," meaning out of the UN Village.
Her words to him were, "Look, the UN is a very isolated institution
and the diplomats hang out with each other. . . . If you want to, you
should get to know a lot more people." He agreed to give it a try.
Picking up on this overture, the Annans began entertaining at their
residence, often to folks outside the village, like heiress Brooke Astor
and her circle. "It was important for Kofi," remarked his New York
friend, "but I thought it was even more important for the United
Nations that it not remain an isolated institution." Socializing outside the village helped make Annan the "rock star of diplomacy," as
Eckhard puts it, and it showcased the UN.

## CHAPTER 9

# Peace Operations

*All members of the United Nations, in order to contribute to the maintenance of international peace and security, undertake to make available to the Security Council, on its call and in accordance with a special agreement or agreements, armed forces, assistance, and facilities, including rights of passage, necessary for the purpose of maintaining international peace and security.*

—UN Charter

Peace-related issues are central to Security Council deliberations, and peacekeeping has been hailed as one of the UN's essential functions. During the 1990s the United Nations launched more peace-related operations than in the previous four decades, and since then, the scale of operations has increased. In May 2013 fifteen peacekeeping missions and one political mission (Afghanistan) led by the Secretariat's Department of Peacekeeping Operations (DPKO) employed 113,057 personnel at an annual cost of about $7.5 billion. The UN's peacekeepers constitute the second-largest deployed military in the world.

The United States has been a strong backer of creating new peacekeeping missions, as in Mali, or expanding existing ones, as in the Democratic Republic of the Congo. A recent State Department report noted that the government "supports peacekeeping operations when they can be an effective means of containing conflict and resolving disputes in support of U.S. national interests." Stewart Patrick characterizes UN peacekeeping and political missions as valuable to the United States. "For every quarter we spend we get a dollar's worth of results. It allows the US to help reduce human suffering and restore peace and hopefully end atrocities in areas where we have a humanitarian concern, to some degree a regional stability concern, but where we, for whatever reason, are not prepared to or are not the right people to have our own troops there. That's a great value when you compare on a dollar-for-dollar basis."

## A Multidimensional Approach

"Today's multidimensional peacekeeping operations are called upon not only to maintain peace and security, but also to facilitate the political process, protect civilians, assist in the disarmament, demobilization and reintegration of former combatants, support the organization of elections, protect and promote human rights and assist in restoring the rule of law."
—UN Department of Peacekeeping Operations

As one of the Permanent Five, the United States can exercise tight control over the whole process, from authorizing a mission to deciding on its size, composition, and level of funding. The United States does not usually provide troops for UN peacekeeping missions, but it is one of the largest financial contributors and is assessed about 28 percent of all peacekeeping costs as part of its treaty obligation at the UN.

## How It Works

UN peacekeeping begins only when the contending parties have agreed to it. The UN does not impose peacekeeping, nor does it regard its peacekeepers as combatants. Rather, it offers peacekeeping as a way of ending a conflict and as a step toward a lasting political or diplomatic settlement. The peacekeeping force is supposed to be impartial, to not take sides but keep contending forces apart and prevent outbreaks of conflict. Peacekeepers may use force, with the authorization of the Security Council, if acting in self-defense or in defense of their mandate.

Once the Security Council authorizes the deployment of a peace-keeping operation, defines its mission, and recommends the way the mission should be carried out, the secretary-general appoints a force commander and, through the DPKO, arranges for management and logistics. The DPKO was originally one entity, but with the rapid growth of peacekeeping missions the General Assembly agreed to split it in two, creating a Department of Field Support (DFS) to look after management and logistics under the supervision of an under-secretary-general. The DFS provides expertise and assistance in personnel, budget and finances, communications, information technology, and logistics for peacekeepers scattered around the globe.

Since the UN does not have a military establishment, it must borrow troops and police from member states. Some have therefore likened UN peacekeeping to a volunteer fire department, but its efforts are not that well organized, according to former secretary-general Kofi Annan, because for every mission it is necessary to scrounge up the fire engines and the money to pay for them "before we can start dousing any flames." Member states are asked to provide personnel, equipment, and logistics. The UN pays member states approximately a thousand dollars for salary and allowances per peacekeeper per month, with supplements for specialists, gear, and weaponry totaling roughly another four hundred dollars, also per peacekeeper per month, but the member states pay the troops according to their own scales. Member states retain control over their units and are responsible for enforcing discipline and punishing any wrongdoing by the troops.

Most of the troops come from developing nations like Bangladesh, India, Pakistan, Nigeria, Jordan, and Egypt, but most of the money to pay for the troops comes from the leading developed nations. As table 2 shows, the top ten contributors to the peacekeeping budget all have large economies and contribute the bulk of funds for peacekeeping. The United States and Japan combined provide almost 40 percent of the peacekeeping budget, while China and Russia combined pay another 10 percent. The formulas by which these contributions are calculated will be discussed in the chapter on UN finances.

Table 2. Top ten providers of assessed contributions to UN peacekeeping
operations, 2013

| Member State | Assessed Contribution (%) |
|---|---|
| United States | 28.38 |
| Japan | 10.83 |
| France | 7.22 |
| Germany | 7.14 |
| United Kingdom | 6.68 |
| China | 6.64 |
| Italy | 4.45 |
| Russian Federation | 3.15 |
| Canada | 2.98 |
| Spain | 2.97 |

*Source:* UN Peacekeeping, "Financing Peacekeeping," http://www
.un.org/en/peacekeeping/operations/financing.shtml.


## An Evolving Concept

Although peacekeeping is one of the quintessential UN functions, the Charter mentions it only briefly. Its full scope and nature have emerged over the decades in response to pressing needs
to help make the peace and keep it. An important distinction is
whether a peacekeeping mission exists solely to monitor a truce,
in which case the observers are unarmed, or whether it is meant to
keep combatants apart, in which case the UN troops carry arms and
function as infantry. In either case, the peacekeepers usually seek to
avoid armed conflict, although that is not always the case, as will be
noted below.

The Security Council's first peacekeeping resolution, in 1948,
established an observer mission, the United Nations Truce Supervision Organization (UNTSO), to oversee the truce between Arabs
and Jews when the British relinquished control over Palestine. As
with peacekeeping today, member states provided the personnel.
UNTSO also set the model for nomenclature: the organization is
invariably referred to by its acronym rather than its full name. Still

Secretary-General Ban Ki-moon greets staff of the United Nations Truce Supervision Organization at Government House in Jerusalem, March 27, 2007. UN Photo / Evan Schneider.

in operation, UNTSO has an expanded mandate that includes supervising the implementation and observance of the general agreements between Israel and its four Arab neighbors.

The nature of peacekeeping has changed as the nature of conflicts has evolved. The norm used to be that conflicts occurred between nation-states, which fought with field armies that targeted combatants, not civilians—that was the theory, anyway. Most operations have involved troops capable of acting as buffers between hostile forces and monitoring truces, troop withdrawals, and borders or demilitarized zones. But these days nation-states have been remarkably well behaved toward one another, and in some places, such as Europe, they have even forged close political ties. Instead, conflicts tend to occur within nations, in the form of civil wars (as in Syria, Sudan, and Libya) or national resistance movements (such as the East Timorese against Indonesian occupation) (table 3).

## UN Peacekeeping Operations

| | |
|---|---|
| UNTSO | UN Truce Supervision Organization |
| UNMOGIP | UN Military Observer Group in India and Pakistan |
| UNFICYP | UN Peacekeeping Force in Cyprus |
| UNDOF | UN Disengagement Observer Force |
| UNIFIL | UN Interim Force in Lebanon |
| MINURSO | UN Mission for the Referendum in Western Sahara |
| UNMIK | UN Interim Administration Mission in Kosovo |
| UNMIL | UN Mission in Liberia |
| UNOCI | UN Operation in Côte d'Ivoire |
| MINUSTAH | UN Stabilization Mission in Haiti |
| UNAMID | African Union–UN Hybrid Operation in Darfur |
| MONUSCO | UN Organization Stabilization Mission in the Democratic Republic of the Congo |
| UNISFA | UN Interim Security Force for Abyei |
| UNMISS | UN Mission in the Republic of South Sudan |
| MINUSMA | UN Multidimensional Integrated Stabilization Mission in Mali |

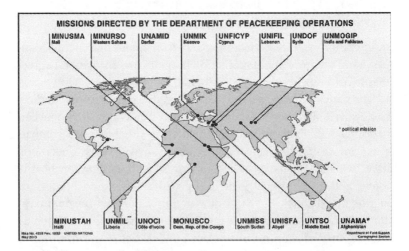

UN peacekeeping operations, February 28, 2014. UN Department of Public Information, March 2014.

Table 3. UN peacekeeping operations, February 2014

| Mission | Year Established | Troops | Military Observers | Police | International Civilians | Local Civilians | UN Volunteers | Total Personnel | Fatalities | Budget (US$) |
|---|---|---|---|---|---|---|---|---|---|---|
| UNTSO | 1948 | 0 | 160 | 0 | 95 | 138 | 0 | 393 | 50 | $74,291,900 |
| UNMOGIP | 1949 | 0 | 42 | 0 | 24 | 44 | 0 | 110 | 11 | $19,647,100 |
| UNFICYP | 1964 | 857 | 0 | 67 | 39 | 110 | 0 | 1,073 | 181 | $56,604,300 |
| UNDOF | 1974 | 1,243 | 0 | 0 | 47 | 99 | 0 | 1,389 | 45 | $60,654,500 |
| UNIFIL | 1978 | 10,200 | 0 | 0 | 315 | 634 | 0 | 11,149 | 303 | $492,622,000 |
| MINURSO | 1991 | 23 | 201 | 5 | 96 | 168 | 15 | 508 | 15 | $60,475,700 |
| UNMIK | 1999 | 0 | 8 | 7 | 114 | 211 | 27 | 367 | 55 | $44,953,000 |
| UNMIL | 2003 | 5,749 | 136 | 1,561 | 420 | 860 | 221 | 8,947 | 181 | $476,329,800 |
| UNOCI | 2004 | 7,957 | 182 | 1,316 | 400 | 762 | 150 | 10,767 | 118 | $584,487,000 |
| MINUSTAH | 2004 | 5,794 | 0 | 2,413 | 373 | 1,242 | 169 | 9,991 | 176 | $576,619,000 |
| UNAMID | 2007 | 14,354 | 330 | 4,508 | 1,060 | 2,957 | 404 | 23,613 | 191 | $1,335,248,000 |
| MONUSCO | 2010 | 19,558 | 502 | 1,185 | 990 | 2,979 | 556 | 25,770 | 70 | $1,456,378,300 |
| UNISFA | 2011 | 3,955 | 133 | 23 | 104 | 59 | 19 | 4,293 | 13 | $329,108,600 |
| UNMISS | 2011 | 7,327 | 152 | 1,015 | 869 | 1,333 | 406 | 11,102 | 25 | $924,426,000 |
| MINUSMA | 2013 | 6,137 | 0 | 956 | 287 | 113 | 58 | 7,551 | 8 | $602,000,000 |
| Total | | 83,154 | 1,846 | 13,056 | 5,233 | 11,709 | 2,025 | 117,023 | 1,442 | $7,093,845,200* |

Source: Adapted from "Current Peacekeeping Operations," prepared by the Peace and Security Section of the UN Department of Public Information, in consultation with the Department of Peacekeeping Operations, Department of Field Support, and Department of Management, DPI/1634Rev. 154—March 2014.

*Adding the requirements for the UN Support Office for the African Union Mission in Somalia (UNSOA), the support account for peacekeeping operations, and the UN Logistics Base in Brindisi, Italy, brings the total to approximately $7.83 billion.

As the focus of peace operations shifted to conflicts within nations, and as the number and scope of operations increased, the Security Council decided it was time for a basic reassessment of peacekeeping. It commissioned a study by Lakhdar Brahimi, the former foreign minister of Algeria, whose final report, presented in 2000, has become a point of reference for most discussions about peace operations. The Brahimi report made many recommendations about updating the concept of peacekeeping to address modern situations and stressed the growing need for better funding and administration. Among its recommendations it urged that military functions be integrated with historically civil functions such as dealing with human rights, policing, food, shelter, and medical services. As we will see, these suggestions have lead to significant changes in UN peacekeeping. Another innovation resulting from the Brahimi report was the creation in 2007 of the Office of Rule of Law and Security Institutions (OROLSI), charged with providing an integrated approach to UN assistance with the rule of law and security. The rule of law is an important component of such integration—hence the creation of OROLSI. The office combines many previously scattered UN entities, such as the police division and the judicial, legal, and correctional units. The goal is to develop a holistic approach by incorporating all aspects of the rule of law and security into a network that includes the police, the judiciary, and corrections, according to the office's director, Dmitry Titov of the Russian Federation.

In addition to the recommendations of the Brahimi report, the UN has also revised its peace operations based on experience in the field, including the need to authorize the use of force in carefully defined situations. The Security Council has on occasion given UN peacekeeping operations broad, "robust" mandates authorizing the use of "all necessary means" to deter forceful attempts to "disrupt the political process, protect civilians under imminent threat of physical attack, and/or assist the national authorities in maintaining law and order." This way of defining "robust" moves the peacekeepers into peace enforcement, a more aggressive stance, which is more likely to involve them in physical conflict. The Security Council supported an even more aggressive stance in 2013 when it directed the establishment of an "intervention brigade" among the twenty thousand peacekeeping troops in the Democratic Republic of the Congo (DRC), whose eastern regions have been the locus of one of the UN's longest-running and most expensive peace operations. After a rebel movement seized part of the eastern regions in 1998, a ceasefire agreement brokered by the Security Council led to the authorization in 1999 of the United Nations Organization Mission in the Democratic Republic of the Congo (MONUC). The Security Council later expanded the mandate from observation of the ceasefire and disengagement of forces to include supervision of the implementation of the ceasefire agreement and other tasks relating to political institutions, the military, and the rule of law. During the approximately ten years of its deployment, from 2000 to June 2010, MONUC cost the lives of 161 UN personnel and required the expenditure of $8.73 billion The UN, through its efforts, helped stabilize the national government in Kinshasa and organized free elections in 2006, when voters elected a national assembly and then a president. In July 2010 the Security Council renamed MONUC the United Nations Organization Stabilization Mission in the Democratic Republic of the Congo (MONUSCO) and authorized it to use "all necessary means" to protect civilians, humanitarian personnel, and human rights defenders under threat of physical violence and to support the government of the DRC in its efforts to consolidate peace.

Despite the presence of the UN force, the DRC's eastern regions have remained contested ground. The Security Council in its 2013 decision therefore made the intervention brigade responsible for actively suppressing Hutu militia groups and other fighters, though only "on an exceptional basis, and without creating a precedent or any prejudice to the agreed principles of peacekeeping." It is uncertain if this decision will set a precedent for future peace operations. Whether it does or not, the word "robust" has become a normal part of peacekeeping terminology. For example, when internal conflict threatened to undermine the government of the Central African Republic in 2013, the Economic Community of Central African States (ECCAS) responded by asking the Security Council for the deployment of a multifaceted peacekeeping mission. ECCAS representatives said that it was necessary "to address the root causes of the conflict," which meant establishing both "a legitimate and representative democracy that served the interests of all and not just a clan or group" and "genuine defence forces that were balanced and representative," not clan-based. The African Union and ECCAS "agreed on the urgent need for the international community to act and that a United Nations peacekeeping mission with a robust mandate would be required." In April 2014 the Security Council accepted the request and authorized creation of a multidimensional UN peacekeeping operation—MINUSCA.

## Police, and Women Too

As peacekeeping mandates like those for the Central African Republic and the DRC become broader, encompassing even elements that might be considered aspects of nation building, the UN finds itself having to expand the nature of the peacekeeping force to include personnel dedicated to keeping civil order—in other words, police. The number of UN police officers in peacekeeping operations and special political missions rose from 5,840 in 1995 to more than 13,500 in 2012. Detachments now may include Formed Police Units, which are more heavily armed than regular United Nations Police (UNPOL) teams and fill the gap between the military component of peacekeeping and the local police. Such units helped reestablish government control in gang-infested parts of Haiti in 2007 and evacuated civilians caught in gun battles in the DRC.

It is also now widely accepted that peacekeeping forces should include women, and in significant numbers. Experience has demonstrated that a female presence in peace operations can help empower women in the host community and address specific needs of female ex-combatants during demobilization. It can also help make the peacekeeping force approachable to women, as well as provide mentors for female cadets at local police and military academies and people who can interact with women in societies where they are discouraged from speaking to men.

Members of the Indian Battalion of the UN Mission in the Republic of South Sudan assisting displaced persons at Juba, December 16, 2013. UN Photo / UNMISS.

The DPKO is working to increase the number of female peace-keepers in the field, but it has been a slow slog. In 1993 women were 1 percent of deployed uniformed personnel. Twenty years later, in 2012, women constituted approximately 30 percent of the civilian peacekeeping staff but only 3 percent of military personnel and 10 percent of police personnel. The issues go beyond percentages. Stefan Feller, police adviser in the DPKO, told correspondents in New York at a meeting in 2013 that "promoting gender mainstreaming is more than just driving numbers." More women were needed, he said, to meet the complex responsibilities of the police, who are "our first-line defense against chaos and instability and our first-line offense toward building safety, security and respect for the rule of law." The UN Police set a target of 20 percent women officers worldwide by 2014, and some peacekeeping missions approached the goal, such as the UN Mission in the Republic of South Sudan (UNMISS), with 19 percent female officers, and even exceeded it, as in the police component of the UN mission in Cyprus (UNFICYP), with 22 percent women.

The more female face of peacekeeping has appeared in Liberia's capital, Monrovia, where Formed Police Units consisting of women from India, dressed in blue uniforms and toting rifles, have patrolled the city streets and enforced curfews, prevented crime, arrested suspects, and in general ensured the safety and security of residents. Haitians and residents of the DRC have seen all-female UN police units from Bangladesh.

## Policing the Peacekeepers

The UN is trying to address an abuse that has plagued peacekeeping missions for a long time: allegations that some troops have sexually exploited civilians. These accusations have become more common as the scale of peacekeeping has grown, leading to calls for a renewed commitment to investigate and prosecute the persons accused and to help the victims. Both the General Assembly and the Secretariat have given sexual abuse issues a high priority.

All personnel deployed in peacekeeping receive DPKO training on the prevention of sexual exploitation and abuse, and countries that contribute troops are urged to cooperate in investigating allegations of wrongdoing. In 2006 the director of DPKO, Jean-Marie Guéhenno of France, briefed the Security Council on his efforts to make troop-contributing countries more sensitive to sexual abuse. In 2007 the General Assembly adopted a strategy on Assistance and Support to Victims of Sexual Exploitation and Abuse by UN staff and related personnel, and in 2008 Secretary-General Ban Ki-moon launched UNITE, a campaign to end violence against women. It was scheduled to run through 2015, a date that coincides with the target date for the Millennium Development Goals (discussed in a later chapter), and all member bodies of the UN were asked to participate, including DPKO. Meanwhile, the Department of Field Support began in 2006 to compile data on allegations of misconduct and subsequent actions. The department launched the Misconduct Tracking System (MTS) in 2008, a global database and confidential tracking system for all allegations of misconduct.

These efforts are offered as one reason for a decline in sexual abuse accusations in at least one peacekeeping operation, in Liberia, in 2007. According to an independent nongovernmental organization, the UN reported 74 allegations of sexual exploitation and abuse by UN peacekeepers in 2011, a considerable decline from the 357 cases in 2006. As the report noted, however, the UN is "limited in how it can prevent and prosecute these allegations due to the organization's size and member state–centric operating system." The problem is that the UN has no authority to punish wrongdoers: only the member state in whose military establishment they serve can do that. Still, the downward trend in sexual abuse allegations is hopeful, and if the UN can leverage it into broader improvement across its operations, it will have made an important advance both in peacekeeping and in human rights.

## Peacebuilding Commission

Traditional peacekeeping is increasingly regarded as an opening move in a process of moving from armed conflict to political dialogue and peace. "Peacebuilding" is a term of recent origin for those UN activities aimed at establishing the foundations of peace and providing the tools for building on those foundations. It includes efforts to strengthen the rule of law, improve respect for human rights, provide technical assistance for democratic development, and promote conflict resolution and reconciliation techniques.

The concept of establishing a separate office devoted to peacebuilding went from discussion to reality in December 2005, when the General Assembly and the Security Council passed resolutions founding a Peacebuilding Commission. The US government backed creation of the new commission, although John Bolton, who was US ambassador to the UN, is skeptical that it was needed. "It's not as if the council is not aware that there are economic, social, and other

## A Peace Glossary

Just as Eskimos are said to have many words for snow, the UN has developed an array of words and phrases for the making and keeping of peace. Here are just a few.

*preventive diplomacy:* Preventive diplomacy seeks to head off disputes before they become full-blown conflicts. The UN prefers this kind of diplomacy but is able to apply it in only some instances. The UN employs its extensive contacts and offices around the world to detect early signs of potential threats to international peace and security.

*peacemaking:* Peacemaking involves the use of diplomacy to persuade belligerents to stop fighting and negotiate an end to their dispute.

*peace enforcement:* Peace enforcement involves the use of force against a belligerent to enforce an end to a fight.

*peacebuilding:* Peacebuilding involves helping nations promote peace before, during, or after a conflict. The UN employs a wide range of political, humanitarian, and human rights activities and programs.

*political missions:* Political missions use diplomacy and mediation to help nations prevent and resolve conflicts peacefully and to avert the suffering and destruction of war.

factors in addition to political and military factors that are critical to maintaining a lasting peace in context after context," he explains. "They don't need a separate commission to do that." Richard Gowan of New York University was even more skeptical when commenting on the commission after it had been in operation for nearly a decade, saying, "Frankly it's junk. It has failed as both a diplomatic initiative and on the ground. I'm not sure that we are very much better at this than we were ten or fifteen years ago."

The commission understandably takes a more positive view. It describes itself as an intergovernmental advisory body that supports efforts to stabilize and rebuild countries emerging from war. It draws resources from the UN Peacebuilding Fund (PBF), established in 2006 to kick-start post-conflict peacebuilding. Some commission projects have encouraged national peace dialogues, while others

have strengthened the rule of law, supported disarmament, demobilization, and reintegration, or provided economic stimulus for
businesses. In Sierra Leone, for example, the PBF helped pay the
salaries of thirty thousand polling staff during national elections,
in addition to funding the purchase of equipment for local police
to control civil disturbances. In 2009, to cite another instance, the
PBF approved a $20 million Peacebuilding Priority Plan package of
support to the eastern DRC. The approach tries to engage all stakeholders in dialogue, which means governments as well as nongovernmental organizations and civil society.

## The Talking Cure

Given the many requests for making or keeping the peace, and
the great expense of putting a peace operation in the field, the Security Council usually begins by looking for a solution that does
not involve the deployment of UN peacekeepers. Conflicts, whether
between nations or within nations, typically run in a cycle, from
initial disagreement through escalation to the threat or actual use
of force, and early intervention by diplomats and other peacemakers
is essential to stop the process. The Department of Political Affairs
(DPA), the lead UN department for peacemaking and preventive
diplomacy, often works behind the scenes to define and plan a mission and to provide UN special envoys and mediators with guidance
and backing from headquarters.

The DPA's director, Jeffrey Feltman, remarked on the centrality
of his organization's work: "Yes, the UN can use troops—and often
needs to—to stabilize and to provide security on the ground. And,
yes, UN humanitarian actors help to diminish the suffering of victims. But lasting solutions to conflicts require working the politics
in tough places. And this is what we are trying to do, with varying
degrees of success, in numerous arenas today, often in evolving and
complex operating environments." The DPA is often the first UN
entity to enter the scene when conflict seems to be in the offing. The
need to respond immediately, with little advance notice, means that
the organization must be able to deploy mediation and other peace-

UN political and peacebuilding missions, February 28, 2014. UN Department of Public Information, March 2014.

making experts rapidly to the field and collaborate with regional organizations at the frontlines of conflicts.

But the role of the DPA varies by situation. Sometimes it is only after the opposing parties have agreed on a truce, and the UN peace-keeping troops have arrived, that the DPA can start its political mission of overseeing longer-term peacebuilding activities. "When people in today's world are at risk or subject to serious violations, they expect and request the United Nations to act—and we do," said Deputy Secretary-General Jan Eliasson before the General Assembly in December 2013. "However, in practice, our response to crisis often comes when a situation has deteriorated to the point where only a substantial political or peacekeeping mission can deal with the problems."

The concept and practice of the political mission has been generally well received by both insiders and outside observers. "Political missions have, just like peacekeeping, turned out to be a remarkable tool for the UN," notes Richard Gowan. "Political missions are a very effective tool and in some ways a more flexible one because they are smaller, lighter, easier to put together than peacekeeping operations." He warns, however, that they are not a panacea. "Sometimes I hear people say, we don't think peacekeeping is working in Sudan, we should think about a political mission. It's not that simple. Political missions lack that leverage that having troops gives you. . . . Sometimes you just need troops, and I think that now and again people support political missions more for cost reasons than good strategic reasons. But all that said, we have seen political missions with regional conflict prevention mandates work as really effective platforms for mediation in cases like Guinea and Kyrgyzstan, where otherwise the UN wouldn't be able to reach."

## Fixing Failed States

"By definition these states lack adequate institutions to function well. We've rescued enough countries from these kinds of conflicts—the East Timors of this world, or the Cambodias or Ugandas or Balkans or Central America—to know it can be done. But often it takes a conflict to mobilize the international will. It's a little bit like the politics of climate change: very hard to do the mitigation in advance, much easier politically to mobilize the response once New York's been flooded."
—Mark Malloch-Brown, former deputy secretary-general of the UN

## Producing Results

Peacekeeping operations have had mixed results. Some have not fulfilled their mission, such as the mission in Rwanda, where the UN force was unable to prevent widespread massacres of Tutsis and others—perhaps as many as a million victims—by members of the Hutu majority, from April through mid-July 1994. The following year saw thousands of civilians massacred in the Bosnian town of Srebenica, in the former Yugoslavia, which had been declared a UN safe area and was defended by a UN protection force. Meanwhile, in

UN peacekeepers from China stand at attention during the visit of
the secretary-general's special representative and head of the UN
Multidimensional Integrated Stabilization Mission in Mali, January
27, 2014. UN Photo / Marco Dormino.

Africa another mission, including forces of the United States, was
attempting to bring humanitarian aid and a measure of peace and
reconciliation to Somalia, where an array of rebel groups were fighting one another after the ouster of the central government in Moga-
dishu. These three missions clearly failed to achieve their mandated
goals.

Another mission failed to achieve its goal, not because of any
shortcoming in the UN's efforts but because the contesting parties could not agree on peace terms. Eritrea, a breakaway province
of Ethiopia that is now an independent nation and a UN member state, in May 1998 ordered its armed forces to occupy a slice
of disputed territory on the border with Ethiopia. A regional body,
the Organization of African Unity (OAU, now the African Union),
worked out an agreement for settling the dispute, but neither side

would commit to it. The Security Council stepped in and urged the disputants to accept the OAU's plan. When they refused and began fighting, the council moved to its next stage of action, which was to tell the combatants to stop fighting, start talking, and arrange a ceasefire. The United States joined the ceasefire efforts, sending former US national security adviser Anthony Lake and an OAU representative to Asmara and Addis Ababa, again to no avail. Finally, once the fighting ended, the Security Council created the UN Mission in Ethiopia and Eritrea (UNMEE) and charged it with monitoring the border and ensuring that the ceasefire provisions were honored. The antagonists accused each other of infiltrating troops into a buffer zone. With no end in sight, the Security Council decided to terminate UNMEE's mission.

Other missions have neither succeeded nor failed, but have continued as permanent features in the local landscape. The Security Council established the United Nations Peacekeeping Force in Cyprus (UNFICYP) in 1964 to prevent hostilities between the Greek Cypriot and Turkish Cypriot communities, and it expanded the mandate after a period of conflict in 1974. Absent a political settlement, UNFICYP has remained on the island to "supervise ceasefire lines, maintain a buffer zone, undertake humanitarian activities and support the good offices mission of the Secretary-General." This is perhaps one of the examples that former US ambassador John Bolton has in mind when he complains about missions that "seem to have gained a degree of immortality" to the extent that they become part of the landscape and may even perpetuate the conflict because the parties can avoid having to negotiate a settlement. "The general problem," he says, is to know when to start a peacekeeping operation and how to finish it. "The Security Council really doesn't fulfill its role, and . . . you're not resolving the underlying dispute but yet you're keeping the peacekeeping operation in the field." Former Ambassador Zalmay Khalilzad, who succeeded Bolton as permanent representative, offered a similar analysis in 2008 when he declared that peacekeeping should not be a substitute for ending conflict. Noting that funds have always been tight, he urged the UN to organize its efforts more cost-effectively. "While we understand

Secretary-General Ban Ki-moon at the ceremony marking the closure of the UN Integrated Peace Building Mission in Sierra Leone and the transfer of its responsibilities to the UN country team, March 5, 2014. The secretary-general (center back) is flanked by the mission head, Jens Anders Toyberg-Frandzen (left) and Ernest Bai Koroma, president of the Republic of Sierra Leone. UN Photo / Eskinder Debebe.

the risks of leaving too soon, we should look to terminate nonviable peacekeeping operations."

Mark Malloch-Brown notes that peacekeeping missions proliferated during the Annan years (1997–2006) and that "not enough of them have gone out of business in the years since. They've become too much a part of the furniture in too many countries." The mission in Darfur, begun under Ban Ki-moon, is an example. There, a complicated internal conflict involving the central government and rebel militias had produced death, misery, and destruction throughout an area larger than France. The usual UN peacekeeping operation consists solely of UN forces, but the government of Sudan refused to accept such a mission. The UN therefore partnered with

## A Peacekeeping Success Story

On March 5, 2014, Secretary-General Ban Ki-moon spoke at the closing ceremony of the United Nations Integrated Peacebuilding Office in Sierra Leone. It marked the end of a decade-long UN effort to end armed conflict and bring the nation to a peaceful state. "Our blue helmets disarmed more than 75,000 ex-fighters, including hundreds of child soldiers," the secretary-general noted. "The UN destroyed more than 42,000 weapons and 1.2 million rounds of ammunition—a potentially deadly arsenal that is now itself dead." Additionally the UN helped the government to end the illicit diamond mining that had fueled the conflict and to hold the nation's first-ever free and fair elections. UN personnel assisted more than half a million refugees and internally displaced persons to return, and trained thousands of police. They also built schools and launched projects that gave jobs to thousands of ex-fighters and basic services to communities. UNIPSIL and the government of Sierra Leone established many peacebuilding precedents:

- the UN's first multidimensional peacekeeping operation with political, security, humanitarian, and national recovery mandates
- the first African country to establish, with UN participation, a tribunal on its own territory to address the most serious international crimes
- the conviction, by the tribunal, of a former head of state, former Liberian president Charles Taylor

Ban concluded that "Sierra Leone has taught the world many lessons, but none more important than the power of people to shape the future."

the African Union to deploy a joint peacekeeping force consisting of military units from both organizations. The African Union–United Nations Hybrid Operation in Darfur (UNAMID) was one of the largest and most complicated peacekeeping missions ever deployed under the UN banner, fielding nearly twenty thousand troops and more than six thousand police. This force has been attempting to establish a secure environment while talks achieve a lasting civil and political settlement. In mid-2014 no settlement was in sight, and the international force remained in place, though hampered by the Sudanese government and opposition groups.

Against the open-ended and sometimes ineffectual missions, there are successes. Both Sierra Leone and Liberia are becoming whole countries again after horrific civil wars, thanks in part to the presence of peacekeeping operations. The Sierra Leone mission fulfilled its mandate and in 2014 closed its doors, eleven years after it was deployed.

Halfway around the world from there, Timor-Leste is now a functioning independent nation largely as a result of UN intervention. When that region sought independence from Indonesia, the Security Council hosted negotiations that led in 1999 to a popular referendum in which the Timorese rejected autonomy within Indonesia and opted for independence. But the council had to authorize a multinational security force after Indonesia-backed militants unleashed a campaign of systematic destruction and violence in response to the Timorese referendum. Many East Timorese were killed, and more than two hundred thousand were forced to flee, most to West Timor.

Acting under Chapter VII of the UN Charter, the Security Council established the UN Transitional Administration in East Timor (UNTAET) in 1999 to restore order and provide administrative services as East Timor prepared for independence. Sérgio Vieira de Mello of Brazil was appointed the Transitional Administrator for East Timor. UNTAET began a program of "Timorization" of key government posts to prepare for transition to full independence. In July, UNTAET established the East Timor Transitional Administration, with a cabinet of nine ministries, five headed by East Timorese. Then UNTAET appointed a thirty-six-member national council representing a wide spectrum of Timorese society and prepared for summer 2001 elections for a national assembly. The assembly drew up and adopted a constitution. David Malone praises Vieira de Mello, who "pulled off the East Timor operation in spite of tremendous problems on the ground and enormous bureaucratic inertia within the UN."

In 2002 the Timorese elected a president and became a new nation, Timor-Leste. Civil disturbances in 2006 led the UN to deploy the Integrated Mission in Timor-Leste (UNMIT) to help preserve order and give the fledgling government time to organize itself. The new country moved quickly to strengthen its national institutions, and in 2012 the citizens elected a parliament and a president. When UNMIT neared its December 2012 completion date, the Security Council's president lauded the new nation's progress. "The Security Council underscores the importance of continued support to Timor-Leste as it embarks on the next stage of its development," he declared, "and notes the willingness of the United Nations and bilateral and multilateral partners to continue, as requested by the Timorese authorities, to play a significant role in this regard."

The success of the missions to East Timor, Liberia, and Sierra Leone may be a reason that outside observers are often impressed with the significance of peacekeeping operations in helping to make the world a safer place. The US government has praised UN peacekeeping. According to estimates by the Government Accountability Office (GAO), UN peacekeeping, on average, is at least eight times cheaper than having the United States undertake its own peacekeeping operations. The White House Office of Management and Budget gave the US contributions to UN peacekeeping its highest possible rating and assessed it to be fiscally effective in achieving its stated goals and in contributing to American objectives.

## CHAPTER 10

# International Terrorism and WMDs

*There is no more urgent threat to the United States than a terrorist with a nuclear weapon. Nuclear weapons materials are stored in dozens of countries, some without proper security. Nuclear technology is spreading. . . . It is essential to strengthen the global nonproliferation and disarmament regime, deal with those states in violation of this regime, and uphold our obligations to work constructively and securely toward the goal of a world without nuclear weapons.*
                    —Susan E. Rice, former US ambassador to the UN

On the day after 9/11, the Security Council officially decreed that acts of international terrorism are threats to international peace and security. The events of September 11, 2001, also pushed the council to act quickly in creating a broad resolution aimed at cutting off all support to international terrorists. "The UN rewrote the law after the 9/11 attacks by stating that countries have an affirmative duty not to give any kind of assistance to terrorist groups [Resolution 1373]," remarks international law expert Ruth Wedgwood of Johns Hopkins University. "It changed the terms of state responsibility. It was a hugely important resolution."

The shocking attacks of September 11 placed the United States at the top of the list of terror-afflicted nations and helped raise international awareness about the urgency of the threat. The media ran stories and editorials about the need to find terrorists and neutralize them before they could mount another major attack, possibly one using weapons of mass destruction, or WMDs.

One immediate response by the United States and many of its friends was to treat terrorism as a variety of military threat, to be countered with the use of force, as in Afghanistan, where al-Qaeda had formed a close alliance with the Taliban government and was using its resources to train recruits. The United States launched an invasion in 2001, with UN approval, that overthrew the Taliban regime and forced al-Qaeda into hiding.

Another response, not only by the United States and its friends but also by the UN, was to treat international terrorism as a form of criminal activity that needed to be made clearly illegal everywhere, both within nations and in international law. As the world's global forum, the UN would seem well suited for this task. The UN has defined several important counterterrorism roles for itself, observes Pakistan's former ambassador Munir Akram, by, for example, shaping "international public opinion, standards, and conventions which have outlawed terrorism and made it possible for countries to cooperate with each other on concrete terms."

## Terrorism and Failed States

"An area where we do spend a lot of our time is the issue of failed states. The breeding ground for terrorism or [nuclear] proliferation or any other manner of ills of this world, whether it's narcotics trafficking or other forms of antisocial behavior, is more likely to develop in a country whose institutions have broken down. . . . That's what Osama bin Laden did when he moved in on the Taliban and used Afghanistan for his own purposes. We at the UN have an interest in states not failing, and we spend a lot of time dealing with states that are threatened in that way."
—John Negroponte, former US ambassador to the UN

An Emerging Consensus

A striking aspect of counterterrorist deliberations is that the major powers all seem to be generally on the same page. The Security Council's permanent members (P5) publicly and officially agree that only through joint efforts can they hope to stop terrorism. They have expressed their unity through a series of resolutions, beginning in late 1999, when the Security Council passed Resolution 1267, requiring the Taliban government in Afghanistan to give up Osama bin Laden, whose al-Qaeda network had been targeting US government and military facilities. Next, Resolution 1269 pledged a "common fight against terrorists everywhere" and specified that member states should share information and refuse to provide a safe haven to terrorists. At the end of 1999, the General Assembly voted to adopt the International Convention for the Suppression of the Financing of Terrorism. This convention makes it a crime to participate in raising funds for terrorist activity, even if no terrorist act ensues.

Then came 9/11. Security Council Resolution 1373, approved on September 28, 2001, requires every UN member state to freeze the financial assets of terrorists and their supporters, deny them travel or safe haven, prevent terrorist recruitment and weapons supply, and cooperate with other countries in information sharing and criminal prosecution.

Resolution 1373 also established the Counter-Terrorism Committee (CTC), a subsidiary body of the Security Council, to strengthen the capacity of UN member states to fight terrorism and coordinate the counterterrorism efforts of regional and intergovernmental organizations both inside and outside the UN system. In 2004 the council adopted Resolution 1535, which created the Counter Terrorism Executive Directorate, designed to give the CTC greater technical capability and expand its ability to help member states implement the provisions of Resolution 1373.

One of the CTC's greatest contributions has been to amass information about the ability of UN member states to fight terrorism. "Of course, the hard work against terrorism on the ground is

done by national governments or international agencies," says former Ambassador Akram, and therefore these governments are the
focus of the CTC's activities. Under Resolution 1373, each member
state must submit an annual report on its antiterrorism activities
and capabilities. The annual reports have revealed that numerous
smaller or less developed nations lack key elements of an effective
strategy such as the legal, administrative, and regulatory capabilities to freeze financial assets, deny safe haven to terrorists, or prevent terrorism groups from recruiting new members and acquiring
weapons.

The CTC's efforts to help these nations get the technical expertise needed to upgrade their capability may have been hindered by
the decision not to sit in judgment of UN member states or to report non-complying governments to the Security Council—a stance
adopted to maintain engagement with all member states. In its annual reports the CTC organizes the analysis by region, not country, making it impossible to determine the antiterrorist measures
and capabilities of any given member state. This preference for
working quietly and not pointing fingers at offenders has brought
criticism from some observers. As one human rights organization
complained in 2013, the CTC "has never named a single terrorist
organization or state sponsor of terrorism." To the contrary, four
states identified by the US State Department as state sponsors of
terrorism "have written reports to the CTC about their compliance
with Security Council Resolution 1373."

## The Debate over Solutions

Another barrier to full implementation of Resolution 1373 has
been the lack of consensus over which possible lines of action are
most likely to eliminate terrorism. In part this derives from disagreement on a definition of terrorism. The General Assembly has
been deliberating on counterterrorism measures to augment the international conventions now on the books. As you might expect, the
assembly's diverse membership has struggled to find consensus,
especially on this question of a definition.

## The UN's Fourteen Counterterrorism Conventions and Protocols

1. Convention on Offenses and Certain Other Acts Committed on Board Aircraft, 1963 (Tokyo Convention)
2. Convention for the Suppression of the Unlawful Seizure of Aircraft, 1970 (Hague Convention)
3. Convention for the Suppression of Unlawful Acts against the Safety of Civil Aviation, 1971 (Montreal Convention)
4. Convention on the Prevention and Punishment of Crimes against Internationally Protected Persons, 1973
5. International Convention against the Taking of Hostages, 1979 (Hostages Convention)
6. Convention on the Physical Protection of Nuclear Material, 1980
7. Protocol for the Suppression of Unlawful Acts of Violence at Airports Serving International Civil Aviation, 1988, supplementary to the Convention for the Suppression of Unlawful Acts against the Safety of Civil Aviation
8. Convention for the Suppression of Unlawful Acts against the Safety of Maritime Navigation, 1988
9. Protocol for the Suppression of Unlawful Acts against the Safety of Fixed Platforms Located on the Continental Shelf, 1988
10. Convention on the Marking of Plastic Explosives for the Purpose of Detection, 1991
11. International Convention for the Suppression of Terrorist Bombings, 1997
12. International Convention for the Suppression of the Financing of Terrorism, 1999
13. International Convention for the Suppression of Acts of Nuclear Terrorism, 2005
14. Convention on the Suppression of Unlawful Acts Relating to International Civil Aviation, 2010

Even the much smaller Security Council has engaged in fruitless debates on a clear definition. To cite one instance, at a Security Council meeting those delegates who stated a position on the matter had differing views on the desirability of even defining terrorism. The Libyan delegate (representing the Gaddafi regime) thought that there was a need for a "clear" definition. The representative from India thought that "there was no need for a philosophical definition of terrorism" because the UN already had plenty of language making terrorism a criminal activity. The representative from Venezuela thought that "in the short run, it was important to create a definition of terrorism" but that terrorism should not be equated with "legitimate struggles for national liberty and self-determination by people under colonial or foreign occupation." The United States and its friends refused to accept the distinction made by the Venezuelan representative.

Former US ambassador John Bolton has a criticism about such debates. "The conclusion you have to draw from the record on terrorism," he says, "where the Security Council creates a committee on terrorism but can't even agree on a definition of what terrorism is . . . is that it's not going to be effective in those areas." Munir Akram is just as impatient with the debates about finding a definition of terrorism, but for quite different reasons. "Perhaps the search for a definition of terrorism is a red herring," he argues. "We all know what terrorism is when we see it, and therefore the search for a legal definition perhaps is not the most urgent effort." Rather, he maintains, it is more important to understand that terrorism takes many forms, divergent from place to place. "We have to address it globally, but we have to act locally."

The Security Council has made international terrorism and its antidotes the focus of numerous meetings. At a special session on terrorism in 2012, for example, Secretary-General Ban Ki-moon opened with a call to strengthen global cooperation against terrorism. He urged an integrated approach providing "education and job opportunities, promoting development and inter-cultural dialogue, and addressing the grievances that terrorists exploited." In the ensuing debate representatives of member states denounced terrorism but without trying to define it. "Terrorism has no justification, no matter how you dress it up," declared Alexander Zmeevsky, a special envoy of the Russian Federation. Li Baodong of China stressed the need to address the "root causes" of terrorism "through integrated measures in development, as well as through a fight against intolerance and extremism," and warned that "relying on military means was counterproductive." Hardeep Singh Puri of India likewise preferred an integrated approach, because "terrorism could not be countered by law enforcement alone"—a view echoed by the representative from South Africa.

## Security Council View on Terrorism

The Security Council has developed language that it typically uses to condemn terrorist acts and terrorism in general. This is an example from Resolution 2133, passed in January 2014:

The Security Council reaffirms that "terrorism in all forms and manifestations constitutes one of the most serious threats to international peace and security and that any acts of terrorism are criminal and unjustifiable regardless of their motivations, whenever and by whomsoever committed and further reaffirm[s] the need to combat by all means, in accordance with the Charter of the United Nations, threats to international peace and security caused by terrorist acts."

The Security Council's increasing willingness to move ahead with a working concept of terrorism, without trying to gain consensus on a carefully devised definition, has been hastened by concerns that time is wasting. During the debate at the special session the representatives often remarked on a growing connection between terrorism and organized crime, as well as rising use of the Internet and other aspects of information technology to recruit terrorists and disseminate terrorist propaganda. The Security Council, and the UN in general, finds itself in a grim race with the terrorists, and winning it requires both reflection and action.

## Weapons of Mass Destruction

Much of the urgency for acting against terrorism comes from the fear that a terrorist group might acquire weapons of mass destruction (WMDs), such as poisonous chemicals, deadly microorganisms, or radioactive or even fissile material that could cause harm on a scale far beyond what happened on 9/11. When the Soviet Union unraveled in the early 1990s, some experts warned about the danger of unauthorized access to nuclear weapons or nuclear materials such as enriched uranium. Meanwhile, the UN had been developing an office to advise on both nuclear and conventional arms. Its name was changed in a series of administrative shufflings going back to the 1980s. In 2007 it became the UN Office for Disarmament Affairs (UNODA), serving as a "focal point" for promoting, assisting, and integrating disarmament efforts and related matters; it is responsible to the office of the secretary-general.

Although UNODA focuses on arms issues, it regards its work as part of a much bigger set of issues. While it acknowledges that disarmament alone will not produce world peace, it maintains that the "elimination of weapons of mass destruction, illicit arms trafficking and burgeoning weapons stockpiles would advance both peace and development goals. It would accomplish this by reducing the effects of wars, eliminating some key incentives to new conflicts, and liberating resources to improve the lives of all the people and the natural environment in which they live."

UNODA's High Representative, Angela Kane, is quick to note that her organization has to rely heavily on persuasion and public support from the secretary-general to accomplish its broad mandate. She is an experienced Secretariat insider, one of her previous posts having been under-secretary for management affairs, and enjoys a close working relationship with personnel at other UN bodies concerned with weapons and disarmament. She is also a realist. "If I were easily discouraged I wouldn't have taken this job," she says half jokingly, "because you can only advocate, only bring pressure, and you cannot easily measure success. If I were in humanitarian affairs and I did X, I could say that I had improved the world to that extent—it's measurable. But I can't do that. I can't say that there is a sudden reduction in nuclear weapons simply because I've advocated." Yet she sees opportunities for positive change. "What I argue for is transparency." For example, she asks, "Why don't we know how many nuclear weapons the nuclear states have? We think we know, we have a figure we toss around, but it's not a confirmed figure." She wants the nuclear states to provide an accurate baseline for assessing the progress of nuclear disarmament, one of her organization's long-term goals.

Nuclear-weapon issues claimed most of UNODA's attention until 2013, when a spreading civil war in Syria raised the specter of another kind of WMD. The many violent encounters between government forces and their opponents included the alleged use of chemical weapons on citizens. At the request of the Syrian and other governments the secretary-general decided to investigate the allegations. Kane led an expert team to Syria, which determined that chemical weapons had indeed been used on a relatively large scale. The Syrian government, in an agreement brokered by the Russian Federation and the United States, declared its willingness to divest itself of its chemical weapons—despite having stated in previous years that it had no chemical weapons—and acceded to the UN-sponsored Chemical Weapons Convention, whose implementation is monitored by the Organization for the Prohibition of Chemical Weapons (OPCW). The OPCW–UN Joint Mission swung into action to locate the weapons and chemical agents and transport the most dangerous chemical materials out of the country for destruction at sea. For its impressive work the OPCW received the Nobel Peace Prize.

Kane marvels at the swift response of the international community and the decisive actions that ensued, attributing much of the success to the collaboration of the Russian Federation and the United States. Other observers saw the Syrian chemical weapons affair as possibly an opening to the reduction or elimination of other kinds of WMDs in the Middle East and other parts of the globe. However, progress in curtailing nuclear proliferation and reducing nuclear stockpiles has not been nearly as impressive.

## Nuclear Threats

During the Cold War the United States and the Soviet Union, which held large nuclear arsenals and their associated delivery sys-

US Secretary of State John Kerry addresses the Security Council after its vote to adopt a resolution on Syrian chemical weapons, September 27, 2013. UN Photo / Amanda Voisard.

tems, negotiated the Nuclear Non-Proliferation Treaty (NPT) in 1970, which addressed both disarmament and proliferation. It obligated the signatories to reduce their atomic arsenals (though without setting a schedule), and it forbade acquisition of nuclear weaponry by nonnuclear states.

The nonproliferation aspect of that treaty held up pretty well for the next few decades, notes Kane, with only India, Pakistan, and Israel never joining and North Korea announcing its withdrawal. But the major nuclear powers have done little, she argues, to reduce their arsenals, and that foot-dragging has led to "increasing dissatisfaction among the nonnuclear states, that the nuclear powers don't want to do anything to change the nuclear status quo." She worries that some nonnuclear member states may decide that they can have bombs if the major powers do. "What really surprises me," she says, "is that nuclear weapons are still seen as status symbols. Excuse me? If you're not going to use them, what status do they have?"

The UN's oldest and best-known agency focusing on nuclear issues is the International Atomic Energy Agency (IAEA), which in the aftermath of September 11 became a lead entity in the UN's efforts to prevent terrorists from acquiring nuclear weapons. It is the world's forum for discussing, debating, and regulating the peaceful, and sometimes not so peaceful, use of atomic energy. Mohamed ElBaradei, the IAEA's director from 1999 to 2009, has noted that because terrorists are willing to take their own lives when committing their violence, the nuclear threat is very serious.

These concerns are shared by his successor, Yukiya Amano, who was Japan's representative to the IAEA when he was elected to become the new director-general in 2009. At a conference on nuclear security in 2013, Amano said that each year more than a hundred incidents of theft and other unauthorized activities involving nuclear and radioactive material are reported to the IAEA. "This means the material is outside regulatory control and potentially available for malicious acts," he declared. "Most of the incidents reported to us are fairly minor, but some are more serious. However, effective counter-measures are possible if all countries take the threat seriously."

The IAEA operates the Incident and Emergency Centre (IEC), the world's only international response system capable of reacting quickly after a nuclear accident or a nuclear terrorist attack. In 2013, for instance, the IEC brought more than forty experts from eighteen countries to conduct measurements in the evacuated areas around Japan's Fukushima Daiichi Nuclear Power Station, which suffered a catastrophic failure during the earthquake and tsunami of 2011. The IAEA also maintains the Incident and Trafficking Database, established in 1995, through which member states share information. As the title suggests, the goal of the database is to identify instances of illegal trafficking in nuclear and other radioactive materials, as well as cases where such materials were lost or disposed of in an unauthorized manner. During 2012 there were 160 incidents reported: 24 involving theft or loss and 119 involving "other unauthorized activities."

Participants at a session of the UN System Chief Executives Board for Coordination in Vienna include Yukiya Amano (second from right), newly appointed director-general of the International Atomic Energy Agency, April 9, 2010. UN Photo / Mark Garten.

## Resolution 1540

The concerns of the IAEA—indeed, of the whole UN family—extend also to information about how to manufacture nuclear and other weapons of mass destruction. The danger came home in 2004, when it was discovered that a Pakistani nuclear scientist, A. Q. Khan, who had helped develop his nation's nuclear bomb, had sold sensitive information to North Korea. It is not hard to imagine that someone else, likewise well placed in a national atomic weapons program, might offer to provide similar information to a terrorist organization.

Recognizing the threat, the Security Council passed Resolution 1540 on April 23, 2004. Among other things, the resolution requires member states to "refrain from supporting by any means non-State actors from developing, acquiring, manufacturing, possessing, transporting, transferring or using nuclear, chemical or biological weapons and their delivery systems." Non-state actors are private persons or groups, whether a secret terrorist ring with international connections or a vigilante coven seeking to destroy some aspect of a government. The resolution also requires member states to "adopt legislation to prevent the proliferation of nuclear, chemical and biological weapons, and their means of delivery, and establish appropriate domestic controls over related materials to prevent their illicit trafficking." Overseeing implementation of the resolution is the 1540 Committee, which was established in 2004 by the Security Council for a two-year period, later extended (Resolutions 1673, 1810, 1977) until 2021. Resolution 1977 (2011) also provides for two Comprehensive Reviews, one after five years and one before the end of the mandate.

## Nonproliferation or Abolition?

Resolution 1540 focuses on the need to prevent the proliferation of WMDs, that is, the acquisition of these dangerous weapons by persons or groups who did not previously possess them. The resolution did not speak of abolishing the WMDs that sit in the arsenals of the United States and several other member states. Some have argued that the surest way of preventing proliferation would be to destroy all WMDs, even those held by member states. The debate about whether to pursue nonproliferation or abolition has continued, sharpened by the fact that nuclear weapons are now within the reach of nations with small industrial and technological bases, as is clear from the situation in North Korea.

One of Kofi Annan's last speeches as secretary-general dealt with precisely this issue. He characterized the Nuclear Non-Proliferation Treaty as a bargain between the nuclear states and the rest of the world. The nuclear states declared they would negotiate in good faith on nuclear disarmament, would prevent proliferation, and would encourage the peaceful use of nuclear energy. In return, noted Annan, the nonnuclear nations agreed not to acquire or manufacture nuclear weapons and to place all their nuclear activities under the verification of the IAEA.

The stability engendered by the agreement lasted until two states that had ratified the treaty were accused of trying to develop nuclear weapons. The government of North Korea started a serious nuclear program in 1989 aimed at producing weapons-grade materials, even though it had agreed to the NPT. Inspectors from the IAEA who visited North Korea under terms of the treaty complained that the government was not providing full information about the nuclear facilities, and the dispute escalated. In 2003 the North Koreans declared they would withdraw from the NPT, and the last IAEA inspections were in 2009. Since then the North Koreans have pushed ahead and tested small nuclear weapons capable of being mounted in long-range missiles, which they are also developing. It is unclear how much the Security Council's sanctions (see chapter 6) have slowed the North Korean efforts to become a nuclear power.

Iran is the other member state that seems poised to develop a nuclear weapons program despite having signed the NPT. The Iranians claim that they are creating a civilian nuclear power industry, but many observers and the US government believe that Iran also aims to make weapons-grade material. Civilian nuclear power programs offer a potential source of enriched uranium, either for processing into fission bombs or for use as "dirty" bombs, which produce massive radiation. The more these civilian programs expand, the greater is the risk of proliferation. Ruth Wedgwood calls this crossover between peaceful and military potential a "fatal flaw" in the Nuclear Non-Proliferation Treaty. "The assumption was that you could segregate civilian and military uses. . . . But enriched uranium is enriched uranium, as North Korea and Iran have shown. The irony is that if you have the proliferation of civilian uses, you're going to have proliferation of weapons uses."

Unlike the North Koreans, the Iranians have continued to accept the NPT and have allowed inspectors to visit some of their nuclear facilities. IAEA inspectors concluded, however, in a report issued in 2013, that they were unable to assess fully the military implications of the nuclear program and urged the Iranians to be more forthcoming with information. The IAEA's director-general put the problem neatly in remarks made in 2012: inspectors were able to track the nuclear material they knew about, but could only guess at what the Iranians were not showing them. As with North Korea, the Security Council has passed sanctions aimed at delaying or preventing Iran from developing nuclear weapons, and they may have had an effect. The Iranians agreed in 2013 to join talks with the P5+Germany aimed at finding a solution to ensure that Iran's nuclear program will be exclusively peaceful.

## Can the UN Do It?

As UN resolutions on terrorism and WMDs have been made, one after the other, some experts believe that the organization's reach may be exceeding its grasp. It is fine to outlaw terrorist acts, they note, but quite another thing to get compliance from member states. Moreover, counterterrorism often requires exactly the kind of stealthy intelligence gathering and quick action that the UN is not known for. According to William Luers, there are "certain issues in global affairs the UN is not equipped to deal with, such as international terrorism, illicit trafficking in humans, and drugs, all flowing out of globalization." The UN, he argues, "has not faced up to terrorism. It has committees and great intentions, but the nature of terrorism doesn't allow for a decisive UN role, though it is seeking to identify what that might be."

Sebastian von Einsiedel, director of the UN University's Centre for Policy Research, argues that the UN was "fairly effective in getting some state sponsors of terrorism out of the terrorism business through Security Council sanctions in the 1990s," referring to measures against Libya (for the bombing of a commercial flight over Lockerbee, Scotland) and Sudan (where al-Qaeda was then lurking), but less successful with respect to Afghanistan (under the Taliban). While "the big Council-mandated terrorism architecture put together after 9/11 [Security Council Resolution 1373 and the Counter-Terrorism Committee] started out promising," it did not lead to as much action as hoped. The Obama administration, in his view, seeing the need for a complementary route, decided to create "new structures outside the UN," such as the Global Terrorism Forum. Von Einsiedel acknowledges the UN's important role in legitimizing multinational intervention in countries such as Mali, where an al-Qaeda cell emerged as a lead element in an insurgency so threatening that it brought intervention by French military forces in 2013.

Unfortunately, the UN has itself become a target of terrorists. The first attack came during the early stages of the US-led occupation of Iraq in 2003, when a car bomb at the United Nations Assistance Mission in Iraq killed at least twenty-two people, including the UN's' special representative in Iraq, Sérgio Vieira de Mello. An al-Qaeda leader claimed responsibility for the blast, which was followed by another bombing a month later. In December 2007 an al-Qaeda–inspired suicide bombing destroyed the UN headquarters building in Algiers and killed nearly forty people, including seventeen UN employees. Al-Qaeda and its affiliates have also threatened or targeted UN officials and peacekeepers in Afghanistan, Somalia, Sudan, and southern Lebanon. In 2011 an Islamist terrorist organization claimed responsibility for a car bombing that killed many staff members at a UN building in Abuja, Nigeria.

The head of a UN team established to monitor the effectiveness of UN sanctions against al-Qaeda and the Taliban stated that "al-Qaeda certainly regards the UN as inimical to its own interests." One of the UN's longtime troubleshooters, Lakhdar Brahimi, was appointed the head of a panel to review security at the organization's facilities worldwide. "I think there are quite a lot of people who do not make a secret that they consider that the UN has become their enemy," he told reporters ominously. "I think the UN has been put on notice that their flag is not anymore a protection."

Despite the UN's limitations and vulnerabilities, it does provide access to information for the counterterrorism effort, and it has a coordinating function as well. Munir Akram puts it this way: "The UN is important because it maintains the international consensus on the issue of terrorism—how to address terrorism and try to take

UN offices in Algiers destroyed by terrorist bombing, December 11, 2007. UN Photos / Evan Schneider.

into account the views and interests of all concerned." In the long term, the UN's greatest contribution may include its social and economic programs, which Akram sees as addressing the root causes of terrorism. "The major focus has to be on economic and social development, on education, on efforts to wean away the appeal of terrorism."

Beyond the terrorism issue lies the huge question of arms reduction by member states, including even the possibility of nuclear disarmament. Here the UN can do little more than persuade, encourage, and use the bully pulpit, but such activities have considerable value, argues Angela Kane. The UN can also do something else: it can help the world community set standards, as in cyber security, "through the patient work of experts sitting around, coming up with results. Even if it's at a low initial level, that's when you build on every single step. It's a normative effort, and that's what the UN does extremely well." Kane admits that "sometimes it takes a long time, but you cannot do this overnight."

## Leading UN Actors

- The International Atomic Energy Agency (IAEA) was established in 1957 and is based in Vienna. It is the global forum for discussing and regulating the uses of atomic energy. Its Department of Technical Cooperation helps countries improve their scientific and technological capabilities in the peaceful application of nuclear technology. Safety and the protection of people from radiation have been important concerns. Inspectors watch more than a thousand nuclear installations worldwide that are covered under the IAEA Safeguards Program. The US government strongly endorses the work of the agency. The IAEA and its then director, Mohamed ElBaradei, shared the Nobel Peace Prize in 2005.
- The Organization for the Prohibition of Chemical Weapons (OPCW) is headquartered at The Hague. Its primary task is to monitor the provisions of the Convention on the Prohibition of the Development, Production, Stockpiling, and Use of Chemical Weapons and on Their Destruction, which entered into force in 1997, which is the first multilateral disarmament and non-

proliferation agreement that addresses the verifiable worldwide elimination of a whole class of weapons of mass destruction. The organization received the Nobel Peace Prize in 2013 for its work in Syria.

- The Preparatory Commission for the Comprehensive Nuclear-Test-Ban Treaty Organization (CTBTO), established in 1996, is based in Vienna. The commission's main job is to refine a verification plan to ensure that the signers of the Nuclear Test Ban Treaty are adhering to its terms.
- UN Office for Disarmament Affairs (UNODA), based in New York City, promotes nuclear disarmament and nonproliferation; encourages disarmament efforts in connection with other weapons of mass destruction and chemical and biological weapons; and advances disarmament programs for conventional weapons, especially land mines and small arms. UNODA had a role in the General Assembly's approval (April 2013) of the Arms Trade Treaty (ATT), which regulates the international trade in conventional arms with the aim of curbing arms flows to conflict regions.

## CHAPTER 11

# Human Rights and R2P

*And so when we respect our international legal obligations and support an international system based on the rule of law, we do the work of making the world a better place, but also a safer and more secure place for America.*

—Condoleezza Rice, former US secretary of state

Rights come first everywhere you look at the United Nations. The purpose of the organization, according to Article 1 of the Charter, is to promote and encourage "respect for human rights and for fundamental freedoms for all without distinction as to race, sex, language, or religion." The Universal Declaration of Human Rights, as we saw earlier, is literally all about rights (see appendix B). Nearly all states that join the UN have agreed to accept its principles by signing and ratifying two international covenants, one addressing civil and political rights and the other economic, social, and cultural rights. The International Covenant on Civil and Political Rights and the International Covenant on Economic, Social, and Cultural Rights, which entered into force in 1976, are legally binding documents. When combined with the Universal Declaration, they constitute the International Bill of Human Rights.

## An Emerging Body of Law

Having rights, real ones that you can actually exercise, requires more than rhetoric and fancy legal language. Rights imply the rule of law, based on the notion that all citizens are equal before the law and that the law will be applied in a rational, consistent manner. You also need mechanisms for protecting and enforcing both the law and the exercise of rights. All of these things are represented in the UN's law and rights establishment, ranging from national tribunals to an associated international court and a council and an executive dedicated to rights issues. "The UN has meant more to the field of human rights than it has to other fields that it works in," declares Felice Gaer, a human rights advocate who directs the Jacob Blaustein Institute for the Advancement of Human Rights in New York City. She says that even though the UN has done a lot in areas like security and development, "in human rights it's been a really big factor."

Other experts offer a similar assessment. Ruth Wedgwood of Johns Hopkins University praises the human rights treaties as being "a great step forward" for many countries. Esther Brimmer of George Washington University makes a similar point when discussing the emerging nations. "The interesting thing about these countries is that most of them are democracies in some way; their publics have connections to their government. So they're actually interesting on topics that are relevant to Western countries, issues like human rights or freedom of speech. You want to talk to these emerging countries because they have views on these topics which have credibility. It's a very different thing than if you're trying to talk to China."

The UN is proud of having helped create a large body of human rights law. Most member states have signed and ratified some eighty treaties (also called conventions or covenants) that address particular aspects of human rights. The International Law Commission is the body that does the actual drafting of text for international conventions. Here are only a few treaties, with the year when the General Assembly adopted them for signing:

- 1948 Convention on the Prevention and Punishment of the Crime of Genocide
- 1951 Convention Relating to the Status of Refugees
- 1965 International Convention on the Elimination of All Forms of Racial Discrimination
- 1979 Convention on the Elimination of All Forms of Discrimination against Women
- 1984 Convention against Torture and Other Cruel, Inhuman, or Degrading Treatment or Punishment
- 1992 Convention on the Prohibition of the Development, Stockpiling, and Use of Chemical Weapons and on Their Destruction
- 2013 Arms Trade Treaty

When a convention enters force, the UN may create a watchdog committee charged with ensuring that its provisions are honored by member states. For example, when the Convention on the Rights of the Child entered into force in 1989, it was accompanied by the creation of the Committee on the Rights of the Child, which meets regularly and has become an international voice for children. All offices and staff of the UN and its peacekeeping operations are responsible for adhering to international human rights law and reporting possible breaches of it to the proper authorities.

## Rights and Security

"There has been a deepening of the understanding that human rights and security are related," notes Esther Brimmer, speaking about an important new way of regarding the role of human rights in the whole UN system. "You can think about the fact that, in history, we tend to put the issue of security in one box and human rights in another box. But actually the argument that you need to have just societies in order to grapple with the issues, so that they don't degenerate to conflicts, makes sense." That insight has implications for how the UN system works because it requires that people and agencies working on different aspects of a problem or issue "should be aware and talking to each other about what they see."

And that is beginning to happen, as Brimmer points out. "So, for example, now the High Commissioner for Human Rights briefs the Security Council. There are times when the human rights commissioner flies in from Geneva and speaks in New York." Beyond that, "look at the Security Council resolutions; there are more places within the peacekeeping resolutions which include human rights elements. . . . There's a sense that the observation of the conduct of human rights is part of the security package. Usually you wouldn't have people even thinking in those terms; that's a different way of understanding, a holistic understanding of security, that you should try to use these tools together for an overall security."

The new perspective makes the rule of law and human rights even more important to the UN system than when it was founded, in 1945.

## The World Court

Americans, when they think of the rule of law, may imagine a courtroom scene, dominated by the imposing figure of the robed judge, seated on high, flanked by the jury box, faced by the prosecutor and the defendant, and with a silent, respectful audience sitting in front. Although the UN is not a government, it does have courts and tribunals, some of them as imposing and solemn as any in the United States.

The International Court of Justice (ICJ), also known as the World Court, is one of the six principal organs of the UN. Based in The Hague, the court offers two kinds of services. It gives advisory opinions on legal questions referred to it by UN organs and agencies, and it settles legal disputes submitted to it by UN member states. Sometimes one member state will bring a case against another member state, but in other situations the two contending states may mutually agree to bring their case before the court. In either event, states that bring a case before the court are obliged to obey its decision. The World Court's first case concerned a boundary jurisdiction involving the United Kingdom and Albania and was filed in May 1947. Between then and July 2013 states brought 153 cases before the court. Among cases in process by then were Peru versus Chile, a maritime dispute; Australia versus Japan, a whaling dispute; and Cambodia versus Thailand, a dispute concerning Cambodia's Temple of Preah Vihear.

The court's fifteen judges, who serve nine-year terms, are elected by the Security Council and the General Assembly through a complicated procedure. No two judges may be nationals of the same state.

## The International Criminal Court

The International Criminal Court (ICC) is solely a criminal tribunal. Established by the Rome Treaty of 1998, the ICC institutionalizes the concept of an international tribunal for crimes against humanity, war crimes, and genocide. Strictly speaking, it is an independent body, and its prosecutors and eighteen judges are not formally part of the UN. They are accountable only to the countries that have ratified the Rome Treaty (which was sponsored by the UN).

The court is not a venue of first resort. Instead, the accused come before the ICC only if their home country has signed the Rome Treaty but is unable or unwilling to act. To prevent malicious or frivolous accusations, the Rome Treaty requires prosecutors to justify their decisions according to generally recognized principles that exclude politically motivated charges.

Before the creation of the ICC there were no international courts for trying persons accused of committing atrocities. The Security Council tried to fill this gap through the creation of special tribunals designed to bring justice to specific nations ravaged by civil war. It created the first such tribunal in 1993 to investigate massacres in the former Yugoslavia. Other tribunals established by the Security Council or with its cooperation have followed, among them one to address alleged genocide and other crimes in Rwanda (1994); another to investigate atrocities against civilians in Sierra Leone (2002); and another focusing on serious criminal offenses in Lebanon (2007).

The United States has applauded the formation of the UN tribunals and has been their most generous donor, but it has been far less enthusiastic about the ICC. When the Rome Treaty came to the United States for ratification, it got a cool reception. The Clinton administration signed it with reservations based on concerns about the possibility of capricious prosecutions. The George W. Bush administration stated that it would not send the treaty to Congress for ratification without major changes aimed at protecting US military and government personnel against "politically motivated war crimes prosecutions." It also removed the US signature from the treaty, to the satisfaction of those in Congress who claimed it violated US sovereignty.

Even though the White House and Congress resisted ratification, the rest of the world made the ICC a reality. The Rome Treaty gained enough signatures to establish the court, officially inaugurated at The Hague in 2003. "The ICC does provide an important place to try to begin to deal with some of the accountability issues," notes Esther Brimmer. "Of course," she adds, "as a judicial process, it's relatively slow, and it's probably a frustration for those who want to move more quickly."

The ICC tried its first case in 2007, with the filing of charges against an alleged militia leader from the DRC for "enlisting, conscripting and using" children to "participate actively in hostilities." In 2008, the court's prosecutor, Luis Moreno-Ocampo of Argentina, began investigating alleged atrocities in the Central African Republic, northern Uganda, and (at the request of the Security Council) the Darfur region of Sudan. The court is also investigating situations that occurred in Côte d'Ivoire, Kenya, Libya, and Mali, and it issued a precedent-setting arrest warrant for Sudan's president, Hassan al-Bashir, for complicity in war crimes in Darfur. In July 2013 the ICC actually requested that the government of Nigeria arrest Sudan's president while he was on a visit to Nigeria.

These cases involve Africans, a fact commented upon by some Africans. Brimmer advises the court's supporters to speak out against "the rather pernicious argument that it only indicts African leaders. I think that's been a convenient argument from the heads of Kenya and elsewhere, and the African Union. I think it's up to member states' parties to try to counter that argument." It should be noted that as of March 2014 most of the court's cases had been brought at the request either of the Security Council (Darfur and Libya) or of an African government (Central African Republic, DRC, Mali, Uganda), and only two by the court's prosecutor.

There are signs that the US government may be softening its stance on the ICC. According to a recent statement by the State Department, the US government supports "the I.C.C.'s prosecution of those cases that advance U.S. interests and values, consistent with the requirements of U.S. law." It goes on to note that "since November 2009, the United States has participated in an observer capacity in meetings of the I.C.C. Assembly of States Parties (ASP). The United States sent an observer delegation to the I.C.C. Review Conference held in Kampala, Uganda, from May 31 to June 11, 2010."

Brimmer also sees a better relationship emerging. "The US is trying to show that it supports the norm of the ICC even though in no time soon will it be able to ratify [the Rome Treaty]." She believes "there's a sense that you would cooperate in terms of providing open-source information when the ICC asks states for relevant information; that you would do that like a normal member state rather than ignoring the request or trying to undermine the request. You respond to the request with your analysis of what's going on, like a normal state," rather than giving, as previously, an "actively hostile response."

## A Council, Not a Commission

Most legal and rights issues do not require a trial in the courtroom. Courts are expensive instruments, and trying cases can consume great amounts of time and money. Both in the United States and the UN, it is usually faster and more efficient to operate through negotiation and discussion to find a mutually acceptable solution that will also be legally and morally sound. In the UN, the Charter places the main burden of examining and resolving human rights issues upon the Commission on Human Rights, created in 1946, and chaired originally by none other than Eleanor Roosevelt.

Secretary-General Ban Ki-moon and Aung San Suu Kyi, Nobel Prize–winning political and rights activist and general secretary of Myanmar's National League for Democracy, at her residence in Yangon, May 1, 2012. UN Photo / Mark Garten.

For decades the commission was the main UN body for making human rights policy and providing a forum for discussion. It met each year in Geneva, Switzerland, and held public meetings on violations of human rights. When necessary, it appointed experts, called special rapporteurs, to examine rights abuses or conditions in specific countries.

Unfortunately, the commission gained a reputation for biases against certain nations, such as Israel and the United States, and for turning a blind eye to gross rights abuses by authoritarian regimes, such as those in China, Russia, and Iran. Observers commented that the commission's members often included nations notorious for their failure to observe the human rights standards that the commission was supposed to be monitoring.

The behavior of the commission became such a scandal among US and European member states that something drastic had to be done. The General Assembly agreed to abolish the commission and replace it in 2006 with a new, improved body called the Human Rights Council (HRC). The new body has forty-seven members, elected to three-year terms through secret ballot by the General Assembly. Seats are allotted by world region: thirteen to Africa, thirteen to Asia, eight to Latin America and the Caribbean, seven to Western Europe and other states, and six to Eastern Europe.

Like its predecessor commission, the council makes frequent use of unpaid representatives, called special rapporteurs, or working groups consisting of one or more independent experts, whom it appoints as monitors and in some cases as investigators for human rights issues, either in specific countries (country mandates) or across the spectrum of member states (thematic mandates). The rapporteurs and working groups rely on the Office of the High Commissioner for Human Rights to provide them with assistance to discharge their mandates.

When the General Assembly appoints members to the council, it is, in the HRC's own words, supposed to take into account "the candidate States' contribution to the promotion and protection of human rights, as well as their voluntary pledges and commitments in this regard." This claim initially drew much attention from critics, who charged that the new council looked and acted a lot like the old commission. Soon after it was inaugurated in June 2006 it began attracting as much criticism as its predecessor, and from the same critics. For starters, its charter members included China, Russia, and Saudi Arabia, whose human rights records were criticized by many Western observers. So unappealing did the new council seem that the US government decided not to seek a seat on it.

That was not what the reformers had planned. "Our original idea, which the Europeans shared," says former US ambassador John Bolton, "was that we would have a whole series of procedural changes to the new Human Rights Council that in the aggregate would result in a divergent kind of membership from the Human Rights Commission, so that you wouldn't have those abusers of human rights or simply countries that didn't much care about human rights and were on the commission just because it was a good thing to be on." Bolton accuses the Europeans of failing to push for reforms that the United States wanted, which meant "that the new body was not going to be that much divergent from the prior body, and in fact that's exactly what happened. That's one reason we voted against it in 2006, because we said it's not much divergent from the Human Rights Commission."

Rights expert Ruth Wedgwood agrees that the Europeans did not push hard enough for meaningful changes in the new council. "The attempted reform was done too quickly," she argues. "The number of countries was only slightly cut down and the predominance of the South was increased. With regional loyalties, even on human rights issues, this made it more likely that the council would spend the bulk of its disposable time on Israel and Palestine." UN insider Jeffrey Laurenti is similarly critical of "this crazy drive to shrink it," which meant the loss of four Western seats. "What were these people thinking?" he asks.

From the other side of the aisle, however, the council didn't look so flawed. According to Pakistan's former ambassador Munir Akram, the old Human Rights Commission was accused of being "a one-sided body, a politicized body, and ineffective in defending human rights," so it was proposed to create a smaller council "to keep the riffraff out so that the major powers could have a smaller body in which they could take the 'right' decisions." According to Akram, the developing countries argued that whatever the size of the proposed council, "it should reflect the actual composition of the General Assembly and the regional groups in the General Assembly." Since, by Akram's math, more than 130 of the 193 UN member nations fall into the developing category, they should arguably constitute the great majority of members of the Human Rights Council.

That is actually how the council was set up, remarks Akram, and "some of our friends in the North are not happy about that." It was mere coincidence, he says, that when the council began its work, unrest and war broke out in Lebanon and Gaza, so the council addressed those events. The Europeans had insisted that a special session of the

John Ashe, president of the sixty-eighth session of the General Assembly, addresses the opening of the twenty-fifth regular session of the Human Rights Council, Geneva, March 3, 2014. UN Photo / Eskinder Debebe.

council could be called by only one-third of the members. "Well, guess what: two can play the game," says Akram, "and therefore special sessions were called by our Arab friends on Palestine and Lebanon, and now it's been said that the council is targeting Israel. But conditions and procedures were dictated by the very same countries that are complaining about it right now."

Ruth Wedgwood saw the council's initial actions as evidence that the old politics were returning. She was especially concerned that North-South issues might tarnish one of the procedural safeguards that the Europeans managed to retain in the new council, the Universal Periodic Review (UPR). That is a regular process of issuing reports on the compliance of each UN member nation with human rights norms, including its obligations under the specific human rights treaties that it has joined. Such reports have value only if conducted in an impartial and rigorous manner, "and they could be positively dangerous if countries lie about their handling of rights."

The Obama administration decided in 2009 that instead of sniping from the sidelines, it was better to join the council and exercise leadership in the proceedings. The State Department's view in a 2013 report was that American leadership had produced significant results in a variety of places, ranging from human rights in Belarus, Syria, and Eritrea to women's rights around the world. "As a member of the Council," notes the report, "the United States' mission remains to highlight key human rights issues while vigorously opposing efforts to shield human rights violators."

UN insiders generally agree that the Obama administration's decision to engage the council had a beneficial impact. Brimmer praises Washington's participation. "The most important thing the United States has done at the UN in the last five years has been to normalize relations in the Human Rights Council, hands down," she says without hesitation. It has been able to move proceedings away from sterile debates about Israel to discussions on current issues like Libya, Syria, and North Korea. Stewart Patrick of the Council on Foreign Relations largely agrees. "One of the things which would have to be counted as a success is the Obama administration's efforts to engage the Human Rights Council and turn it into a useful instrument," he declares. "That statement remains controversial. There are those who continue to believe that the Human Rights Council is a den of abusers—and it does include abusers, of course—but not in the sense that it puts the foxes in charge of the hen house." Rather, he asserts, "if you look at the success that the administration has had in rolling up its sleeves, they got a bunch of resolutions condemning the actions of particular governments including Syria, while the Security Council wasn't doing very much. At least it's managed to keep a number of abusers . . . off of the Human Rights Council, and through the system of Universal Periodic Review it's managed to shed light on some of the abusers. It's made things better so that the glass is half full as opposed to before," when it was "most certainly half empty, more than half empty."

However, the improvements came after an initial period of chaos, argues Hillel Neuer of UN Watch, and have only returned things to the generally "depressing" level of the old Human Rights Commission. He notes that while recent Human Rights Council resolutions had indeed targeted rights abusers like Iran, other nations, like Saudi Arabia and China, have totally escaped discussion. The United States and other Western nations are unwilling to challenge those member states, he says. They have received "a free pass."

## The High Commissioner

Criticisms of the council sometimes obscure the presence of another force in the UN rights establishment. In 1993 the General Assembly established the post of UN High Commissioner for Human Rights, responsible to the secretary-general. The high commissioner's office is charged with being a secretariat for the Human Rights Council, overseeing the UN's human rights activities, helping develop rights standards, and promoting international cooperation to expand and protect rights. The office does not control the Human Rights Council, nor does it have much influence over it or its special rapporteurs.

"The high commissioner's role is not defined, so it's up to each high commissioner" to define it, says Wedgwood. "Part of the work of the overall job is to help coordinate the development of the jurisprudence of the human rights treaty bodies. This has been a challenge because each of the committees is made up of volunteers and has its own trajectory. You also have the problem of countries having to report on multiple topics to multiple treaty bodies and of the committees potentially taking divergent views of issues."

The first high commissioner was José Ayala-Lasso of Ecuador, who was succeeded in 1997 by Mary Robinson, former president of Ireland. Her successor was Sérgio Vieira de Mello of Brazil, who in 2004 was succeeded by Louise Arbour of Canada. In 2008, Ban Ki-moon named Navenethem (Navi) Pillay, a South African judge and the former president of the International Criminal Tribunal for

A Security Council debate on the promotion and strengthening of the rule of law in the maintenance of international peace and security, February 19, 2014. Linas Antanas Linkevičius, foreign minister of the Republic of Lithuania and president of the Security Council for February, chairs the session. On his right is Secretary-General Ban Ki-moon. UN Photo / Evan Schneider.

Rwanda, as the next commissioner. She was succeeded in fall 2014 by Prince Zeid Ra'ad Zeid al-Hussein of Jordan.

## The Responsibility to Protect (R2P)

Everyone is "for" human rights, but people may not agree on how to enforce rights when they seem to conflict with national sovereignty. If mass atrocities are being committed within a nation—something that has happened with lamentable frequency—does the world community have the obligation or the right to intervene to stop it? The usual response over the decades has been no.

Kofi Annan proposed to alter the historical approach by arguing that international human rights law must apply in each member state and that certain acts, such as genocide, war crimes, and crimes against humanity, cannot be allowed to occur with impunity. He based his view, no doubt, on his own bitter recollection of events in places like Rwanda and Bosnia, where the UN was accused of doing too little to prevent mass murders. Annan was under-secretary-general for peacekeeping during those years (1992–96).

Annan formally stated his new approach to intervention in an address at the General Assembly in September 1999, in which he asked member states "to unite in the pursuit of more effective policies to stop organized mass murder and egregious violations of human rights." Conceding that there were many ways to intervene, he asserted that not only diplomacy but even armed action was an acceptable option. Many leaders in Africa were coming to the same conclusion. Representatives of nations drafting the Charter of the African Union (AU) in 2000 declared in Article 4(h) that it is the "right of the Union to intervene in a Member State pursuant to a decision of the Assembly in respect of grave circumstances, namely war crimes, genocide and crimes against humanity."

At Annan's urging the Canadian government established the International Commission on State Sovereignty, whose report, issued in 2001, laid out the basic principles of what became known as the responsibility to protect (R2P). In 2005 world leaders at the UN World Summit endorsed the concept, and in 2009 Secretary-General Ban Ki-moon issued a report, *Implementing the Responsibility to Protect,* that sought to make the concept into a working principle. This basic document set forth the three pillars of R2P:

1. States have the primary responsibility for protecting their citizens from genocide, war crimes, crimes against humanity, and ethnic cleansing.
2. The international community is responsible for helping states protect their citizens from these crimes.
3. The international community is responsible for acting decisively and in a timely manner to prevent or halt these crimes when a state is evidently failing to protect its citizens.

Since the secretary-general's report, R2P has been invoked by various parties, including the UN and human rights NGOs. The Security Council has embraced it and incorporated it into numerous resolutions. The council first mentioned the term officially in 2006, in Resolution 1674, on the protection of civilians in armed conflict, and later referred to the resolution when passing Resolution 1706, authorizing deployment of a peacekeeping mission to Darfur. Later council resolutions and statements mentioned R2P as an issue—for example, in Libya (Resolutions 1970 and 1973), Côte d'Ivoire (Resolution 1975), South Sudan (Resolution 1996), Yemen (Resolution 2014), and the Central African Republic (Resolution 2121).

Edward Luck, an expert on R2P, praises Annan for "putting humanitarian intervention on the map" and expressing "the dilemma facing the international community." He also recognizes that R2P is a controversial issue. Pakistan's former permanent representative Akram, like some other observers, sees R2P as merely a "slogan," and not even a necessary one. "International humanitarian law already allows the international community to act in cases where there are such crimes—war crimes, genocide, crimes against humanity," he maintains. "You don't need new decisions or new conventions for that purpose." He elaborates. "Wherever there has been genocide—in Srebrenica or Rwanda—in recent years, it has been because of the failure of the great powers to allow the international community to act. Srebrenica, we know what happened: the Security Council would not send troops to protect those defenseless people, who we knew were going to be slaughtered, and the Dutch troops stood by while the slaughter happened. So where is the R2P?" Akram maintains that responsibility for failing to protect lies not with the developing countries but with the major powers, "and therefore this is an exercise to salve their conscience."

The controversy over R2P has also brought complaints that it could be used as a pretext for other aims. That charge has been made in connection with the Security Council's decision to intervene in the Libyan civil war that toppled dictator Muammar Gaddafi. Civil unrest became overt in 2011 and soon moved to open conflict between rebels and the government. Speeches by Gaddafi and the actions of his military forces suggested that the government would try to suppress the uprising brutally.

Attempts by the United Kingdom, the United States, and other nations and regional groups, including the African Union, to encourage a political resolution did not bring peace. The Security Council decided to intervene, first with Resolution 1970, passed unanimously in February 2011, which declared that the Libyan government had a responsibility to protect its citizens. It also imposed an arms embargo and other sanctions and asked the International Criminal Court to investigate allegations of crimes against humanity. When the Libyan government seemingly ignored the resolution, the Security Council passed a much stronger one, Resolution 1973, in March that, among other items, authorized UN member states to impose a no-fly zone over Libya and apply all measures necessary to protect civilians in threatened areas.

Proponents of Resolution 1973 argued that peaceful attempts to prevent crimes against humanity had failed and that there was no alternative to the use of military force. A significant minority of council members—China, Brazil, Germany, India, and Russia—had reservations about the resolution, though instead of opposing it, they simply abstained from voting. Some skeptics wondered whether all peaceful means really had been exhausted. The African Union thought more could be done. Moreover, the application of military force raised serious issues: How much force, and for how long? Should it be aimed solely at protecting civilians, or could it be applied to advance the cause of the rebels?

NATO air forces immediately began airstrikes to stop the Gaddafi regime from sending tanks against civilians. They also helped the rebels counterattack the government forces and eventually take control of the country. According to Mark Malloch-Brown, the airstrikes went beyond the scope of the Security Council resolution. "Somehow this correlation was being introduced between R2P and the right to intervene," he remarks. "In fact the R2P doctrine was always meant to assume a lot of pre-intervention effort to mitigate, head-off, or resolve conflict, and was not meant to be a rush to arms." As he sees it, "R2P rests on a concept of individual rights vs. state rights that is very European and not universally accepted." To make it work requires "a clear framework of agreed action" that will not be exceeded. "It's got to become a code of interstate conduct which is fully respected even when it means that some jerk doesn't lose his presidential palace. The purpose is to prevent him from hurting his citizens, not to open up a generalized effort to remove him, even though logic may often—and Gaddafi was an example—impel the idea that the only way to remove the threat is to remove him."

Part of the fallout from the Libyan intervention, in Malloch-Brown's view, has been a loss of trust among the five permanent members of the Security Council. The Chinese and Russians may, he says, now see R2P as simply a device to justify intervention that may involve regime change and other goals not directly related to protecting civilians. That concern, he argues, was a major reason why China and Russia prevented attempts by the Security Council to intervene strongly in the Syrian civil war. The United States and its allies, however, may take a different view of R2P.

Caught in the middle is the secretary-general, who must satisfy all P5 members if he is to attain his objectives. Ban Ki-moon shows no sign of wavering. Rather, he has been a staunch supporter of R2P since the day he took office in 2007. Madeleine Albright thinks Ban is doing the right thing. "The secretary-general keeps pushing," she says, "and ultimately we have to show that the concept of national sovereignty and the responsibility to protect can work together."

## CHAPTER 12

# ECOSOC and NGOs

*The Economic and Social Council may make or initiate studies and reports with respect to international economic, social, cultural, educational, health, and related matters and may make recommendations with respect to any such matters to the General Assembly, to the Members of the United Nations, and to the specialized agencies concerned.*

—UN Charter

The Economic and Social Council, or ECOSOC, established as a principal organ of the UN, is one of those organizations that may work better on paper than in practice. It was intended to function as a forum for discussing international social, economic, and humanitarian issues, as well as to coordinate the work of UN agencies and bodies concerned with those issues. As part of its coordinating role, ECOSOC commissions studies, writes reports, and makes policy recommendations to the General Assembly and other parts of the UN on a wide range of issues, from rights to international finance. The Charter also authorizes it to draft General Assembly resolutions and even to convene conferences. Every spring, for example, it hosts a high-level conference of the Bretton Woods Institutions (the World Bank and the International Monetary Fund), the World Trade Organization (WTO), and the UN Conference on Trade and Development (UNCTAD) focused on international finance and development.

Perhaps because its mission is so broad it has struggled to define a clear identity and has been accused of a lack of focus. Insiders have remarked on ECOSOC's talent for fostering debate that leads to little apparent action. Some diplomats, like Canadian David Malone, have found the organization's fuzziness and long discussions hard to endure. This has spawned recommendations for reworking the body, some of which have been adopted, including a full-time move to New York. Under the previous confusing arrangement it alternated between New York and Geneva.

Despite the criticisms, membership in ECOSOC is coveted, owing to the body's central role in the UN universe. Its fifty-four members, elected by the General Assembly, serve three-year terms.

## Counting the Hours

"The worst two years of my professional life, 1990 to 92, were spent as Canada's representative of ECOSOC. A complete waste of time."
—David Malone, former Canadian ambassador to the UN

## Looking for Focus

Pakistan's former ambassador Munir Akram believes that ECOSOC would be very functional and relevant if it had the same kind of binding authority on economic decisions that the Security Council has for political and security issues. "You have to empower ECOSOC," he asserts. "You have to see how to make it work in a system that is relevant to the real world." One can imagine Malone nodding in agreement but asking, How?

In 2005, the UN adopted proposals by several member states to update ECOSOC through two mechanisms. One is the Annual

Delegates attending a special event of the Economic and Social Council on "security sector reform," November 4, 2013. UN Photo / Paulo Filgueiras.

Ministerial Review (AMR), and the other is the Development Cooperation Forum. The AMR enables ECOSOC to hold annual meetings for reviewing international policies about trade and development, including the Millennium Development Goals (MDGs). The first AMR, which convened in Geneva in July 2007, focused on "strengthening efforts to eradicate poverty and hunger, including through the global partnership for development." For 2013 the topic was "Science, technology and innovation (STI) and culture for sustainable development and the MDGs." The Development Cooperation Forum, in contrast, reviews the status of development cooperation within the UN system. Since its launch in 2007 the forum has met in alternate years, beginning in 2008.

David Malone is skeptical that the reforms will make a big change in the organization's corporate culture and mode of thinking. Esther Brimmer comments simply that of all the parts of the UN system "ECOSOC shows the least amount of real change."

## Working with the NGOs

An irony of ECOSOC's difficult evolution is that one of its most important and delicate tasks today was barely on the radar screen back in 1945, when the organization was created. ECOSOC is the intermediary between the General Assembly and nongovernmental organizations. NGOs are independent, nonprofit groups. In the United States they are usually known as "nonprofit organizations" because Americans distinguish between private enterprise (which is profit-making) and civil society (which is not), but in most of the world, where the crucial distinction is between governmental and nongovernmental, NGO makes more sense as a category. (Outside the United States, business is often included in civil society, again because the crucial distinction is between governmental versus nongovernmental.)

There were few NGOs decades ago when the UN was founded, but their number worldwide has multiplied many times over since then. The UN has taken a growing interest in NGOs because they represent the interests of civil society, which is gaining visibility as a foundation of democracy. Kofi Annan acknowledged the importance of creating partnerships between the UN and civil society to achieve "a new synthesis between private initiative and the public good, which encourages entrepreneurship and market approaches together with social and environmental responsibility."

### A Public-Private Partnership

"NGOs play a more and more important role not only in the policy debates but equally important, maybe even more important, are critical in implementing many of these policies. A lot of the aid and emergency humanitarian assistance, like food distribution by the World Food Program, is done through the NGOs. There really is a public-private partnership, or a public-NGO partnership, that is very important. NGOs are effective, and part of the reason is they are private and they are accountable, they watch their pennies. People have a choice as to whom to give their money."          —John Negroponte, former US ambassador to the UN

ECOSOC negotiates the agreements that define relations between the UN and more than thirty-one thousand NGOs in addition to nearly four thousand that hold "consultative status," which gives them the right to participate in certain UN meetings, studies, and projects and to submit reports to ECOSOC. Nongovernmental organizations may also serve as technical experts, advisers, and consultants to governments and the Secretariat. As advocacy groups, they may support UN plans of action, programs, and declarations. Organizations qualifying for General Category consultative status may even propose new items for ECOSOC's consideration.

NGOs have their own liaison body, the Conference on Non-Governmental Organizations in Consultative Status (CONGO), to represent their interests before ECOSOC and hold meetings about issues of common interest. Those NGOs holding consultative status remain independent bodies and do not become actual parts of the UN. To the contrary, their influence often depends on their reputation for independence from outside authority.

## Civil Society Matters

"Civil society matters not because it will always validate the opinions we hold, but because it has the capacity to test, prod, and stretch our way of looking at the world so that we will understand more tomorrow than we do today. That is how civilization progresses. It is how we alleviate the immense pain we see around us. And it is how we translate the abstract promise of democracy into a world constantly renewed by lively debate, innovative ideas, and accountable government."
—Samantha Power, US ambassador to the UN

NGOs have become important in helping advance many UN efforts and programs, such as those related to human rights, literacy, health care, and economic development. Insiders generally acknowledge that NGOs have expanded the UN's reach and technical competence and serve a useful watchdog function.

## CHAPTER 13

# The UN to the Rescue

*Each of these crises is about people. It's about the people who are affected, it's about the children, it's about the families, and part of the job that I have to do is to make that real for the world. To make it clear that it's not just about numbers. It's not just about the millions, the thousands. It's about every single person.*
—Valerie Amos, under-secretary-general for humanitarian affairs

The UN has always regarded disaster aid as one of its primary missions, defining "disaster" in both natural and human-made terms. It helps after earthquakes and floods and with disease, famine, and armed conflict, to name just a few disasters. Typically the UN seeks to find partners in government and civil society. Humanitarian aid organizations operate in collaboration with the UN Emergency Relief Coordinator and a committee of representatives from UN agencies and such NGOs as the Red Cross.

To the UN's chief of humanitarian relief, Valerie Amos, under-secretary-general for humanitarian affairs and emergency relief coordinator (ERC), the world body faces three major assistance challenges. "One is how do you make our system, our humanitarian response system, as effective as possible. How do we collectively do the best we can to reach the people who need the help." The response system she mentions is actually many systems, tied together through the Office for the Coordination of Humanitarian Affairs (OCHA). "Secondly," she continues, "how do I make sure that the people that we are there to help and support, that their voice is heard . . . in a way that touches the hearts of the people across the world so that we can raise the money that we need to raise to give people that support." Much of the money needed to support the UN's relief efforts comes from voluntary donations by governments, foundations, and other organizations. "The third major challenge," she concludes, "is how do we make sure as crises are more complex, as there is more politics, if you like, in those crises, as we see in Syria right now, as we see in Mali right now" that "the work that we are doing on the humanitarian side . . . is kept separate from those broader political agendas."

## A Global System Emerges

No single plan governed the evolution of the UN's humanitarian agencies and organizations. Instead they were established to meet immediate needs, and they tended to operate individually and with their own methods and priorities. Such was the UN Relief and Works Agency for Palestine Refugees in the Near East (UNRWA), founded in 1949 to provide emergency humanitarian aid to Palestinians displaced during the creation of the state of Israel. UNRWA became a permanent social services agency providing health, education, and social services to nearly five million registered Palestinian refugees in the Middle East.

As the UN's humanitarian responsibilities and organizations grew in number, during the 1960s and 1970s, and then kept growing during the 1980s and 1990s, it became evident that more could be accomplished through better coordination. Some UN agencies were responding to crises with immediate aid in the form of food, shelter, or medical care. Others saw their role more broadly to include planning and preparation designed to prevent crises or manage them more effectively. In 1992, the General Assembly sought to provide coordination for these efforts by establishing what was to become the Department of Humanitarian Affairs (DHA) and then later OCHA. Reminiscing in 2014 about those early days, Deputy Secretary-General Jan Eliasson notes that the impetus for change came with the end of the Cold War. "We were some ambassadors who met. We saw the beginning of the end of the Cold War and we saw the risks that this period would turn into civil wars, in Africa, for example. We had humanitarian crises coming, when tensions which had been held up in the Cold War came to the surface. We felt the vibrations in the ground."

The looming challenge required a response. "We created the DHA, as it was later called. The decision was made at 1:00 in the morning, the 18th of December 1991, and it resulted in a resolution which I'm still proud of. It was as difficult to achieve as the Magna Carta." General Assembly Resolution 46/182 (1991) created the new office, and based on the General Assembly's decision, Secretary-General Boutros Boutros-Ghali established the Department of Humanitarian Affairs, with Jan Eliasson as under-secretary-general for humanitarian affairs. When Kofi Annan became secretary-general, he began a significant administrative reform program that included a reorganization of humanitarian affairs. In 1998, DHA became the Office for the Coordination of Humanitarian Affairs (OCHA), with an enlarged mandate that included the coordination of humanitarian response, policy development, and humanitarian advocacy. Today a staff of nearly two thousand works in more than thirty offices worldwide.

## Collaborating UN Bodies

As director of OCHA, Under-Secretary-General Amos can mobilize the expertise and capability of many UN bodies, selecting those that are most appropriate for a given situation. Her work involves travel to crisis spots around the world, where she speaks with people affected by the disaster, with personnel from local organizations and governments, and with staff from those UN agencies that are en-

At a Security Council meeting on Syria, Bashar Ja'afari (right), permanent representative of the Syrian Arab Republic to the UN, speaks with Valerie Amos, under-secretary-general for humanitarian affairs and emergency relief coordinator, April 18, 2013. With them is Vitaly I. Churkin, permanent representative of the Russian Federation. UN Photo / Devra Berkowitz.

gaged in that particular place. She briefs the media, both to inform the world and to draw the attention of potential financial donors to the need for assistance.

For acute needs of food and shelter the World Food Program (WFP) might be the lead agency in a disaster-struck region. Although the

WFP engages in social and economic development, its main focus is on helping disaster victims, long-term refugees, and displaced persons. During the Syrian civil war, for example, the WFP's executive director, Ertharin Cousin (a native Chicagoan), visited Damascus for high-level talks with government officials about the need to supply food to residents isolated by the conflict. She also toured a food-distribution center and spoke with families receiving monthly rations. "This month, we scaled up our food assistance to reach 4.25 million people inside Syria," Cousin told the media. "The challenge is gaining access to the hot spots and besieged areas. Without access we cannot reach the increasing number of families trapped by the fighting and in desperate need of food assistance." So dire was the overall situation in Syria that WFP launched an appeal in 2014 for nearly $2 billion to provide food for more than seven million Syrians (about one-third of the total population), many of them refugees in camps in neighboring countries. It was WFP's "most challenging, complex and largest emergency."

Often the WFP collaborates with other UN bodies, such as the High Commissioner for Refugees (UNHCR) and the UN Children's Fund (UNICEF), as well as with NGOs that help distribute aid and ensure that it goes where most needed. The UNHCR was recognized for its efforts helping and protecting refugees with Nobel Peace Prizes in 1954 and 1981. It has developed "quick impact projects," or QIPs, to bridge the gap between emergency assistance for refugees, including refugees returning home, and longer-term development aid undertaken by other agencies. Typical QIPs rebuild schools, repair roads, or restore water supplies.

Media coverage has made the UNHCR's blue plastic tents familiar to people around the world as they view media coverage of conflicts in Asia (Afghanistan), Africa (Democratic Republic of the Congo, Somalia), and elsewhere. Each year the agency finds itself called on to assist ever more refugees. A recent enumeration lists 34 million people of concern: 14.7 million internally displaced, 10.5 million refugees, 3.1 million returnees, 3.5 million stateless, more than 837,000 asylum seekers, and more than 1.3 million others. The

A World Food Program convoy in Darfur, Sudan, is protected by Ethiopian and Rwandan troops from the African Union–UN Hybrid Operation in Darfur, February 10, 2014. UN Photo / Albert González Farran.

budget has grown, of course, from a minuscule $300,000 in its first year (1951) to more than $3.59 billion in 2012.

Not surprisingly, the UN has a humanitarian organization devoted solely to protecting the interests of children. It created the International Children's Emergency Fund in 1946 to provide food, clothing, and health care to European children in the aftermath of World War II. Seven years later the General Assembly extended the fund's mandate indefinitely, deleting "International" and "Emergency" from the name but retaining the "I" and the "E" in the acronym: UNICEF.

Though UNICEF retained its largely hands-on, field-based focus (e.g., immunization programs), it soon expanded its activities from acute emergency relief to addressing the needs of the whole child, including education, and to pursuing even longer-term goals, such as global monitoring and assessment. It has been a principal actor in generating public discussion about children's issues, both within the UN, through debates and treaties, and globally, through movies, videos, its famous holiday cards, and Goodwill Ambassadors.

In 1989, UNICEF sponsored the Convention on the Rights of the Child, which passed in the General Assembly and soon entered into force. Ratified by all the world's nations (except the United States and Somalia), it lays out a bill of rights for children and encourages governments to adopt internationally recognized ethical standards assuring that citizens have the basics to survive. UNICEF's advocacy has given children's issues a highly visible place in the world body. The Security Council has since 1998 often debated issues related to children and armed conflict; in 2002 the General Assembly held a special session on children that included children as official delegates.

The list of UNICEF's interests and program ranges from adolescent and childhood development and hygiene to immunizations, nutrition, sanitation, and water. UNICEF protects children in times of crisis, whether natural or human-made. Its work on statistics and monitoring is valued by experts for providing national and global data and assessments on key child-related issues. Each year it publishes the *State of the World's Children,* an assessment of the condition of children from a specific perspective. In 2013 the focus was on children with disabilities. "In many countries," the report's authors note, "responses to the situation of children with disabilities are largely limited to institutionalization, abandonment or neglect. These responses are the problem, and they are rooted in negative or paternalistic assumptions of incapacity, dependency and difference that are perpetuated by ignorance." The authors warn that "unless this changes, children with disabilities will continue to have their rights neglected; to experience discrimination, violence and abuse; to have their opportunities restricted; to be excluded from society."

Most crises have an unwelcome accomplice, illness, and in some cases, the illness itself is the crisis, as with the HIV/AIDS epidemic, malaria, and bird flu. That is when the World Health Organization (WHO) steps in. Responding to health crises figures large in

WHO's broad mandate to protect the health of the world's peoples. In 2014 the organization's "Humanitarian Health Action" listed eleven health crises that had occurred in recent years, from Afghanistan (typhoid and other communicable diseases) to Mali (disruption of health care owing to armed conflict) to Yemen (schistosomiasis). WHO's response varies depending on the need. Sometimes it consists of medications; at other times it involves sending health specialists to the affected region. And in other cases, as with swine flu and Ebola Virus Disease, it provides the monitoring essential to tracking the outbreaks and isolating and treating the victims.

From its headquarters in Geneva, WHO coordinates the work of more than seven thousand personnel in 150 offices worldwide. Its staff include not only medical doctors, public health specialists, scientists, and epidemiologists but experts in the management of information systems, health statistics, and emergency relief. Each year WHO issues a world health report on a specific issue. For 2013 the issue was access to health care. The argument in *Research for Universal Health Coverage* is that "everyone should have access to the health services they need without being forced into poverty when paying for them," and the report marshals evidence to claim that universal health coverage is the solution.

## Moving from Crisis to Recovery

At some point a crisis ends and the next stage begins. What is that next stage, and when does it succeed the crisis? The decision about when a crisis has ended is a judgment call, and the timing may vary even among the experts.

That is a huge challenge for the UN system, and it seems to have no simple answer. "I think there are promising signs," says Eliasson. "You see it in the Sahel strategy, how the two areas come together in the humanitarian crisis and development." He is referring to a precedent-setting attempt by the UN and its partners to address the acute problems affecting millions of people in the vast geographical region that separates the Sahara to the north from tropical Africa to the south. The "triple crisis," as it is called, involves high food prices

## From Crisis to Recovery

The transition from crisis or disaster aid to recovery or development assistance is a big issue within the UN system. Direct crisis aid is expensive and only alleviates immediate problems. If the transition to recovery is delayed, the UN finds itself obligated to spend money on food or shelter that it would rather devote to education or the procurement of tools, computers, or other productive technologies. "What I hope to see," says Deputy Secretary-General Jan Eliasson, "is to make sure that we don't get stuck in the humanitarian stage for a longer time. When I was in Darfur I noticed that there were too many people in the camps. It cost $800 million every year, and I said there has to be an element of recovery or reintegration and development and the possibility of returning to the villages. We must have a continuum between relief and development."

and diminished harvests owing to the severe drought in 2011, the sapping of human resilience owing to chronic food shortages and malnutrition, and a political crisis in Mali that has produced large numbers of refugees and internally displaced people.

Since the Sahel region extends across many countries, a national approach is not workable. Nor is crisis management sufficient by itself, because of the complex interweaving of acute problems with long-term underlying factors. Similarly, the acute needs make long-term development methods insufficient by themselves. The solution is to combine the two in an integrated approach.

The UN's strategy, as summarized in table 4, is to apply crisis methods where appropriate while also recognizing the need to move to recovery and development. This is perhaps easiest to see in the second goal, dealing with food insecurity and malnutrition. In the right-hand column, 2.1 addresses the acute need for basic social services, while 2.2 describes a development goal: ensuring "sustainable livelihoods and environmental practices with the aim of mitigating and adapting to environmental shocks."

Eliasson sees the integrated approach beginning to appear elsewhere too. "You see it in Syria," he notes, "where we've had discus-

Table 4. The Sahel humanitarian strategy and strategic objectives

| Regional Goals | Regional Strategic Objectives |
|---|---|
| Households are appropriately supported to rebuild after the 2012 crisis. | 1.1. Livelihoods of the people affected by crises are ensured by, among other things, providing support to agriculture, income-generating activities. food and cash. |
| | 1.2. A target number of "most vulnerable" households have improved access to basic social services and social protection coverage. |
| | 1.3. The nutritional status of the most vulnerable population, including children, has improved. |
| Chronic levels of food insecurity and malnutrition have been addressed through integrated programming to build resilience. | 2.1. The effective coverage of basic social services is improved and social protection coverage is extended for the most vulnerable population. |
| | 2.2. Sustainable livelihoods and environmental practices with the aim of mitigating and adapting to environmental shocks are ensured. |
| | 2.3. Positive behavioral practices, particularly in health, nutrition and sanitation, that encourage risk reduction and adaptive capacities are adopted. |
| | 2.4. Analysis, coordination and preparedness capacities are strengthened at local, national and regional levels. |
| | 2.5. Early warning and disaster risk reduction measures are implemented. |
| Humanitarian actors respond effectively to the needs of refugees, displaced people and host communities resulting from both the complex emergency in Mali and other emergencies. | 3.1. The basic assistance needs of refugees and displaced populations have been met. |
| | 3.2. Excess mortality and morbidity in crisis situations is eliminated. |
| | 3.3. Humanitarian access to and the protection of people is ensured. |
| | 3.4. A harmonized and coherent humanitarian response across Sahel countries is ensured through efficient coordination. |

*Source:* Adapted from the UN report *Sahel Regional Strategy, 2013,* p. 18, http://reliefweb.int/sites/reliefweb.int/files/resources/SahelStrategy2013_Dec2012.pdf.

sions about the strains and tensions in the societies, particularly Lebanon and Jordan, with a million or two million refugees outside, half of them children. You have enormous strain on schools, health clinics, the job market—the whole infrastructures of Jordan and Lebanon are affected. We cannot only deal with this as a humanitarian problem; it's an infrastructure challenge, and we have to enroll other actors to deal with that situation."

This integrative approach expresses a new method of providing humanitarian assistance, a new way for the UN to come to the rescue, and it is also another aspect of Ban Ki-moon's plea that "no organization, no country, however powerful . . . can do it alone."

## Leading UN Actors

- The Office of the United Nations High Commissioner for Refugees (UNHCR) is based in Geneva. Its staff of about 7,685 work in 126 countries and look after nearly thirty-four million people. In 2012, almost all of the $3.59 billion budget came from voluntary donations from governments. The General Assembly and ECOSOC oversee UNHCR, and the assembly appoints the chief executive officer, the high commissioner. UNHCR's executive committee approves the biennial programs and budget, and the high commissioner presents them to the General Assembly and ECOSOC for approval.

- The United Nations Children's Fund (UNICEF) is headquartered in New York. Its main task is to help children in developing countries achieve their full potential as human beings, which it does by focusing on rights, needs, and opportunities. A thirty-six-member executive board, representing the regional groups of member states, governs UNICEF and reports to the General Assembly and ECOSOC. The US government has invariably been UNICEF's largest single donor.

- The World Food Program (WFP) was created in 1963 to provide emergency food and shelter in crisis areas around the globe. Headquartered in Rome, the WFP is the world's largest humanitarian agency focused on the alleviation of hunger. The US government has praised the program for its lean and cost-effective performance.

- The World Health Organization (WHO), founded in 1948, is based in Geneva. One of the largest specialized agencies, WHO is charged with improving world health and eradicating or controlling diseases. The eradication of smallpox is considered one of its most significant accomplishments. With six other UN agencies, WHO belongs to the Joint United Nations Program on HIV/AIDS, described as "the leading advocate for a worldwide response aimed at preventing transmission, providing care and support, reducing the vulnerability of individuals and communities, and alleviating the impact of the epidemic."

## CHAPTER 14

# Sustainable Development in the New Millennium

*Development, after all, is about people. Their aspirations and ambitions must shape our policies and goals. I am determined to make sure that what a farmer says in Tanzania, or a student says in Vietnam, or a mother says in Honduras, will be heard at UN Headquarters.*
— Ban Ki-moon, secretary-general of the UN

From its beginning the UN has been committed to improving the lives of poor, disadvantaged, and neglected people, no matter where they may live. The Universal Declaration of Human Rights describes access to adequate food, housing, education, and employment as rights, not privileges or commodities. The UN's development focus is to "help nations work together to improve the lives of poor people, to conquer hunger, disease and illiteracy, and to encourage respect for each other's rights and freedoms." Given the large number of poor member states in the UN—they are actually a majority—this expansive notion of rights, which includes social and economic aspects, is pretty much taken for granted at the world body.

## Millennium Development Goals (MDGs)

So varied and numerous are the UN's social and economic development efforts that they sometimes seem to operate in their own individual worlds, leading to a dispersion of effort that may reduce or limit their impact. It was to help bring cohesion to development efforts that in 2000, Secretary-General Kofi Annan urged the member states to create a single campaign that would highlight the UN's development efforts and provide realistic long-term goals. That, he argued, could help make the best use of the limited funds and staff at the UN organizations, commissions, funds, and other entities. The world's leaders accepted his challenge at the General Assembly in New York City on September 8, 2000, when they launched the Millennium Development Campaign. It was defined as a fifteen-year campaign focused on improving living standards by targeting eight goals:

- Eradicate extreme poverty and hunger
- Achieve universal primary education
- Promote gender equality and empower women
- Reduce child mortality
- Improve maternal health
- Combat HIV/AIDS, malaria, and other diseases
- Ensure environmental sustainability
- Develop a global partnership for development

All members of the UN family were expected to address the goals of this, the UN's most ambitious development effort. World leaders reconvened at a follow-up summit in New York in 2005, and again in 2010, to review progress in reaching the goals by 2015.

In brief, member states resolved that during the campaign they would reduce by half "the proportion of the world's people whose income is less than one dollar a day and the proportion of people who suffer from hunger and . . . to halve the proportion of people who are unable to reach or to afford safe drinking water." They also pledged to ensure that "children everywhere, boys and girls alike, will be able to complete a full course of primary schooling and that girls

Josaia V. Bainimarama, prime minister of the Republic of Fiji, addresses the opening of the special event "Towards Achieving the
Millennium Development Goals (MDGs)," organized by the president of the General Assembly, September 25, 2013. UN Photo / Rick
Bajornas.


and boys will have equal access to all levels of education." Other
pledges focused on health care: to reduce "maternal mortality by
three quarters, and under-five child mortality by two thirds, of their
current rates," and to stop and begin to reverse "the spread of HIV/
AIDS, the scourge of malaria and other major diseases that afflict
humanity."

The member states acknowledged the key role of women in addressing these problems, and they declared their commitment to
"promote gender equality and the empowerment of women as effective ways to combat poverty, hunger and disease and to stimulate
development that is truly sustainable." The need for addressing the
interrelatedness of issues appears in another pledge: "to develop
strong partnerships with the private sector and with civil society

organizations in pursuit of development and poverty eradication." And this in turn tied in with the establishment of free and open political systems. "We will spare no effort to promote democracy and strengthen the rule of law," declared the member states, "as well as respect for all internationally recognized human rights and fundamental freedoms, including the right to development." This led them inexorably to their promise "to respectfully uphold the Universal Declaration of Human Rights. To strive for the full protection and promotion in all our countries of civil, political, economic, social and cultural rights for all."

## The UN Development Program (UNDP)

A good place to start when considering the Millennium Development Goals is the UN Development Program (UNDP), which has existed almost since the beginning of the world body and is recognized as a leader in social and economic development efforts around the world. One of the important services rendered by the UNDP is the publication of data about the status of social and economic development across the globe. The annual *Human Development Report* has been issued since 1990, and each report focuses on a theme. For 2013 the theme was "The Rise of the South: Human Progress in

### A Vision for Progress

"The first *Human Development Report* in 1990 laid out a vision of economic and social progress that is fundamentally about people enlarging their choices and capabilities. Since then, there has been substantial progress: many developing economies continue to grow rapidly and raise standards of human development. The rise of the South is a feature of a rapidly changing world. The South now accounts for almost a third of world output and consumption. Without the robust growth in these economies, led by China and India, the global economic recession would have been deeper."                    —UNDP, *Human Development Report 2013* a Diverse World." The report noted the rapid improvement in living standards and other key indicators for residents of many developing countries, often referred to as the South to distinguish them from the generally well-developed nations, most of which lie north of the equator. Progress was made despite the worldwide recession of 2008.

The *Human Development Report* also includes the Human Development Index (HDI), which rates each country's place on a scale of social and economic development. The index addresses a wide range of sectors, from health to education to environmental quality, but it also presents a single HDI rating that ranks nations from most to least developed. Not surprisingly the United States sits very high, in third place (table 5).

The UNDP sees itself as a partner with nations that want to reduce poverty, achieve democracy, prevent disasters and recover from them when they occur, protect the environment, and gain adequate access to energy for sustainable development. In pursuing that broad agenda the UNDP encourages "the protection of human rights, capacity development and the empowerment of women." We can pull at the last three items to reveal what lies underneath the words.

The first item is the protection of human rights, which the UNDP seeks to advance through the building of "effective and capable states that are accountable and transparent, inclusive and responsive—from elections to participation of women and the poor." One of its programs attacks official government corruption, which involves public servants accepting bribes to give preferential treatment to the citizens who offer the bribes. Corruption abridges human rights because it gives one citizen an unfair advantage over another: it subverts the democratic belief in equal access to rights and opportunities. Corruption is pervasive in many countries, especially poorer ones where the demand for services (like education or licenses to do business) may outstrip the ability or willingness of the government to provide them.

The UNDP chose Thailand for launching an innovative anticorruption program, one aimed at changing the basic perception of corruption from something that "everyone does" to something that

Table 5. Selected national rankings from the Human Development Index, 2012

| HDI Rank | Life Expectancy at Birth (years) | Mean Years of Schooling | Gross National Income per Capita in Purchasing Power Parity (US$) |
|---|---|---|---|
| 1 Norway | 81.3 | 12.6 | 48,688 |
| 2 Australia | 82.0 | 12.0 | 34,340 |
| 3 United States | 78.7 | 13.3 | 43,480 |
| 5 Germany | 80.6 | 12.2 | 35,431 |
| 10 Japan | 83.6 | 11.6 | 32,545 |
| 16 Israel | 81.9 | 11.9 | 26,224 |
| 18 Singapore | 81.2 | 10.1 | 52,613 |
| 26 United Kingdom | 80.3 | 9.4 | 32,538 |
| 39 Poland | 76.3 | 10.0 | 17,776 |
| 45 Argentina | 76.1 | 9.3 | 15,347 |
| 55 Russian Federation | 69.1 | 11.7 | 14,461 |
| 57 Saudi Arabia | 74.1 | 7.8 | 22,616 |
| 69 Kazakhstan | 67.4 | 10.4 | 10,451 |
| 85 Brazil | 73.8 | 7.2 | 10,152 |
| 90 Turkey | 74.2 | 6.5 | 13,710 |
| 101 China | 73.7 | 7.5 | 7,945 |
| 114 Philippines | 69.0 | 8.9 | 3,752 |
| 121 South Africa | 53.4 | 8.5 | 9,594 |
| 136 India | 65.8 | 4.4 | 3,285 |
| 145 Kenya | 57.7 | 7.0 | 1,541 |
| 153 Nigeria | 52.3 | 5.2 | 2,102 |
| 161 Haiti | 62.4 | 4.9 | 1,070 |
| 171 Sudan | 61.8 | 3.1 | 1,848 |
| 175 Afghanistan | 49.1 | 3.1 | 1,000 |
| 184 Chad | 49.9 | 1.5 | 1,258 |

*Source:* UNDP, *Human Development Report, 2013.*

*Note:* Data are from 2012.

shouldn't exist at all. It partnered with Khon Kaen University's College of Local Administration in 2012 to organize the Thai Youth Anti-Corruption Network, a student-led group that began with thirty-six students from fifteen Thai universities. The UNDP held anticorruption camps across the country to educate student leaders about the dangers of corruption and to promote responsible citizenship and civic knowledge. This led to a rally by two thousand students at the Bangkok Art and Culture Center on International Anti-Corruption Day (December 9), aimed at showing that every part of Thai society needs to fight corruption. Pleased at the results of its work, the UNDP has decided to continue its university-based anticorruption efforts by fostering the growth of campus activist organizations with links among students, academics, journalists, and civil-society organizations.

The second item is capacity building, which is development-speak for the improvement of a government or organization's ability to function, whether through improved information technology, staff development, or some other enhancement. It is a major issue in many developing countries owing to government indifference, shortages of funds for adequate equipment and services, and low educational attainment among large segments of the population. "Among countries with well-designed and well-funded poverty reduction plans," the UNDP notes, "the ability to reduce poverty is still being hindered by in-country leadership and knowledge gaps, a shortage of technical and managerial know-how, and difficulties retaining talented staff in an environment with few incentives."

The UNDP has expertise related to addressing these gaps. In Liberia, for example, it helped the government create a "national capacity development strategy" that assesses the ability of ministries and other key organizations to define and fulfill their mandates and to manage and support talented staff. The government of Tanzania asked the UNDP to partner with a foundation to establish an online information management system that could track official development assistance and link it to MDG-related results. In Namibia the UNDP helped devise guidelines for collaborative arrangements between local governments and private entities for the delivery of municipal public services. It "helped to identify the capacity gaps and to reframe the roles, rights, responsibilities, and incentives of all involved in a public-private partnership."

The third item is the empowerment of women. A consensus has emerged among development experts that many key social and economic problems can be addressed only if women join as equal partners with men in defining the issues and fixing them.

## The Women's Century

Deputy Secretary-General Jan Eliasson predicts that "this is going to be the century of the women. It has never happened before and it will happen, and that is a tremendous potential. We have women in the UN, but the empowerment of women politically, economically, there's still a long way to go, but it will happen during the century. It is hopefully unstoppable."

The UN has merged several of its women-related organizations under a new office, UN Women, the United Nations Entity for Gender Equality and the Empowerment of Women. To some extent, the growing emphasis on women reflects the feminist movement, which has expanded beyond the United States and Europe to all parts of the globe, but it also reflects something even bigger: the interrelatedness of so much of what happens in the social and economic spheres. When the field of development arose decades ago, its practitioners often worked on a fairly narrow range of issues or factors. Single-focus projects were the norm, as in providing basic farm equipment or teaching simple but more effective agricultural techniques.

Such single-focus projects remain important for promoting development, but increasingly they share the stage with projects and campaigns that address a range of interrelated issues. So, for example, the UNDP began a program in Egypt's Siwa Oasis that brought literacy to girls and women. Many of the local girls came from families too poor to provide even limited education, and there was also a traditional community bias against female education, leading to a female illiteracy rate of 40 percent. In 2008 the UNDP, using one of its funds and acting in collaboration with the Egyptian Ministry of Communication and Information Technology and several partners, including the World Health Organization (WHO), Vodafone Foundation, and a local community development association, started a program to teach girls and women literacy skills and in that way give them opportunities for new or better employment.

In addition to teaching eighty-eight hundred women how to read and write and training some to be literacy instructors, the initiative put a special emphasis on computer skills, even giving participants their own personal computers. As a result, women learned to read and write, improved their agricultural and handicraft production abilities, and acquired online marketing skills. Siwa women began to promote their products through an online store. As one woman remarked, "I found in computers life itself. Now I can read and write. I can earn my living and give my children a better life. And as a mother, I am a better role model for them to follow." In her words we can see the connections among education, women's empowerment, economic development, and family life—just the kind of linkage that now characterizes thinking among development experts in the UN. The development landscape is changing.

## A New Development Landscape

The MDGs exist in a changing world, where international status and clout now seem less concentrated in a few nations than previously. A similar dispersion is occurring in the social and economic spheres, as economic growth in Brazil, China, India, Korea, and other so-called emerging nations are redrawing the global financial picture and creating large new middle classes that long for the quality of life enjoyed in the developed nations.

### Hard-Core Contraction

"Development assistance is changing. The hard-core poverty is contracting and getting focused down to a smaller group of countries."
—Mark Malloch-Brown, former director of the UN Development Program

Consumer-based societies are popping up all over and, with them, new markets for telecommunications, health care, transportation, education, recreation—basically all the accoutrements of modern life. "It's all good news," remarks Malloch-Brown, who directed the UNDP before becoming deputy secretary-general under Kofi Annan. "It shows development works." He acknowledges that older forms of development, by which governments made large financial grants to poorer nations' governments, are not as useful as before, nor as necessary, owing to the enlarged financial wealth and capital of many developing nations. Nowadays, he explains, government-to-government grants are largely for technical assistance "rather than the large transfer kind." Increasingly, development assistance is coming through hybrid arrangements involving public-private partnerships or even private-private ones. "In a whole array of countries, poor and middle-income, there remains plenty of space for the new kinds of hybrid arrangements of public-private collaboration, roles for the private sector, domestic and international, in development."

The new landscape has posed challenges for Malloch-Brown's former agency. "UNDP is struggling with resources," he observes, "squeezed by the rise of the very targeted single-issue global funds, whether it's around public health or education. There is more private-sector capital now, including large foundations and NGOs, who are new actors in development."

David Malone agrees that UNDP is feeling pressure. A former Canadian diplomat, now rector of the United Nations University in Tokyo, Malone knows the UN system from both the outside and the inside. He sees major shifts occurring as a result of the great global financial meltdown of 2008, including reduced contributions to the world body. "The Europeans are lately preoccupied with their own affairs" and are "not providing their usual energy at the UN." Lamenting that "there are new issues but no new money," Malone says that "a number of agencies are shrinking very fast," among them the UNDP. Even the World Bank now faces "major operating budget cuts."

Malone's comment on the World Bank is significant. The World Bank Group is a major source of financial support and services to developing countries seeking to improve their social and economic conditions. Its motto is "Working for a world free of poverty," and it pursues its goals through various strategies. One of its five components is the International Bank for Reconstruction and Development (IBRD), which lends to "governments of middle-income and creditworthy low-income countries." Another is the International Development Association (IDA), which provides grants and credits, that is, interest-free loans, to governments of the poorest countries. The International Finance Corporation (IFC), a third component, focuses exclusively on the private sector; it offers financial and advisory services to businesses and governments. The fourth component, the Multilateral Investment Guarantee Agency (MIGA), promotes foreign direct investment by offering political risk insurance to investors and lenders. The fifth component, the International Centre for Settlement of Investment Disputes (ICSID), provides international facilities for conciliation and arbitration of investment disputes.

Secretary-General Ban Ki-moon (left) meets with Jim Yong Kim, president of the World Bank, during the annual World Economic Forum in Davos, Switzerland, January 23, 2014. On the right is Deputy Secretary-General Jan Eliasson. UN Photo / Eskinder Debebe.

Historically the World Bank has been generously funded by the developed nations, especially the United States, and usually an American sits as its director, though the current director, Jim Yong Kim, is a Korean. He faces challenges in moving the bank through the new development landscape. Many developing nations now are creditworthy enough to draw on new sources of development capital and no longer have to rely as heavily on the World Bank. Some national economies are growing so fast that their capital needs are outstripping the bank's ability to lend. The financial meltdown of 2008 only made things worse, especially when the leading developed nations cut their financial contributions to the bank. Perhaps feeling the heat, the bank has refocused itself on a campaign to end extreme poverty by 2030, with particular emphasis on raising the incomes of the poorest 40 percent in every country, even the richer ones. By doing so it is aligning itself with the poverty-reduction goals of the Millennium Development Campaign, just when the UN is trying to decide what to do for an MDG encore.

## Evaluating the MDGs

Has the Millennium Development Campaign succeeded? Like so many grand enterprises, it had its ups and downs, but on the whole it was well received. Certainly it led to more improvements in global well-being than many observers expected in 2000, when it must have seemed yet one more well-intentioned UN scheme.

During the span of the Millennium Development Campaign, global rates of extreme poverty fell by half, and two billion more people gained access to safe drinking water. The first MDG addressed the need to eradicate extreme poverty and hunger and was the first to be met. Maternal and child mortality dropped considerably (though not as much as hoped), and a record number of children were in primary school, with the number of girls equaling the number of boys for the first time. The battle with killer diseases such as malaria and AIDS made real gains. On the other hand, much work remained to be done. Global carbon emissions, a factor in climate change, rose, and forests and fisheries continued to suffer from overexploitation.

Child mortality fell, but not enough. The eighth goal, creating a global partnership for development, seems to have met with the least success, except for the greater availability of essential medicines.

Despite the limitations, many observers rate the MDGs a success in providing generally acknowledged benchmarks of progress and in helping focus international development efforts (table 6). Deputy Secretary-General Eliasson rates the MDGs as "extremely useful both for global aspirations in the area of development but also translating to the national and even local levels. They have become a very effective instrument, a very effective tool of measurement of progress."

As the MDGs neared their target date, 2015, stakeholders and others from the UN and elsewhere began reflecting on next steps. Secretary-General Ban Ki-moon commissioned a panel of notable persons from around the world to offer thoughts on the post-2015 agenda. In 2013 they issued their report, *A New Global Partnership: Eradicate Poverty and Transform Economies through Sustainable Development.* They praised the accomplishments of the Millennium Goals Campaign while also enumerating the many shortfalls and failures. A new approach was needed, they argued, based on a global partnership that would eradicate extreme poverty by 2030 and help achieve sustainable development. Despite the world's economic growth in recent decades, they continued, the 1.2 billion poorest people accounted for 1 percent of world consumption, while the richest 1 percent accounted for 72 percent.

The authors stressed the importance of integrating various approaches into a coherent plan. The MDGs "fell short by not integrating the economic, social, and environmental aspects of sustainable development as envisaged in the Millennium Declaration, and by not addressing the need to promote sustainable patterns of consumption and production." As a result, "environment and development were never properly brought together. People were working hard—but often separately—on interlinked problems."

Out of this and other discussions and reports there emerged a

Table 6. Millennium Development Goals scorecard, 2013:
Selected highlights

| Goal | Progress |
| --- | --- |
| 1. Eradicate extreme poverty and hunger | • The target of reducing extreme poverty rates by half was met five years ahead of the 2015 deadline.<br>• The global poverty rate at $1.25 a day fell in 2010 to less than half the 1990 rate.<br>• The hunger reduction target (to halve the proportion of people who suffer from hunger) is within reach by 2015. |
| 2. Achieve universal primary education | • Enrollment in primary education in developing regions reached 90 percent in 2010, up from 82 percent in 1999.<br>• Progress on primary school enrolment has slowed. Between 2008 and 2011, the number of out-of-school children of primary age fell by only 3 million.<br>• Gender gaps in youth literacy rates are narrowing. Globally there were 95 literate young women for every 100 young men in 2010, compared with 90 women in 1990. |
| 3. Promote gender equality and empower women | • The world has achieved equality in primary education between girls and boys, but only 2 out of 130 countries have achieved that target at all levels of education.<br>• Globally women held 40 out of every 100 wage-earning jobs in the non- agricultural sector in 2011, a significant improvement since 1990.<br>• In many countries gender inequality persists and women face discrimination in access to education, work and economic assets, and participation in government.<br>• Violence against women continues to undermine efforts to reach all goals |

*continued*

Table 6. *continued*

| Goal | Progress |
|------|----------|
| 4. Reduce child mortality | • Despite population growth the number of deaths among children under five worldwide declined from 12.4 million in 1990 to 6.9 million in 2011.<br>• Since 2000 measles vaccines have averted over 10 million deaths.<br>• An increasing proportion of child deaths are in sub-Saharan Africa, where one in nine children die before the age of five, and in Southern Asia, where one in 16 die before age five. |
| 5. Improve maternal health | • Maternal mortality has nearly halved since 1990. An estimated 287,000 maternal deaths occurred in 2010 worldwide, a decline of 47 percent from 1990. In Eastern Asia, Northern Africa, and Southern Asia maternal mortality has declined by around two-thirds. But the maternal mortality ratio in developing regions is still 15 times higher than in the developed regions.<br>• The rural-urban gap in skilled care during childbirth has narrowed.<br>• In developing regions prenatal care increased from 63 percent in 1990 to 81 percent in 2011.<br>• Fewer teens are having children in most developing regions, but progress has slowed.<br>• Official development assistance for reproductive health care and family planning remains low. |
| 6. Combat HIV/AIDS, malaria, and other diseases | • New HIV infections continue to decline in most regions. Nevertheless, comprehensive knowledge of HIV transmission remains low among young people, along with condom use.<br>• Access to treatment for people living with HIV increased in all regions. By the end of 2011, eleven countries had achieved universal access to antiretroviral therapy.<br>• The global estimated incidence of malaria has decreased by 17 percent since 2000, and malaria-specific mortality rates by 25 percent. |

Table 6. *continued*

| Goal | Progress |
|------|----------|
| | • Countries with improved access to malaria control interventions saw child mortality rates fall by about 20 percent.<br>• Treatment for tuberculosis has saved some 20 million lives between 1995 and 2011. |
| 7. Ensure environmental sustainability | • Forests, a safety net for the poor, continue to disappear at an alarming rate. South America and Africa saw the largest net losses of forest areas between 2000 and 2010.<br>• Global emissions of carbon dioxide, a greenhouse gas, have increased by more than 46 percent since 1990.<br>• In the 25 years since the adoption of the Montreal Protocol on Substances that Deplete the Ozone Layer, the consumption of ozone-depleting substances has fallen by 98 percent.<br>• At Rio+20, the United Nations Conference on Sustainable Development, world leaders pledged more than $513 billion for sustainable development initiatives.<br>• The world has met the target of halving the proportion of people without access to improved sources of water, five years ahead of schedule. Over 40 percent of all people without improved drinking water live in sub-Saharan Africa.<br>• The share of urban slum residents in the developing world declined from 39 percent in 2000 to 33 percent in 2012. More than 200 million of these people gained access to improved water sources, improved sanitation facilities, or durable or less crowded housing, thereby exceeding the MDG target. |
| 8. Create a global partnership for development | • Only a small proportion of trade restrictions introduced since the end of 2008 have been eliminated, despite pledges by G20 members following the global financial crisis. |

*continued*

Table 6. *continued*

| Goal | Progress |
|------|----------|
|  | • Tariffs imposed by developed countries on products from developing countries have remained largely unchanged since 2004, except for agricultural products.<br>• Initiatives have somewhat reduced the external debt of certain very poor countries, but 20 developing countries remain at high risk of debt distress.<br>• Resources available for providing essential medicines through disease-specific global health funds increased in 2011, despite the global economic downturn. |

*Source:* Compiled from *The Millennium Development Goals Report 2013* (New York: United Nations, 2013), http://www.un.org/millenniumgoals/pdf/report-2013/mdg-report-2013-english.pdf.

vision for global development in the post-MDG years, from 2015 to 2030. Sustainable Development Goals—SDGs—have replaced the MDGs and will continue and expand the work already done by governments and the UN's many development organizations and partnerships. Eradicating extreme poverty and hunger remains a prime focus, but increasing emphasis now falls on the need for sustainability. The UN's Open Working Group on Sustainable Development Goals has stated that the eradication of poverty is one part of an overarching goal that also includes replacing unsustainable modes of production and consumption with sustainable ones, and protecting and managing the natural world, which is the resource base of economic and social development. The working group also remarked on how experience with the MDGs revealed the need for defining goals and outcomes carefully in order to draw useful conclusions about the effectiveness of global development efforts. Clearly, the analysts at the UN see the MDGs as a laboratory that has helped improve and refine international development.

All parts of the UN system are expected to advance the SDGs.

"People across the world have mobilized for the MDGs, the most successful anti-poverty push in history," the secretary-general has declared. "Now we must finish the job and tackle a new generation of development challenges." The intent of the UN, he said, is to create "the most inclusive global development process the world has ever known," with the goal of empowering people and building "a better life for all while protecting our planet. This is the essence of sustainable development."

## Leading UN Actors

- The Food and Agriculture Organization (FAO), based in Rome, is the lead UN agency for agriculture, forestry, fisheries, and rural development. In November 2013 the FAO employed 1,795 professional and 1,654 support staff. For 2014–15 the total budget was $2.4 billion, including voluntary contributions by members and other partners to support technical and emergency (including rehabilitation) assistance to governments as well as directly support the FAO's core work.
- The International Fund for Agricultural Development (IFAD), founded in 1977, is a specialized agency of the UN based in Rome. It is mandated to combat hunger and rural poverty in developing countries by providing long-term, low-cost loans for projects that improve the nutrition and food supply of small farmers, nomadic herders, landless rural people, poor women, and others. IFAD also encourages other agencies and governments to contribute funds to these projects. The United States is one of the agency's largest contributors.
- The International Labour Organization (ILO), created in 1919, is based in Geneva. The ILO formulates international labor standards through conventions and recommendations that establish minimum standards of labor rights, such as the right to organize, bargain collectively, and receive equal opportunity and treatment. One of the ILO's most important functions is to investigate and report on whether member states are adhering to the labor conventions and treaties they have signed. The United States, which has a permanent seat on the ILO's governing body, considers

the organization vital for addressing exploitative child labor. A US government report claims that the programs have "removed tens of thousands of children" in Central America, Bangladesh, Pakistan, and elsewhere "from exploitative work, placed them in schools, and provided their families with alternative income-producing opportunities." On its fiftieth anniversary, in 1969, the ILO received the Nobel Peace Prize.

- The UN Center for Human Settlements (Habitat), created in 1978, is headquartered in Nairobi. Habitat describes itself as promoting "sustainable human settlement development through advocacy, policy formulation, capacity-building, knowledge creation, and the strengthening of partnerships between government and civil society."

- The UN Development Program (UNDP), founded in 1945, is based in New York. The UNDP concentrates on four aspects of development: poverty, the environment, jobs, and women. A US government report observed that the UNDP gives the United States an "important channel of communication, particularly in countries where the US has no permanent presence." The United States has been the organization's biggest donor.

- The UN Industrial Development Organization (UNIDO), which became a specialized agency in 1985, is based in Vienna. UNIDO helps developing nations establish economies that are globally competitive while respecting the natural environment. It mediates communication between business and government and works to encourage entrepreneurship and bring all segments of the population, including women, into the labor force. Its staff include engineers, economists, and technology and environment specialists.

- UN Women, the United Nations Entity for Gender Equality and the Empowerment of Women, was established in 2010 as part of the UN reform agenda. It merged the efforts of four previously distinct entities: Division for the Advancement of Women (DAW); International Research and Training Institute for the Advancement of Women (INSTRAW); Office of the Special Adviser on Gender Issues and Advancement of Women (OSAGI); and United Nations Development Fund for Women (UNIFEM). The

General Assembly gave UN Women responsibility for assisting in the formulation of policies, global standards, and norms and helping member states to implement these standards. An example of its work is the *Millennium Development Goals Gender Chart*, published in 2014, which assesses progress in meeting those MDGs relating to the status of women, including employment, education, maternal health, and empowerment. UN Women is also charged with holding the UN system accountable for its own commitments to gender equality.

- The World Bank was established in 1945 with the goal of reducing global poverty by improving the economies of poor nations. In recent years the bank has tried to ensure that local organizations and communities are included in projects in order to increase the chances for success. The World Bank consists of five parts, all based in Washington, DC:

1. The International Bank for Reconstruction and Development began operations in 1946. It offers loans and financial assistance to member states, each of which subscribes an amount of capital based on its economic strength. Voting power in the governing body is linked to the subscriptions. Most of its funds come from bonds sold in international capital markets.

2. The International Development Association offers credit to countries with low annual per capita incomes. Most of the funds come from the governments of richer nations.

3. The International Finance Corporation is the developing world's largest multilateral source of loan and equity financing for private-sector projects.

4. The Multilateral Investment Guarantee Agency provides guarantees to foreign investors in developing countries that protect against losses from political factors and such other factors as expropriation and war.

5. The International Center for Settlement of Investment Disputes provides arbitration or conciliation services in disputes between governments and private foreign investors.

# CHAPTER 15

# Global Connections

*The United States is a global power. Global political, economic, and social power needs to have a certain amount of global standards. There's a set of UN technical agencies, including things like the ICAO, that are the bedrock of this structure; there are whole sections of the United States which benefit from global technical norm-setting.*
          —Esther Brimmer, Elliott School of International Affairs,
                                   George Washington University

We live in a world of interconnections. A single computer, sitting by itself, can perform impressive computational and information-management functions, but it doesn't begin to reach its full potential until it is connected with other computers. Each new connection makes the computer far more useful, not just to process information but to obtain it, create it, and disseminate it. Connectivity gives the machine a whole new dimension. The UN plays a vital role in facilitating and managing the world's many forms of interconnectedness, whether over the Internet, through financial markets and currency exchanges, over the airwaves, across shipping lanes, on postal routes, or along the avenues of international trade and commerce. All of these important areas of human interconnectedness depend upon rules, standards, norms, and agreements between nations that are facilitated by various UN-related treaties, organizations, and agencies

## Helping Make Things Work

Although the UN is not the only player fostering connectivity, it is a very important one owing to its unique position in the world community. As some observers have remarked, the UN can act as honest broker in mediating and enabling discussions about how to regulate, monitor, or define major global issues and functions. Because of their international perspective, UN bodies can take a broader view that is helpful in reaching agreement among national governments, transnational industries, and businesses. They have become valuable as monitors, administrators, and facilitators of the many "soft infrastructures" that enable complex international systems to work reasonably well most of the time. They have provided assistance to governments trying to cope with the fast pace and intensity of modern economic relations—rapid swings in currency and capital flows can send a seemingly sound national economy into sudden crisis. The UN is especially effective in setting standards for the world's soft infrastructure of laws, procedures, and other intangible but essential elements.

Oldest of all the UN bodies is the International Telecommunication Union (ITU), founded in 1865 in Paris as the International Telegraph Union. Its original purpose was to help standardize telegraph services, which at that time were the world's only means of electronic communication. It became the ITU in 1934 and joined the UN as a specialized agency in 1947, by which time telephones, radios, and televisions had greatly broadened the nature of telecommunications and created additional needs for standards and compatibility.

Today the ITU helps governments and the private sector coordinate and improve global telecommunication networks and services. It develops standards for enabling networks and technologies to interconnect, seeks to improve electronic telecommunications access for underserved communities, and assigns global radio spectrum and satellite orbits. Satellite orbits? That's taking connectivity pretty far from regulating the telegraph. Alone among UN agencies, the ITU has both government and nongovernment members. In addition to the 193 UN member states, its members include regulators, academic institutions, and approximately 700 private companies. In an increasingly interconnected world, notes the organization, "ITU is the single global organization embracing all players in this dynamic and fast-growing sector." Its director, Hamadoun Touré, has been pushing member states to pay more attention to the risks inherent in a computer-based world. He sees cyberwar as a current reality and, when discussing solutions, offers a mantra that would warm the heart of Secretary-General Ban Ki-moon: "No one single entity can do it alone. We have to change the mindset."

Next in seniority is the Universal Postal Union (UPU), established by the Bern Treaty of 1874, to help create standards for and compatibility among the world's postal systems. Before the electronic age, the delivery of physical letters, documents, and packages was the primary means of communication among individuals, businesses, government entities, and indeed all organizations. It was essential that the various national systems be able to work with one another to ensure that the mail would reliably reach its destination, no matter where that might be. The UPU took on the job. It became a UN specialized agency in 1948, charged with regulating and assisting cooperation among international postal services, as well as providing advice, mediation, and technical assistance. Every five years it convenes the Universal Postal Congress.

As you might imagine, any organization devoted to the world's postal systems is grappling with the effects of the telecommunications revolution and the panoply of digital communications media. Why send a letter when you can send email? The UPU's director-general for 2013–16, Bishar A. Hussein, acknowledged the challenge in the 2012 annual report. "While much has been achieved, much more must be done to lift the public postal sector out of the doldrums," he wrote. "The Union must focus its efforts on ensuring that the use

Hamadoun I. Touré, secretary-general of the International Telecommunication Union, speaks at a high-level panel on cyber security and cyber crimes in Geneva, January 31, 2012. UN Photo / Jean-Marc Ferré.

of new technologies permeates the postal business and on breaking down barriers impeding the flow of mail across the globe. It must boldly face the rising volumes of e-commerce parcels in the network, improve customer-service levels and respond quickly to rapidly changing client needs." Surely the leaders of the US Postal Service are rooting for the UPU's success in this quest.

Postal services deliver many kinds of packages, but not human beings. Airplanes deliver pretty much anything that they can lift, including millions, even billions, of passengers each year. Four decades after the Wright brothers made their historic flight at Kitty Hawk, the International Civil Aviation Organization (ICAO) was created, in 1944, upon the signing of the Convention on International Civil Aviation, also known as the Chicago Convention, a treaty that ICAO oversees. A UN specialized agency since 1947, ICAO is responsible for setting international standards and regulations necessary for the safety and efficiency of civilian air transport. It does this by establishing international standards for aircraft, pilots and flight crews, air traffic controllers, ground and maintenance crews, and security in international airports. ICAO and the signatories of the convention, along with global industry and aviation organizations, establish international standards and recommended practices (SARPs), which nations use to create their civil aviation regulations. The nineteen annexes of the Chicago Convention currently have more than ten thousand SARPs. The organization boasts that these SARPs and ICAO's policy, auditing, and capacity-building efforts ensure that "today's global air transport network is able to operate over 100,000 daily flights, safely, efficiently and securely in every region of the world."

In the year following ICAO's founding, another organization fostering connections came into existence. The International Monetary Fund (IMF) was established at the Bretton Woods Conference and became an agency of the UN, charged with facilitating international monetary cooperation and providing financial capital, fiscal and monetary advice, and policy recommendations to national governments. Unlike the World Bank, the IMF's writ runs to all nations, not just the developing ones. In times of crisis, if a member nation is unable to meet its foreign obligations or its financial system becomes unstable, the IMF can offer essential aid in the form of large loans. The IMF has occasionally generated controversy, however, owing to the terms it has imposed on some nations caught up in regional or international financial crises and unable to pay their international obligations.

Critics have complained that the IMF's emphasis on government fiscal restraint has sometimes made national financial emergencies worse rather than better, especially for less developed countries, and that there is a need for less rigorous measures.

One of the UN's most creative approaches to promoting interconnections dates to 1945 with the founding of the United National Educational, Scientific, and Cultural Organization (UNESCO) "in order to respond to the firm belief of nations, forged by two world wars in less than a generation, that political and economic agreements are not enough to build a lasting peace. Peace must be established on the basis of humanity's moral and intellectual solidarity." The organization explains that it "strives to build networks among nations that enable this kind of solidarity." UNESCO focuses on four general areas. First is ensuring that children have access to good-quality education "as a fundamental human right and as a prerequisite for human development." Second is building intercultural understanding through the protection of cultural heritage and diversity. UNESCO invented the concept of the World Heritage Site, which has become an accepted part of our discourse about cultural heritage. Third is advancing scientific cooperation "to strengthen ties between nations and societies," and fourth is protecting freedom of expression as "an essential condition for democracy, development and human rights." The organization's director-general, Irina Bokova, has captured the mandate's essence in two concise sentences: "We are living in a new age of limits—in terms of material resources, in terms of the planet. This calls for greater investment in the most powerful renewable energy we have, that is, human ingenuity."

As for what UNESCO actually does, one example comes readily to mind. The use of the World Heritage Site label has enabled UNESCO to bring certain cultural treasures to special public attention and in that way help protect them and ensure that they are available for future generations. Some of these sites are in cities; others are in jungles or deserts or other out-of-the-way places; and some of them are underwater. "Underwater Cultural Heritage encompasses all traces of human existence that lie or were lying under water and have a cultural or historical character," declares UNESCO. But even treasures lying out of sight under water need protection from treasure hunters and looters. UNESCO drafted the Convention on the Protection of the Underwater Cultural Heritage in 2001, which provides an international legal framework for protecting underwater sites. When signed by twenty member states, it came into force in 2009.

Many of the underwater treasures that UNESCO wants to protect are vessels from decades ago (the *Titanic,* for example), or centuries or even millennia ago, that sank while engaged in commerce. Maritime commerce did not have a UN connection until 1959, with the creation of the International Maritime Organization (IMO). That's a rather late date considering that maritime commerce has a history dating back thousands of years and that today ships carry about 90 percent of international trade.

The IMO's mandate is to make shipping goods for international trade safe and unlikely to pollute the seas. Immediately upon starting operations, the IMO revised the International Convention for the Safety of Life at Sea (SOLAS), a treaty made after the sinking of the *Titanic* in 1912, which IMO labels "the most important of all treaties dealing with maritime safety." Regarding pollution by ships, IMO has introduced measures aimed at preventing oil tanker accidents, minimizing their effects, and limiting the environmental damage caused by the cleaning of oil cargo tanks, the disposal of engine room wastes, and other routine operations. The most important of these efforts, according to the IMO, is the International Convention for the Prevention of Pollution from Ships of 1973 as modified by the Protocol of 1978. It covers accidental and operational oil pollution as well as pollution by chemicals, goods in packaged form, sewage, garbage, and airborne contaminants. Through its meetings, forty conventions, and one thousand codes and recommendations, IMO has helped develop common standards of safety and efficiency in navigation, technical regulations and practices, and pollution control. That is no small task given that a ship's ownership may be separate from its management and may involve more than one country, and that the ship's itinerary may take it to many different countries, none of which might be its place of ownership or management. "There is, therefore, a need for international standards to regulate shipping," notes the IMO, "which can be adopted and accepted by all."

Ships are big and physical, but a lot of today's infrastructure is intangible and soft, such as the rules and standards for the creation, ownership, and development of intellectual property. Soft infrastructure includes laws and regulations about the ownership of intellectual property, which can be anything from songs and novels to inventions, pharmaceuticals, and even genes. As with any form of property, disputes arise about ownership and use. The World Intellectual Property Organization (WIPO) provides such services as helping nations harmonize their laws and procedures about intellectual property, so that creators in each country can more easily be protected in other countries. It administers eleven treaties that set out internationally agreed-on rights and common standards, which the signatory states promise to enforce within their own borders.

The agency's global patent system, which processes more than two hundred thousand applications every year, enables inventors to protect their intellectual property in multiple countries with a single filing. Similarly, the International Trademark System gives coverage in more than ninety countries with a single application. Countries sometimes need protection too, so WIPO maintains a database relating to an article of the Paris Convention that protects the flags and emblems of states that are party to it against their unauthorized registration and use as trademarks. In other words, it prevents someone from claiming the French flag as a trademark. A more useful WIPO service, for us ordinary folk, may be the Arbitration and Mediation Center, which is available to resolve Internet domain-name disputes without resort to litigation.

## Crime and Drug Trafficking

Criminals have learned to exploit the interconnections common in modern life. Air travel, electronic communications, and global financial connections are not only vulnerable to attack but are in some instances being used for nefarious purposes. Drug trafficking is one of these illegal use that has drawn special attention from the UN, which has concentrated its efforts on monitoring drug use worldwide, compiling statistics, and offering expert analyses to assist policymakers and law enforcement officials. The Commission on Narcotic Drugs (CND), a functional commission of ECOSOC, is the UN's main source of drug-related policy and is the governing body of the UN's International Drug Control Program.

Three international conventions form the basis for the CND's policies. The Single Convention on Narcotic Drugs (1961) tries to confine drugs to medical use; the Convention on Psychotropic Substances (1971) seeks to control synthetic drugs; and the UN Convention against Illicit Traffic in Narcotic Drugs and Psychotropic Substances (1988) deals mainly with drug trafficking and related issues like money laundering. However, the CND does not actually monitor implementation of these treaties. That task is the responsibility of the International Narcotics Control Board, an independent panel of thirteen persons elected by ECOSOC and financed by the UN.

The rapid growth of the international narcotics trade has led the UN to coordinate its antidrug operations under the UN Office on Drugs and Crime (UNODC), established in 1997. The UNODC has two components, the Crime Program and the Drug Program. The Crime Program focuses on corruption, organized crime, trafficking in human beings, and terrorism. The Drug Program offers an integrated approach that begins with the farmer and ends with the drug dealer and money launderer. It compiles and disseminates information about illicit drugs, monitors illegal drug-related agriculture, fights the laundering of drug-related money, and helps governments write antidrug legislation.

Among UNODC's major efforts are the Global Assessment Program, which provides accurate information about the international drug problem; the legal Advisory Program, which assists governments in writing laws against the drug trade and helps train judicial officials; and the Illicit Crop Monitoring Program. The Alternative Development Program tries to nip the drug problem at its source by offering farmers alternative crops that will enable them to earn a decent, and legal, living.

The agency's 2013 World Drug Report states that global markets for illicit drugs were largely stable, although opium production in Afghanistan remained too high, and new psychoactive drugs were being developed with alarming rapidity and sold in large quantities: "The multitude of new psychoactive substances and the speed with

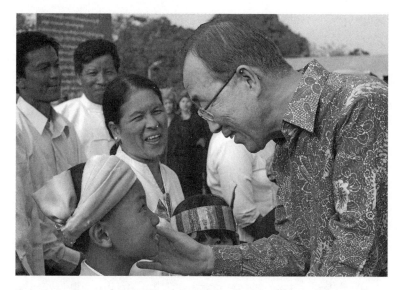

Secretary-General Ban Ki-moon meets local villagers in Kyauk Ka Char, Myanmar, where he visited the Drug Alternative Development Project, cosponsored by the government and the UN Office on Drugs and Crime, April 30, 2012. UN Photo / Mark Garten.

which they have emerged in all regions of the world is one of the most notable trends in drug markets over the past five years." Some countries have adopted innovative approaches to curb the emerging problem, notes the report, "but the global nature of the problem requires a response based on international cooperation and universal coverage." After remarking on the adverse health impacts of drug use, the report calls pointedly for "an interconnected re-balancing of drug control efforts," including "more serious efforts on prevention and treatment, not only in terms of political statements, but also in terms of funds dedicated for these purposes."

The UN's efforts, like those of law-enforcement agencies across the globe, aim at identifying and breaking the connections that enable international crime, including the illicit drug trade, to flourish. But this is proving to be a slow and difficult process.

## Leading UN Actors

- The Commission on Narcotic Drugs (CND) was established in 1946 and has its headquarters in Vienna. It makes UN policy about drugs and is the governing body for the UN Drug Control Program.
- The International Civil Aviation Organization (ICAO) is based in Montreal. ICAO sets the international safety and efficiency standards and regulations for civil aviation. The United States is a strong supporter of organization.
- The International Maritime Organization (IMO) is headquartered in London. Its focus is shipping that is safe and nonpolluting. The IMO founded the World Maritime University in 1983 in Sweden and has also established the IMO International Maritime Law Institute and the IMO International Maritime Academy.
- The International Monetary Fund (IMF) is based in Washington, DC. Member countries subscribe to the IMF through contributions to the budget and can draw on IMF loans according to the level of their subscription. The IMF publishes two important reports: *World Economic Outlook* and *International Capital Markets*. The 188 member nations are each represented on the board of governors, which sets policy and has general oversight. Regular operations are managed by a twenty-four-member executive board.
- The International Telecommunication Union (ITU), located in Geneva, helps governments and the private sector coordinate and improve global telecommunication networks and services. Its responsibilities include developing standards to enable networks and technologies to interconnect. It also offers technical assistance to developing countries.
- The UN Office on Drugs and Crime (UNODC) is based in Vienna. It was established in 1997 through a merger between the United Nations Drug Control Program and the Centre for International Crime Prevention. UNODC operates in all regions of the world through an extensive network of field offices. Some 90 percent of its funding comes from voluntary contributions by member states.

- The United Nations Educational, Scientific, and Cultural Organization (UNESCO), founded in 1945, is based in Paris. Its programs are aimed at promoting the free flow of ideas, open access to education, the transfer of scientific knowledge, and the protection of cultural and natural heritages. With a staff of 2,160, it includes 191 national commissions and some 3,600 UNESCO associations, centers, and clubs.
- The Universal Postal Union (UPU) is headquartered in Bern and charged with helping postal systems deliver the world's mail. The UPU's funds are independent of the UN system and come from the member countries. The organization claims to have the smallest annual budget in the UN system.
- The World Intellectual Property Organization (WIPO), based in Geneva, helps protect intellectual property worldwide. Among its services it offers WIPO Academy, a distance-learning option that assists innovators in developing countries use information about advanced technology. WIPO raises its annual budget largely through earnings from registration systems.

CHAPTER 16

# Climate Change

*This generation, which we represent, is the first in history that has to think about the future of the planet. If I ask myself how many of my generation's parents even mentioned climate change, I don't think that anyone can say yes. It's a new issue; the fact that sustainability is part of the public discussion now is a sign of this.*
—Jan Eliasson, deputy secretary-general of the UN

We all know the saying "People talk about the weather but no one does anything about it." That's only partly true nowadays. Not only do we talk about the weather, especially that part of it called global warming, but we are even trying to do something about it. The effort to halt human-induced climate change is actually part of a much broader discussion about the global environment and the plants and animals within it: the biosphere. Like the canary in a cage, climate change can offer warning about changes across the entire global space of air, land, water, and living beings. Perched next to the canary is the UN, in the middle of the whole effort. When Ban Ki-moon became secretary-general, he made climate change his number one priority, and he has continued to emphasize it. After returning from a tour of the typhoon-ravaged Philippines in 2013, he declared, "I saw yet again how climate change is—quite literally—an existential threat."

## Establishing the Facts

Talk about climate change has been around for more than half a century. Scientists began debating a theory that modern industrial society is capable of transforming the weather through its rising emissions of so-called greenhouse gases. Carbon dioxide and methane are among the gases that have a curious property: like the glass panes in a greenhouse, they are barriers to the radiation of heat. When humans burn carbon-based fuels and increase the level of heat in the vast greenhouse we call the earth, they also raise the level of greenhouse gases in the atmosphere. These gases trap more of the heat instead of letting it radiate into outer space, and over time the atmosphere becomes noticeably warmer. Eventually, says the theory, average atmospheric temperatures will rise enough to alter weather patterns.

Global climate change through human action remained a provocative but obscure theory until the 1980s, when scientists developed sensing mechanisms and computer programs sophisticated enough to track worldwide temperature changes and began analyzing how the warming might someday play out in real-time weather. Mounting evidence was so persuasive that by the new millennium most scientists accepted some kind of link between rising global temperatures and the emission of greenhouse gases.

One of the most influential groups in this discussion is the UN Intergovernmental Panel on Climate Change (IPCC). Established in 1988 by the UN Environment Program (UNEP) and another UN-related body, the World Meteorological Organization (WMO), the IPCC began to review the world's scientific literature to make an impartial assessment of human impacts on the climate. Its official reports, issued in 1990, 1995, 2001, and 2008, are now seen as decisive in changing how the world thinks about climate change.

In sober and reasoned prose, the IPCC's reports laid out the facts—

Secretary-General Ban Ki-moon visits Ilulissat Icefjord, Greenland, to see the impact of global warming, March 27, 2014. UN Photo / Mark Garten.

based on the research and analysis of thousands of scientists world-wide—and concluded that human activity was indeed changing the climate and would continue to do so if current conditions persisted. For its impressive work, the IPCC was awarded the 2007 Nobel Peace Prize jointly with environmental activist, writer, and former US vice president Al Gore.

The consensus position is that continued global warming will disrupt many aspects of life and possibly bring social and economic upheaval. It is clear, for example, that a warmer earth will cause the melting of glaciers and polar ice sheets, leading to a rise in sea level. Coastal cities like Shanghai, New York, and Mumbai and low-lying island nations might have to plan for a very wet future. Other effects seem likely, too, such as the drying out of the American Midwest, which might be extreme enough to limit large-scale agriculture in the famous Corn Belt. Alongside the losers there would probably be some winners, as clouds moved to new latitudes and brought rain to today's deserts, but these improvements would be small compared to the harm suffered in densely populated regions.

## Mobilizing the Response

The UN has been urging the world's governments to curb the emission of greenhouse gases. The first step was a UN-sponsored meeting in 1992. The Conference on Environment and Development, commonly known as the Earth Summit, met in Rio de Janeiro and adopted Agenda 21, a plan for global sustainable development that is now being monitored by a UN body, the Commission on Sustainable Development. Delegates at the Earth Summit got the opportunity to sign the UN Framework Convention on Climate Change, which urged industrialized nations to reduce their emission of greenhouse gases to 1990 levels by 2000. The need for action was documented in 1995 in a report by the IPCC. Five years after the summit, the General Assembly held a special session, Earth Summit+5, to assess progress (which was very uneven) and suggest further action. To push matters along, the UN sponsored a meeting in Kyoto, Japan, in December 1997, where major industrialized nations signed a protocol setting hard-and-fast targets for decreasing the emission of six greenhouse gases by more than 5 percent by 2012. Developing nations were exempted from the reduction target, although the largest of them, China, became the world's biggest emitter of carbon dioxide in 2006.

The effectiveness of the UN's efforts to move from identifying the problem to fixing it has gotten mixed reviews. Richard Gowan finds it worrying that the UN process on climate change, a "big universal discussion," "failed to deliver in Copenhagen," a UN-sponsored climate change meeting in 2009: "it's only crawling along." A major limiting factor, argues Gowan, is the UN's preference for acting through consensus. "That whole negotiating format with every single state having a voice and every single state being able to block progress is not working."

Undeterred by critics, the UN has convened meetings of stakeholders and sought to raise public awareness of the need for global

## A Call to Action

"The science of climate change is leaping out at us like a scene from a 3D movie. It's warning us; it's compelling us to act. And let there be no doubt in anybody's mind that the science is absolutely certain. . . .

"I am pleased to tell you that the leaders of China agree that it is time to pursue a cleaner path forward. China is taking steps, and we have already taken significant steps together through the U.S.-China Climate Change Working Group that we launched in Beijing last year. Just yesterday, we announced a new agreement on an enhanced policy of dialogue that includes the sharing of information and policies so that we can help develop plans to deal with the UN climate change negotiation that takes place in Paris next year, in planning for the post-2020 limit to greenhouse gas emissions. These plans are a key input into UN negotiations to develop a new global climate agreement, and we have hopes that this unique partnership between China and the United States can help set an example for global leadership and global seriousness.

"Make no mistake: this is real progress. The U.S. and China are the world's two largest economies. We are two of the largest consumers of energy, and we are two of the largest emitters of global greenhouse gases—together we account for roughly 40 percent of the world's emissions. But this is not just about China and the United States. It's about every country on Earth doing whatever it can to pursue cleaner and healthier energy sources. . . . This is going to require us to continue the UN negotiations and ultimately finalize an ambitious global agreement in Paris next year. And nations need to also be pursuing smaller bilateral agreements, public-private partnerships, independent domestic initiatives—you name it."

—US Secretary of State John Kerry speaking in Jakarta, Indonesia, February 16, 2014

action. Secretary-General Ban places a lot of importance on getting the business and financial sectors behind the climate change issue. "With the private sector's well-known ingenuity harnessed in the battle against climate change, we can leverage costs into economic gain. That's good corporate citizenship—but it also makes sound economic sense. I've personally met with business leaders in major cities across the United States and elsewhere to drive home this point." At the World Economic Forum on Climate, Growth and Development, held in Davos, Switzerland, in 2014, he urged his listeners to "go green" and to invest "trillions" of dollars in low-carbon energy and stop investing in high-carbon energy.

Ban sees the United States as a key player in the effort and has urged Washington to lead the effort against global warming, declaring that "the whole planet Earth is at a crucial juncture." The cost of inaction, he warns, "will be far greater than the cost of action." While noting that the UN accepted responsibility for helping to muster the political will to address climate change, he says the United States is "in the best position to bring change" because of its advanced technology and its status as one of the largest producers of greenhouse gasses. He declares, "If you take leadership, I think we can save this planet earth from plunging into a very difficult situation."

When President Obama unveiled a US action plan to curb greenhouse emissions, in June 2014, the secretary-general responded immediately and positively, calling the plan "a significant step toward reducing greenhouse gas emissions that are disrupting the climate, exacerbating extreme weather patterns, and threatening human health, sustainable economic growth and development." Among other things, the Obama plan ordered the US Environmental Protection Agency to establish carbon emission standards for all power plants and to permit the construction of a specified amount of wind- and solar-generating capacity on public lands.

Additionally, the Obama plan sought to expand climate change initiatives with other nations. Many developing nations in Africa and elsewhere have become increasingly concerned about the threats of human-induced climate change. Attention has focused especially on China. Beijing's heavy air pollution is only the most immediately visible aspect of the massive environmental changes sweeping China's air, rivers, lands, and shores. Clearly undesirable, the pollution has nevertheless raised public and official awareness of China's major contributions to climate change. China's planners responded to the threat in their Five-Year Plan, adopted by the government in March

Secretary-General Ban Ki-moon (right) meets with Michael Bloomberg, former mayor of New York City and his special envoy for cities and climate change, February 21, 2014. UN Photo / Eskinder Debebe.

2011, which established new targets and policies for 2011–2015, including efforts to reduce fossil energy consumption and eventually to establish a market for the trading of rights to emit carbon. Common concerns about climate change led the Chinese and US governments to state publicly their desire to work together in addressing the issue.

## Protecting the Biosphere

Talk of developing a green economy draws immediate interest from environmentalists and others concerned about the state of the natural world. Use of fossil fuels typically exacts large environmental costs. Coal mining, to name one culprit, is notoriously polluting to waterways, and the burning of coal emits both greenhouse gases and toxic substances, like mercury, that ride the winds and spread far beyond the point of emission. This is only one example of how the campaign against climate change can also be viewed as an attempt to preserve and restore the natural world.

Concern for the natural environment has moved up on everyone's agenda over the past five decades as rapid population increases and economic development have strained the world's forests, farmlands, atmosphere, rivers, and oceans. These are areas where the UN's global reach and ability to act as an honest broker have produced impressive results. One of the UN's first efforts to take the lead in addressing a global environmental issue concerned the thinning of the atmosphere's ozone layer. Scientific analysis showed that certain manufactured chemicals, especially chlorofluorocarbons (CFCs), can catalyze the breakdown of ozone in the upper atmosphere and thus increase the amount of harmful ultraviolet sunlight reaching earth. In response to the threat, the world community took decisive action under the leadership of the UN Environment Program. Following the terms of the Montreal Protocol of 1987, the industrialized countries banned production of CFCs beginning in 1996; developing countries were granted a grace period for compliance. All signs indicate that the plans are helping to avert an environmental and human catastrophe.

Within the UN system, UNEP takes the lead on environmental issues, acting as a "catalyst, advocate, educator and facilitator to promote the wise use and sustainable development of the global environment." It claims a vast mandate: "To be the leading global authority that sets the global environmental agenda, that promotes the coherent implementation of the environmental dimensions of sustainable development within the United Nations system and that serves as an authoritative advocate for the global environment." The breadth of the mission and activities shows how a green economy, protection of wildlife, and sustainable social and economic development are increasingly being understood as related parts of a much bigger picture. They also lend strength to the statements of Secretary-General Ban Ki-moon and others that no single nation or organization "can do it alone."

## Leading UN Actors

- The United Nations Environment Program (UNEP), founded in 1972, is based in Nairobi. UNEP acts as the UN's voice for the environment and describes itself as an "advocate, educator, and facilitator to promote the wise use and sustainable development of the global environment." The US government values UNEP's function as a global catalyst of ideas and action and has been the program's biggest donor from the beginning. According to the US Environmental Protection Agency, "EPA has had a long and very successful relationship with UNEP, including numerous substantive partnerships." In the Mercury Emissions Study, for example, both organizations compiled data about the sources and scale of mercury emissions and the cost and effectiveness of control options, all with an eye to providing guidance in negotiations for "a legally binding global agreement on mercury." Their efforts helped lead in 2013 to adoption of the Minamata Convention on Mercury, a global treaty to protect human health and the environment from the adverse effects of mercury.
- The World Meteorological Organization (WMO), founded in 1951, is based in Geneva. A specialized agency of the UN, it provides scientific information about the atmosphere, freshwater, and climate, including depletion of the ozone layer, global warming, droughts, and El Niño. Its staff of more than two hundred serves 182 member states and six territories. Beyond that the agency contributes to policy formulation in these areas at national and international levels.

## CHAPTER 17

# Keeping Tabs on How Nations Vote

*A country's voting record in the United Nations is only one dimension of its relations with the United States. . . . Nevertheless, a country's behavior at the United Nations is always relevant in its bilateral relationship with the United States, a point the Secretary of State regularly makes in letters of instruction to new U.S. ambassadors.*

—US Department of State

Because the United States is the biggest player at the United Nations, its words, actions, and nonactions are parsed in a hundred divergent ways by the world's media, governments, and analysts. But people are not generally aware that the US government does its own parsing of member states' behavior, especially their voting records. The US government places such great importance on positioning itself strongly within the UN system that it monitors how other nations vote in the 193-member General Assembly and the 15-member Security Council. Section 406 of Public Law 101-246 requires the State Department to inform Congress annually about how UN member states have voted in comparison with the United States. As the report's introductory section notes, the Security Council and the

Table 7. Voting activity of the Security Council, 2003–12

| Year | Meetings | Resolutions Considered | Resolutions Adopted |
|------|----------|------------------------|---------------------|
| 2012 | 199 | 55 | 53 |
| 2011 | 235 | 68 | 66 |
| 2010 | 210 | 59 | 59 |
| 2009 | 194 | 49 | 48 |
| 2008 | 244 | 66 | 65 |
| 2007 | 202 | 57 | 56 |
| 2006 | 272 | 89 | 87 |
| 2005 | 235 | 71 | 71 |
| 2004 | 216 | 62 | 59 |
| 2003 | 208 | 69 | 67 |

*Source:* Adapted from US Department of State, *Voting Practices in the United Nations, 2012,* http://www.state.gov/p/io/rls/rpt/c57662.htm.

General Assembly are "arguably the most important international bodies in the world, dealing as they do with such vital issues as threats to peace and security, disarmament, development, humanitarian relief, human rights, the environment, and narcotics—all of which can and do directly affect major U.S. interests."

Each year, the State Department's UN analysts tote up how member states vote on the issues, whether with or contrary to the US voting position. For the Security Council, there is usually little suspense about the numbers. The tight club almost always acts through consensus (table 7). In 2012 the council considered fifty-five resolutions and adopted fifty-three, many of them unanimously. The sole vetoes were cast by China and Russia on resolutions about Syria. Only four resolutions were not adopted unanimously, one each on Cyprus, Sudan, children in armed conflict, and the International Criminal Tribunal for the former Yugoslavia. Former US ambassador John Negroponte sees the strong consensus numbers as clear proof that "for all the talk about our being unilateral, the number of resolutions and issues that we succeed in dealing with on a totally consensus basis is really quite striking."

The General Assembly passes most of its resolutions by consen-

The Security Council chamber before a meeting on Afghanistan, December 17, 2013. UN Photo / Amanda Voisard.

sus and the rest by tallied vote. When you factor in all the resolutions passed, both by consensus and by tallied vote, it turns out that in 2012 the member states and the United States voted the same way 83.9 percent of the time. The percentage has been stable in recent years: 84.3 percent in 2009; 85.4 percent in 2010; 85.9 percent in 2011. That may be unexpected, given the wide spectrum of perspectives, agendas, and interests in the assembly.

Votes on non-consensus issues, however, show a much different pattern. During the fall 2012 session the Sixty-Seventh General Assembly held eighty-nine tallied votes on resolutions. The United States voted yes twenty-nine times, voted no forty-nine times, and abstained eleven times. Did other countries vote substantially the same way as the United States on those resolutions? Only 42.5 percent of the time, according to the State Department's tally.

The numbers become more interesting in the State Department's tabulation of voting coincidence by country. We can see, for example, that Afghanistan voted with the United States 36.5 percent of the time. Other percentages are Australia, 71.0 percent; Brazil, 35.1 percent; China, 30.3 percent; Germany, 60.0 percent; Saudi Arabia, 29.2 percent; and the United Kingdom, 73.8 percent.

Other tabulations show voting coincidences by region, bloc, and "eight important votes," meaning votes on issues that the United States holds especially close to its national interest. In 2012 these eight were votes on:

- ending the US economic blockade of Cuba
- four resolutions concerning the Palestinians and Israel
- the status of human rights in Iran
- the status of human rights in Syria
- entrepreneurship for development

In table 8 we can see that US interests often differ from those of other governments or blocs, such as the Asian and African Groups, and to that extent we can see how the United States sits within the broader world community.

Table 8 lists basic groups. For Africa, whose fifty-four nations run from Algeria to Zimbabwe, the average voting coincidence with the United States in 2012 was 25.7 percent. After reaching a low with the Arab Group (12.4 percent), which includes Egypt, Morocco, Saudi Arabia, and Tunisia, among others, the numbers improve. The Asian Group, a conglomeration of fifty-three nations stretching from India to Indonesia, voted with the United States 26.6 percent of the time. Europeans were far more likely to vote with the United States: the twenty-three nations in the Eastern Europe Group, 60.8 percent of the time, and the nations in the Western Europe and Others Group, 63.3 percent. The Latin America and the Caribbean Group represented another drop in coincidence. The thirty-three members, on average, voted with the United States 32.1 percent of the time.

Another way to parse the voting is by political grouping. UN member states belong to various affinity groups, such as the OIC (Islamic Conference), ASEAN (Association of Southeast Asian Nations), the Nonaligned Movement (NAM), and the North Atlantic

Table 8. Voting coincidence of General Assembly groups on "eight important votes," Sixty-Seventh General Assembly (2012)

| Region or Group | Number of Members | Share of Coinciding Votes (%) |
|---|---|---|
| African Group | 54 | 25.7 |
| Arab Group | 20 | 12.4 |
| Asian Group | 53 | 26.6 |
| Eastern European Group | 23 | 60.8 |
| Western European and Others Group | 28 | 63.3 |
| Nordic Group | 5 | 57.7 |
| Latin America and Caribbean Group | 33 | 32.1 |
| Association of Southeast Asian Nations (ASEAN) | 10 | 15.3 |
| Nonaligned Movement (NAM) | 118 | 22.3 |
| Organization of Islamic Conference | 57 | 17.9 |
| NATO | 27 | 64.8 |
| European Union | 27 | 63.3 |

Source: Adapted from US Department of State, Voting Practices in the
United Nations, 2012, http://www.state.gov/p/io/rls/rpt/c57662.htm.

Note: Some nations belong to more than one group.

Treaty Organization (NATO). The State Department annually exam-
ines how these blocs vote on issues that the United States considers important. Voting coincidence among the ten ASEAN nations
averaged 15.3 percent in 2012, while for the NAM, a collection of
member states ranging from little Barbados to oil-rich Saudi Arabia
to the subcontinent of India, the coincidence was a little higher, 22.3
percent. NATO and the European Union were three times as likely
to vote the same way as the United States.

The number of nations voting with the United States has generally risen after the marked decline during the George W. Bush administration. General Assembly voting coincidence with the United
States was 18.3 percent in 2007; 25.6 percent in 2008; 39 percent in
2009; 41.6 percent in 2010; 51.5 percent in 2011; and 42.5 percent
in 2012.

European nations, most of which are affluent and developed, are more likely to vote with the United States, whereas developing nations are not. In other words, the North-South divide seems to be in play. The divide's influence may be exacerbated by another factor suggested by insider Jeffrey Laurenti. "Developing country democracies do not behave the way Washington does by dint of being democracies, or see things by dint of being democracies," he says. "The thing that is striking, and very hard for many in Washington to understand, including many liberal voices, is that India, South Africa, and Brazil tend to see international crises more like China does than the United States does." Laurenti's explanation is that compared with rich and powerful countries, poorer countries "have a divergent optic. . . . So they have a tug of claims: the claim of solidarity among the poor of being able to understand things that wealthier countries don't instinctively get, and a sense of doubt about the motivations perhaps of the rich and powerful—in many cases the rich and powerful that have colonized those same countries within living memory."

Stewart Patrick of the Council on Foreign Affairs likewise remarks on the difference in perception. "The US loves it when the emerging powers do more in the UN as long as they agree with the US." Often they don't. "The difficulty is, of course, these countries actually have minds of their own and they aren't always aligned with the US. So it's one thing to ask them to shoulder a greater burden of global order and international good. It's another to expect that they're going to align with the United States." This has caused frustration on the US side. "One US official actually said that the US sees some of these countries 'cross-dressing.' In some venues they'll be in bilateral conversations with the US and they'll be very aligned, but when you get them in the UN General Assembly they'll play to the galleries. A lot of it has to do with the ambivalence and split political identity of some of these emerging regional and potentially global powers."

However we interpret lesser degrees of coincidence, we are left with yet another question: What do these numbers mean in terms of American foreign policy? As the State Department's annual report observes, although a nation's UN voting record "is only one dimension of its relations with the United States," it is nevertheless a significant factor and "always relevant in its bilateral relationship with the United States." A particular aspect of that relationship is foreign aid, which some experts have argued should be linked to how a nation votes in the UN (something that Congress has not required).

Even without any formal linkage it is possible that the State Department's report may have an effect on how other nations vote. The department sends copies to the foreign ministries and missions of UN member states as a friendly reminder that Uncle Sam is watching.

## CHAPTER 18

# The Call for Reform

*When I return to Washington, and when other permanent representatives return to their capitals, we want to be able to report to our taxpayers that the UN has entered a new era and that governments can be confident that the resources they invest will be used wisely.*
— Samantha Power, US ambassador to the UN

Reform is a loaded word, especially in the UN. The call for making improvements may imply that better things are coming, but it also raises the prospect that some people or groups may lose privileges or coveted status. "In theory," observes Edward Luck, "all the member states want reform; in practice they all mean very different things by it. So it's very hard to get a consensus among the members for change in the organization." He adds that "the big powers are afraid that they'll lose some degree of control; the small powers are afraid that whatever pledges they've received regarding the bureaucracy will be lost in a more sweeping reform controlled by the bigger powers and bigger contributors." Predictably, when Ban Ki-moon became secretary-general in 2007 and presented his ideas for reform, they met resistance from many directions.

In the Name of Efficiency

Speaking broadly, the calls for reform fall into two categories: a more up-to-date alignment of status and authority and better management of the system. Security Council restructuring, considered in chapter 6, represents the push for a realignment of status and authority. The management aspect of reform , which is less overtly political and philosophical in nature, is a favorite topic among Western analysts and politicians, who believe that the UN system could be much more effective, efficient, and accountable than it is. The most outspoken proponents of reform have usually come from the large donor nations, which say they want to make the organization better.

An Obvious Choice

According to former US ambassador Richard Holbrooke, the UN "is the flawed but indispensable institution that we have two choices with: weaken it by undermining it or [try] to strengthen it by getting it to correct its flaws." For him, the choice was obvious: "In America when we discern flaws we try to fix them. We should do the same with the UN because in the end, it's a highly leveraged organization that helps America and the nation's interest and world. But what a mess it is."

When Kofi Annan took office in 1997, he launched what he called his "quiet revolution" to streamline the organization and make it both more efficient and more effective without raising costs. The quiet revolution managed to stop the Secretariat's budget creep for a few years, beginning in 1998, and even reduced it a little. Although the UN claimed that the total number of all staff in the UN system (about fifty-two thousand) was much smaller than the number of employees at many large corporations, it nevertheless tried to keep staff numbers from growing too fast. Former UN ambassador Nancy Soderberg thinks that Annan tossed out a lot of the dead wood. "I would say that 90 percent are terrific. You have the young

people who are very enthused about it and the senior people who
have worked their life in the UN and loved it, and then you have a
few people scattered around who are there for life."

Mark Malloch-Brown makes a different criticism of the bureaucracy, citing a pervasive "disconnect between merit and reward." It's
"rational," he notes, "that if you work hard and do well, you get pro-
moted, and if you don't work hard you don't. In parts of the UN that
doesn't happen." He advocates "reconnecting merit to make the UN
again an international meritocracy." To do this, however, Malloch-
Brown believes that the UN must stop advancing its personnel on
the basis of political correctness, which encourages promoting staff
disproportionately from certain regions of the world. Asia, Africa,
and other so-called less developed regions now offer a large pool of
talented, skilled, and highly motivated professionals, which, in his
view, the UN ought to make more use of. These individuals are so
highly qualified, he believes, that they will readily move up through
the UN system without need of the "cultural relativism which is
used to promote incompetents."

A related point is often made by UN member states from the
developing world who complain that some of the most desirable
senior posts within the Secretariat are filled under a "tradition"
of regional representation that favors the United States and other
affluent nations. The point has been made forcefully by former ambassador Munir Akram of Pakistan, who was once head of the G-77.
"The major countries, the major powers, hold very high positions
in the Secretariat and support their national interests and refuse
to allow the secretary-general to cut departments," he claims. And
when they do ask for budget cuts, they do it "where it does not affect
their national interests." He labels this "a double standard which
is applied or is thought to be applied in the Secretariat, and we as
overseers of the G-77 do not accept this double standard."

Malloch-Brown comments on the importance of UN agencies
and departments being able to cooperate smoothly with one another. He "saw very clearly how the system doesn't really want to
allow that to happen." He found the General Assembly suspicious
that the secretary-general was "ceding certain management respon-

sibilities to a Western deputy"—Malloch-Brown, when he was deputy secretary-general—and yet "the powers were those which in any corporate setting would be seen as the powers not of a chief executive but of a chief operating officer." The division of responsibility was necessary and reasonable, says Malloch-Brown, "unless you assume a secretary-general is to do everything, from turning off the lights at night to signing off on payroll every month."

## Fixing What's Broken

One of the UN's first substantive efforts to address criticism of its administration came in 1994 with the establishment of the Office of Internal Oversight Services (OIOS), charged with making the bureaucracy more effective and efficient. Creation of the office pleased the US government, which described it as "one of the most significant management reforms adopted by the General Assembly in many years." The Secretariat gained a new reform tool in December 2000, when the General Assembly authorized it to start "results-based budgeting." Long urged by the United States as a way of rationalizing the allocation and spending of funds, results-based budgeting establishes objectives for each department or program and develops "performance indicators" to measure progress in reaching them.

### Worth Fixing

"The UN continues to be vital to the functioning of the international system, but it needs reform. It needs a lot of support by nations. It needs to really keep revitalizing itself. I am a great believer in the UN but there have to be some very serious reforms."
—Madeleine Albright, former US ambassador to the UN

Many observers credit Annan's quiet revolution with making real improvements. It was pushed along by the Procurement Task Force, established in January 2006, largely at the urging of the under-secretary-general for management at the time, Christopher Burnham. The task force was charged with looking for corruption and abuse and providing information for prosecutors. Burnham, a former official in the US State Department, was appointed in May 2005 and left the UN in fall 2006. During his brief but energetic tenure he pushed for the creation of a UN Ethics Office, which officially opened in 2007. He is also credited with establishing a whistle-blower protection policy for UN staff; introducing international public-sector accounting standards for the UN; and modernizing the UN's information and communication technology infrastructure.

Esther Brimmer of George Washington University sees reform succeeding in some parts of the system, like the UNDP (more transparency), but she complains that the information technology is "woefully behind" and that the standardization of budgeting across the system is "only fair." Similarly, reports by a respected US government body, the Government Accountability Office (GAO), usually give mixed reviews of UN reform efforts. They often speak of progress in various aspects of the UN's operations, from the practice of professional ethics to oversight and efficient management, but the favorable comments are invariably tempered by warnings that the pace of change is often too slow, owing to various factors, including a lack of interest by many member states. A GAO report in 2011 noted progress in improving the effectiveness of the UN's internal oversight body but also identified key areas of weakness, such as understaffing and insufficient audit authority, and called for further action.

## Seeking Organizational Discipline

The experiences of Malloch-Brown and other insiders suggest that UN staff must operate in a highly politicized environment, where the Security Council and the General Assembly, which make the rules, can ignore them if they so choose. UN analyst Shepard Forman criticizes the UN precisely on this point: unlike the US government, he argues, "the UN doesn't have an effective system of checks and balances." Budgets, for example, may be treated as entitlements rather

Secretary-General Ban Ki-moon speaks during an informal thematic debate on management reform at the General Assembly, April 8, 2008. UN Photo / Paulo Filgueiras.

than limits to spending and in that way become vulnerable to uncontrollable growth.

US Permanent Representative Samantha Power referred to the arbitrariness of the budgeting arrangements in December 2013, when she spoke at the General Assembly's Fifth Committee, the one that shapes the biennial budget. "Under the leadership of Secretary-General Ban Ki-moon," she began, "the UN has taken some important steps to improve the organization's relevance and performance. Over the past two years the Secretariat has operated within its budget allocation for special political missions; that is a laudable break from the past, and one that my government commends." Unfortunately, she continued, in the proposed budget for 2014–15, "promises of future change are simply not enough."

Power reviewed recent history to make her point. "Recall that two years ago, we approved a budget based on the understanding that if some costs exceeded expectations, others would be reduced to keep the overall level roughly the same. This pledge has not been kept." Instead, after approval of the budget "we have already agreed to two separate additions, totaling $200 million for recosting, and we have funded add-ons made necessary by new mandates, such as special political missions in Yemen and the Sahel." And that was not the end of the additions, for "the current report seeks an additional $160 million in recosting costs above and beyond the approved budget." She admonished her audience, pointing out that "such a request is not typical of how most businesses and organizations function."

The problem, Power continued, is that "we are essentially budgeting by looking backward, saying the UN budget is what we spent, rather than saying a UN budget is the envelope defining what we have available to spend." The solution is to realize that something can be done about it. "There is an unfortunate tendency to act as if none of these cost increases are within our control—that it is all the result of methodologies that are written in stone and that cannot be altered or countered. The truth is that each of these increases and these methodologies is the product of choice. And what we have the power to choose, we do have the ability to work together to change." At the conclusion of her remarks Power reminded the committee members that in the final analysis the UN budgets depend on the willingness of the more affluent nations to pay the greater part of the organization's expenses.

Undoubtedly, many members of the US Congress would agree with her assessment and her suggestions for improvement, but the question remains whether the UN can actually reform its corporate culture, which is more bureaucratic than entrepreneurial and ill-suited to the kind of dispassionate self-examination and self-discipline that Power seeks. Reform is possible at the UN, as Burnham's efforts show, but within limits, as Malloch-Brown's experience demonstrates. Malloch-Brown admits that progress on reform "is generally quite low." He explains: "My problem always is, the demands on the UN grow exponentially; the rate of reform is a much lower trend line. It's a gentle uphill move, whereas the demands on the UN rise vertically, so the gap between expectations and performance continues to grow."

## CHAPTER 19

# Paying for It All

*I'd like to have a Ferrari, but since I can't afford it, I'm probably going to get a cheaper car when I leave this job. So therefore, we have to work hard with the Secretariat, with the other member states, to do what we must, what we can afford, but the whole budget process needs to be looked at to make it more rational, to make the presentation a single comprehensive budget so the members can make a determination.*
—Zalmay Khalilzad, former US ambassador to the UN

There is no free lunch, not even at the United Nations. Each month the UN's financial office sends out millions of dollars' worth of checks to pay for staff salaries, computer services, electricity, technical consultants, housekeeping for its big New York City headquarters, and a thousand other things. When you add all these costs from all the members of the UN family, including the various agencies and committees, as well as peacekeeping costs, the total runs to many billions each year. Where does the money come from? Not from taxes. The UN is not a government, so it cannot levy taxes. The bulk of the dollars comes from the UN members themselves.

Think of the UN as a condo apartment building—we'll call it

Global Towers—located on prime real estate on the east side of Manhattan in New York City, with a breathtaking view of the cityscape and the East River. Periodically the condo owner-members (nation-states) meet to vote on setting a budget for the coming years, based on regular membership fees, voluntary contributions, and occasional special assessments. Discussion invariably focuses on how big the expense budget should be and how the costs should be allocated among the owners, who vary widely in wealth, outlook, and commitment to keeping the condominium safe, comfortable, and solvent.

As in any condo where the owners are well known to one another, the budget debate inevitably runs along ruts worn during decades of meetings, with occasional sharp exchanges when opinions clash. Something of this sort unfolds in the General Assembly's Fifth Committee (Administrative and Budgetary) every three years as it deliberates on the size of the assessments that each country must contribute. That is when the General Assembly can really flex its muscles, because its decisions affect all parts of Global Towers, from the airy thirty-eighth-floor office of the secretary-general to the stuffy basement, where the building engineers make their daily rounds. It is estimated that the annual operating budgets of the Secretariat, other UN organs, peacekeeping operations, and the UN agencies, funds, and programs, excluding the World Bank and the International Monetary Fund, come to some $30 billion each year.

## Money Talks

"The test of the American commitment to the UN, above all, is financial. That's what tests it, and whether we seek to strengthen the UN through a combination of resources and reform or weaken it through neglect and punishment." —Richard Holbrooke, former US ambassador to the UN

## The Budget Process

Membership in the UN comes with the obligation to help pay for its support—something that has never been questioned. In-

stead, the focus has been on the size of each member state's contribution. Financial support takes three basic forms. First is the mandatory assessment for the general UN budget, also referred to as
the "regular" or "administrative" budget, which funds the Secretariat and related bodies. There is also the mandatory assessment
for the peacekeeping budget. In addition are the assessed contributions that member states make for specific UN agencies and
organizations, such as the International Atomic Energy Agency
(IAEA) and the World Health Organization (WHO). Second are
voluntary donations to such UN programs as the United Nations
Children's Fund (UNICEF) or the World Food Program (WFP). And
third are occasional special assessments, like the $2-plus billion
that the members had to pay to renovate the New York City headquarters.

Discussions in the media often relate to the "regular budget,"
which pays for activities, staff, and basic infrastructure but not
peacekeeping. In 2013, the budgeted amount was slightly less than
$2.6 billion. (The regular budget is for a two-year period, a bien-
nium, so $2.6 billion is simply half of the $5.2 billion that the General Assembly approved when it voted on the budget.) The formulas
for calculating a nation's assessed contributions for the regular budget and the peacekeeping budget are based largely on the country's
share of the world economy. In other words, the rich pay more than
the poor do. Nations with a low per-capita income get a discount, as
do those with a high level of foreign debt. The United States, having
the world's largest economy by a wide margin, naturally pays the
largest share, about 22 percent, and very poor nations pay a nomi-
nal amount. The poorest nations have to pay a minimum of about
$25,000 annually for their UN dues.

The regular budget is the product of a complicated process designed to ensure that all interested parties have their say in how
funds are obtained and spent. The secretary-general proposes a
draft budget and gives it to the Advisory Committee on Administrative and Budgetary Questions (ACABQ) for review. The advisory committee consists of sixteen individuals nominated by their
governments, usually including a US national, and elected by the

General Assembly. The Committee for Program and Coordination (CPC), consisting of thirty-four experts elected by the General Assembly, reviews the program aspects of the budget. Unlike the advisory committee, in which the experts serve in their personal capacity, the program committee experts represent the views of their governments. The revised draft is sent to the General Assembly's Fifth Committee for approval. The Fifth Committee makes a final adjustment and votes to approve the budget, which it then sends to the General Assembly for a vote by the full membership of the UN. That vote makes the document the official UN regular budget for the next biennium. Each country has the opportunity to suggest changes in the draft budget, but the changes may not necessarily be adopted.

Peacekeeping is treated separately from other budgets. The scale used to make peacekeeping assessments has ten levels of support, with the least-developed countries paying 10 percent of what they would have owed according to the assessment scale for the regular budget, and the five permanent Security Council members paying a surcharge of about 25 percent. The US share of peacekeeping costs is about 28 percent.

The UN's agencies, commissions, and programs have their own budgets. Each director draws up a budget and sends it to the secretary-general, who incorporates the information into the overall UN budget, which is sent to the General Assembly's Fifth Committee. Most agencies, commissions, and programs also raise funds independently from member states and other sources. When Mark Malloch-Brown was head of the United Nations Development Program (UNDP) he answered a query about his organization's budget this way: "I call it $1.2 billion, and there are two other numbers which others use. One is $750 million, which is core contributions. I call it $1.2 billion because that's core plus donor contributions to special trust funds for special issues. Some call it $2 billion because that includes what we call cofinancing, where developed countries kick in a huge volume of resources because they like us, in many cases, to spend their money for them. I count that out because for various reasons not dealt with it's a little misleading. So I say $1.2 billion, pessimists say $750 million, the optimists say $2 billion or $2.1." Is that perfectly clear?

## Sharing a Growing Burden

One of the most surprising fiscal events at the UN was the large and rapid escalation of budgets between 2002 and 2011. For example, annual peacekeeping costs peaked at $3.5 billion in 1994, during the large-scale operations in the former Yugoslavia, dropped to $1.3 billion in 1997, and rose toward the $3 billion level in 2002. After that they climbed steeply as the United States and other Security Council members authorized the creation of more peacekeeping missions. The budget for 2012–13 was just over $7 billion.

The UN's general, or regular, budget experienced a similar increase, from $2.5 billion for the 2000–2001 biennium, to $3.6 billion in 2004–5, $4.1 billion in 2006–7, and $5.2 billion in 2008–9. It peaked at $5.4 billion in 2010–11 before declining slightly to $5.2 billion in 2012–13. The increase occurred largely during the George W. Bush administration and was alarming to many. Former US ambassador John Bolton calls 'it "a breakdown of a twenty-year-long effort to rein in UN spending."

Even these escalating budget figures are pretty small potatoes in today's world of trillion-dollar economies. The UN once noted that "the budget for UN worldwide human rights activities is smaller than that of the Zürich Opera House." That may be true, but not every member state can afford the cost of the Zürich Opera House, so questions often arise about how to allocate fiscal obligations.

Most discussions about excessive burdens have focused on some of the richest member states. The top fourteen nations, including the United States and Japan, paid a total of $1.9 billion, or nearly 80 percent of the 2012 general budget of $2.4 billion, leaving the remaining 179 member states to pay the balance of about 20 percent.

The United States and Japan, the largest contributors to the UN budgets, have each asked for downward adjustments in what they pay. As listed in table 9, the United States and Japan together paid

Table 9. Top fourteen funders of the UN regular budget, 2012

| Member State | Assessed Contribution (US$) |
|---|---|
| United States | $569,000,000 |
| Japan | $296,000,000 |
| Germany | $189,000,000 |
| United Kingdom | $156,000,000 |
| France | $145,000,000 |
| Italy | $118,000,000 |
| Canada | $76,000,000 |
| China | $75,000,000 |
| Spain | $75,000,000 |
| Mexico | $56,000,000 |
| Republic of Korea | $53,000,000 |
| Australia | $46,000,000 |
| Netherlands | $44,000,000 |
| Brazil | $38,000,000 |
| Total | $1,936,000,000 |

*Source:* Compiled from UN Secretariat, *Assessment of Member States' Contributions to the United Nations Regular Budget for 2012* (December 27, 2011).
*Note:* Total budget, US$2,412,000,000.

$865 million, about 36 percent of the 2012 general budget. In FY 2010, the United States contributed some $7.691 billion to the UN family, including $2.648 billion to peacekeeping, and was a major donor to the World Food Program (36.3 percent of the agency's budget) and the UN High Commissioner for Refugees (37.0 percent), to name just two agencies.

The United States has negotiated several reductions in its share of the general budget. For example, in 1974 the UN agreed to place a cap of 25 percent on the size of a member state's assessment, effectively lowering the United States' share in subsequent years. Another change came in 2001, when the General Assembly reduced the US share of the regular budget to a maximum of 22 percent and its share of peacekeeping costs from 31 percent to about 28 percent. Both reductions came at the urging of the US government in response to a law stipulating that the United States would pay nearly $1 billion in assessment arrears if the UN met certain conditions, such as a reduction in the assessment rate.

The Japanese government took another approach to trying to reduce its assessed share of the general budget. In 2006, it unsuccessfully proposed that the UN put a floor of 3 or 5 percent under the regular-budget contributions of the P5. In other words, a permanent member of the Security Council would have to pay an annual assessment of at least 3 or 5 percent of the total general budget. When the Japanese made this proposal, China was paying only 2 percent and Russia 1 percent of the general budget, compared with 19 percent for Japan and 22 percent for the United States. Raising the Chinese and Russian assessments would permit reductions in those of other nations, including Japan's.

As a concession to some of the wealthier and more highly assessed members states, the assembly and its Fifth Committee began passing UN budgets by consensus in 1988. This was intended to give the wealthier states some leverage in the budget process. Additionally, the Japanese were able to negotiate reductions in their share of the general budget, from more than 19 percent in 2006 to roughly 16 percent in 2007, and then again to about 12 percent in 2010.

The G-77 and the NAM, blocs consisting largely of the less affluent member states, have voting power in the General Assembly beyond what one would expect based on their financial contributions to the UN, and the discrepancy has led to friction in the assembly. Complaints about process and equitable sharing of burdens have led some US foreign-policy experts and some critics in Congress to urge that the United States withhold funds for specific UN bodies that need reform or fail to meet US expectations. Former UN ambassador John Bolton is among those who would like to go even further. He proposes that the leading nations lobby for a fundamental revision in the nature of UN funding. "What we really need is not additional effort for marginal change but a major change in the way the whole UN is funded, to move toward voluntary contribu-

Fifth Committee members in informal negotiation during a meeting break, April 28, 2006. UN Photo / Mark Garten.

tions. That's the only way to get people interested [in UN reform]." He accepts the need for the United States to take the lead but is sure that other donors, such as Japan, will welcome it. "They will fall in behind us," he says, "but as usual at the UN we would have to be the ones who really press it."

## Budget Arrears

Ideally, each member state accepts its assessment as being appropriate and immediately sends a check to the UN for the full amount. Reality is more complicated. Even for routine and predictable budgets, like the regular budget, the UN has a hard time getting everyone to pay fully and on time. Some member states delay their payments for various reasons, often unrelated to their ability to pay, while others (like the United States) pay on their own schedule, depending on when their legislature or national assembly votes the funds.

The Charter (Article 19) permits the UN to penalize a member that is two years in arrears by taking away its vote in the General Assembly. This has been done infrequently, as a last resort. The United States has found itself in danger of penalization during years when it was withholding its dues or paying them slowly to express its unhappiness with the UN. In fact, of all member states the United States typically has the largest payments in arrears to the general and peacekeeping budgets. (It also makes the largest contributions to the UN.) For 2007 the United States accounted for about half of all arrears for the combined regular and peacekeeping budgets. By 2010 the US arrears, amounting to some $1.2 billion, constituted only a quarter of payments owed by all member states because the global financial crisis of 2008 had led to late payments by an especially large number of member states. The Obama administration worked with Congress to authorize payment of arrears in late 2010 and pledged to pay the annual assessments "in full and on time." The United States has done so and as of 2014 was in good standing at the world body.

## The General Assembly

*From the UN Charter, Chapter IV*

ARTICLE 19

A Member of the United Nations which is in arrears in the payment of its financial contributions to the Organization shall have no vote in the General Assembly if the amount of its arrears equals or exceeds the amount of the contributions due from it for the preceding two full years. The General Assembly may, nevertheless, permit such a Member to vote if it is satisfied that the failure to pay is due to conditions beyond the control of the Member.

The discussions about budget assessments and arrears have generated suggestions about possible fixes, including a global tax on currency transactions and even one on international air travel, but they haven't gone beyond talk. One observer, Shepard Forman of

New York University's Center on International Cooperation, has offered his own solution. "I once suggested rather facetiously," he says, "that there should be a reverse scale of assessments in which countries that act badly and therefore cost the UN more . . . should have to pay more dues." Getting those nations to pay, however, might be a true "mission impossible."

CHAPTER 20

# Action in the Field with UNHCR

A Staffer's Challenging First Assignment

*We were dealing with actual human beings, and I could put my head to the pillow at night knowing that what I did made a real difference in people's lives—people I could see and feel and meet and touch and actually talk to. That kind of direct connection, that's something that UNHCR affords that's truly extraordinary.*

—Shashi Tharoor, former UN under-secretary-general
for communications and public information

To put a face on the UN, it's helpful to listen as one of its former staff members talks about his early years in the UN as an idealistic young administrator out to learn about the world. Shashi Tharoor, who was born in London and educated in India and the United States, in 1978 became a staff member of the UN High Commissioner for Refugees (UNHCR), which assists refugees in resettling. He was posted to Singapore from 1981 to 1984 to help organize efforts to aid the thousands of Vietnamese fleeing their homeland in the aftermath of the collapse of the Saigon government and the takeover of the country by the communists in 1975. From 1989 to 1996, Tharoor was part of the peacekeeping office of the Secretariat as

Under-Secretary-General Shashi Tharoor addresses a United Nations forum on the information age, November 29, 2006. UN Photo / Paulo Filgueiras.

a special assistant to the under-secretary-general for peacekeeping operations. He then served as a senior adviser to Secretary-General Kofi Annan before becoming under-secretary-general for communications and public information in 2002. He made a bid to succeed Kofi Annan as secretary-general in 2006 and left the UN early the next year. In an interview at his UN office, Tharoor recalled his challenging work as a new staff member of the UNHCR.

"The High Commissioner for Refugees was a great place to begin my career because it really attracts a lot of idealists, in those days in particular. What really brought me to a conviction of the indispensability of the UN was working for UNHCR in the field. I arrived in Singapore at the peak of the Vietnamese boat-people crisis. There were four thousand refugees living at the camp, sleeping twenty-five, thirty to a room this size. The situation had become totally unmanageable. When refugees left Vietnam by boat, they were picked up by boats sailing into Singapore. The Singapore government was very unhappy about having refugees come in, and they manifested this by making difficult the disembarkation of some of these refugees and having nothing to do with the camps themselves. Other countries who were receiving Vietnamese refugees ran their own camps, usually with their military, whereas in Singapore the UN was asked to run their camps.

"UNHCR in those days believed it was not an operational agency, so we weren't supposed to be running camps. It was an extraordinary challenge for someone who was in their twenties as I was. I essentially invented operational partners by going to churches and church groups and saying, 'Put your label on us and say you're the operational partner, and I will raise money to get the staff and we will run the camp.' I got volunteers from the city, including wives of diplomats, to come in and teach refugees and run camps. I took donations from the community for the benefit of the refugees. I got refugees to run their own democracy, elect their own camp leader.

"On the diplomatic side, there was dealing with a tough government, trying to use the power of my office to get them to cooperate. Church groups can go and help refugees, volunteers can go and help refugees, but only the UN can go to a government. I would tell officials, 'You have an obligation to honor your international commitment to this organization.' Even if they're not signatories to the UN convention, as a member of the General Assembly they're bound by the statute of the organization, which is a General Assembly resolution. We expect them to honor their role as a government and a member of the UN.

"We had to invent whole new procedures. For example, when ships came in, [the authorities] insisted that every ship that had refugees had to provide a guarantee that the refugees would be resettled. Then they realized that some of the guarantees were worthless because some of the ships were from Bangladesh and India and flag-of-convenience ships flying the Liberian flag or the Panamanian flag. What use was a letter of guarantee from Liberia that they will resettle their refugees?

"The Singaporeans then wanted a letter from a country of resettlement. We had to invent a scheme, where we had looked into the ownership of a ship and got a country of registration to actually provide the guarantees, and then there were the weekly meetings in my office with the immigration chiefs of embassies. It's a sobering thought that there are kids growing up French, or Canadian, or American today because of my skill or lack thereof in persuading an immigration officer to bend the rules.

"Every month more were arriving. I would imagine somewhere between twelve thousand and twenty thousand refugees passed through my hands in Singapore. In one case, for example, a family left for Singapore on a tiny boat with a cannibalized tractor engine. It wasn't a proper motor, and sure enough, it conked out, and they were drifting on the high seas. They ran out of food, out of water, and they were subsisting on rainwater and hope. What do the parents do? They slit their fingers to get their babies to suck their own blood in order to survive. They were finally rescued by an American ship, and they were so weak they couldn't stand up; they had to be lifted out of the boat. We rushed them into intensive care in the hospital as soon as we could disembark them. Now, to see that same family three or four months later, healthy, well fed, well rested, well dressed, heading off to new lives in the United States, there is simply no job that could compare with that sort of thing—pure human satisfaction.

"When Poland declared martial law in December 1981, do you remember the Solidarity movement [labor union] and all of that? A Polish ship docked in Singapore on a Saturday, and four or five Polish seamen jumped ship and looked up the UN in the phone book and came to my office and wanted asylum. I had no authority to grant asylum. I woke up the director of international protections of the UNHCR and said, 'What do I do?' The guy said, 'Follow the convention, interview these people, and determine if in your view they should have refugee status. If you do, they are refugees.'

"It was quite a drama. I interviewed them. I felt that they had a credible case. They said they were supporters of Solidarity, and if they went back they would be locked up, so they jumped ship. I said, 'I recognize you as refugees,' and basically said to the Singaporeans, 'You've got to let these people stay.' The Singaporeans were furious, but I contacted some embassies and said, 'Could you try and take

these people?' We worked out a scheme. The Singaporeans retali-
ated by banning shore leave for all Polish seamen. They kept saying,
'You are only here to look after the Vietnamese.' And I said, 'No, I'm
with the UN High Commissioner for Refugees. Vietnamese happen
to be my caseload, but anybody else who comes in, I'm legally mandated under the statute of the office to help them.'

"A couple of months after this first episode, I got a frantic call
from the Singaporeans and the Americans, one after the other. A
Polish sailor had jumped ship and swum to an American destroyer
in the port. Singapore naval police and immigration police said he
had to be handed over because he was illegal. The American captain
said that the sailor was fleeing communism and he would not sur-
render him. There was a diplomatic standoff. Neither side wanted
this to hit the press, but the Singaporeans wouldn't let the American
ship sail with the Polish seaman on board, and the Polish seaman
couldn't go back to his ship. The Americans allowed the Singaporeans to take him off the ship under the condition that he be brought
to me. He was brought to the US consul's office in the embassy,
where it was determined he had refugee status, at which point we
took charge and put him in a little hotel in Singapore (where it's not
an inexpensive proposition for the UN, I can tell you).

"Then I started putting heat on the Americans, saying, 'Take him
because we solved the problem for you and you have to resettle him.'
It dragged on for a couple of months before the United States agreed
to take him. A new consul arrived and was very helpful and said that
he would take charge.

"I got a lovely postcard from San Diego from this Polish seaman,
saying, 'I never will forget you, Mr. Shashi.' One of the precious
souvenirs of my career!

"Singapore was such an extraordinary period, and among other
things, it convinced me about the indispensability of the UN cause.
Most things I've done under the UN, only the UN could have done.
The UN has a hell of a lot of advantages in dealing with authorities.
There are so many stories in which the governmental influence that
the UN can bring to bear changes the lives and fortunes of people
who are in danger or distress."

Diplomat for a Day: The Model UN

In a Model UN conference, students role-play delegates to the UN and participants of UN committees, the Security Council, and the General Assembly. As delegates of a given member state, they debate, write position papers, negotiate resolutions, and do all the other things that diplomats do, while observing UN diplomatic protocols. Many organizations offer Model UNs, at a variety of venues across the United States, ranging from high schools to college campuses and even the UN headquarters in New York City. The Model UN is an international phenomenon, with meetings in more than fifty countries each year. Sponsoring organizations may be local or national, large or small. Some of them offer handbooks and other useful tools for participants.

One of the most comprehensive Model UN websites is Best Delegate (bestdelegate.com), which provides a database of US and foreign current and recent Model UN conferences with dates, locations, and contact information. Extensive listings are also offered by the United Nations Association of the USA (www.una-usa.org), sponsor of many Model UNs. Another useful site is that of the Na-

tional Model United Nations (www.nmun.org), also a sponsor of
Model UN conferences in the United States and abroad. Its par-
ent organization is the National Collegiate Conference Association
(NCCA).

## GETTING STARTED

Participation in a Model UN is a group activity. A participant will
be one of several colleagues from a school or university. After the
group has registered, the meeting organizers will make country assignments, which may include a single country or several. Typically
the members of a group will be asked to form delegations, each one
representing a country. The organizers will also assign the members of delegations to specific UN bodies, like the General Assembly
or ECOSOC, and to committees within them.

Model UN conferences often require that each delegation prepare
and submit a position paper that presents the delegation's views on
the topics listed for discussion in committee. Writing the position
paper will require research into the designated country and the
issues being discussed, and it will also require that members of the
delegation agree on their position and present it clearly in writing.

The event itself consists largely of simulated formal and informal
meetings. Within the formal meetings the goal is to agree on the order
of agenda items and then discuss them so that the committee can
write a resolution. Finally, committee members vote on the resolution.
Committee members may also choose to meet in a caucus, which is
an informal setting that can be useful in working out common positions among the delegations. The format of the committee meetings
and caucuses puts a lot of emphasis on the ability to speak, both from
prepared materials and in the back-and-forth that typifies any meeting of people grappling with common issues. To maintain an orderly
discussion the committee members are expected to follow established
procedures and protocols for presentation and discussion.

## GAINING HANDS-ON EXPERIENCE

What sorts of experiences might come out of participating? The following remarks are drawn from a video produced by the National

Model UN. The moderator, Richard Reitano, of Vassar College and Duchess Community College, is a former president of NCCA, which sponsors the Model UN. He is speaking with two former Model UNers. One is Joseph Melrose of Ursinus College, who has enjoyed a decades-long career as a UN diplomat. His Model UN posts include that of US ambassador to Sierra Leone and acting US representative for management and reform at the UN. He, too, is a former president of NCCA. At the time of the video Carolyn Smith was a graduate student at New York University and an intern at the US Mission to the UN. She has attended seven model UNs. The audio transcript, provided courtesy of the National Model UN, was edited for publication in this book.

Reitano: What are some of the characteristics of a good and effective diplomat?

Smith: The first thing I think of with a diplomat is definitely discretion. You are more likely to listen to what someone else has to say than to force your opinion or to broadcast it. Also very friendly. Diplomats from countries you would consider not very friendly with each other, at the UN I see these people shake hands with each other every day, asking about each other's kids. Definitely very personable, very discreet, and ready to listen, and just very patient also, not forcing an issue.

Melrose: Most of the really skilled professional diplomats separate the policy issues from the personalities. I might disagree with the position you're taking but that doesn't mean I'm rude to you or in any way insulting. We expect mutual respect, cordiality, because after all the UN seeks to achieve consensus.

Reitano: Some of the historically bad examples include Nikita Khrushchev, the Soviet premier, banging his shoe in the General Assembly's Great Hall in 1960. Some even cite the president of Iran and remarks he made at a 2012 General Assembly meeting. Do you think the permanent UN representatives act that way?

Smith: Absolutely not. Those speeches were during the general debate, where heads of state, heads of government, come to talk to the UN. A lot of the time those are done for show. Those are the ones where the presidents are able to make a statement often more to their own people than to the international community. The permanent representatives and certainly the people who work for them on the different specific issues are never so dramatic. As Joe said, there's an understanding that you don't create a policy, you are a civil servant to your government, you are representing your government's policy, it's not a personal issue. Even the diplomats who represented the USSR at the time and even Iran, they are not as difficult as their heads of state are in these very public, showy general debates.

Melrose: You get some speeches that are clearly more assertive than others. You're playing to a combination of the UN audience and your own national population. When you get into the committee sessions, with the First Committee, Second Committee, through the Sixth Committee, I can recall only one instance where a representative protested vocally by banging his placard on the desk, which broke and flew in the air.

Reitano: How would you describe the behavior and actions of a good diplomat? What advice could you give to students, to delegates participating in the Model UN is this regard?

Smith: The first thing I would say is do not try to model the way you act as a diplomat on a general debate speech. I understand there's always been a draw to represent a country like Iran or, say, North Korea because they have very clear policies on things and they are very interesting and very different from what you might deal with. But the way you see their head of state behave in the general debate is not the way that their diplomats behave on a day-to-day basis, especially in the different committees. My first advice is never take it to an extreme, do not bang your shoe on the table. Of course there is certain language that they are more likely to use. I would say definitely look at speeches they have given in different committees—those are always on record. Look for that kind of language, and use that kind of language, but also keep in mind that even if you do not have good relations with that country, that doesn't meant that you don't say hello and introduce yourself and ask the person what their opinion is, because that's what works in the real General Assembly.

Reitano: How does Model UN assist you in understanding global issues and in your career choices?

Smith: Model UN gave me a very good understanding of the UN system, which is much more complicated than I ever imagined. I can't say that I was very well informed when I was in high school. Most people think of the United Nations, maybe the General Assembly and the Security Council. The reality is that there is such a broad spectrum of issues that they deal with. It's not just questions of Do you send a peacekeeping crew here. Model UN gave me a really good idea of the issues, from development to human rights to gender issues, that the international community deals with on a daily basis that I never would have imagined getting done in a forum like the UN. Model UN really prepared me for my internship. It gave me the knowledge of how committees work and also the types of issues that they deal with and what powers they have and where their limitations are. It gives students a well-rounded view of how our country interacts with other countries, not just in the UN but also at a bilateral level, using the UN as a forum for that.

Reitano: Some of my students have described their experience with Model UN as life-changing. Do you think that's a valid observation?

Smith: Definitely. The first Model UN I did, I was a freshman, and we went to a Model UN in Washington, DC. I was representing our country in the Security Council. The life-changing thing about that was the idea, at least at that Model UN, that sticks out for me, is that everyone was there working toward a common goal. You're given an issue and your job is to come up with an answer that all your countries can accept. It wasn't about someone winning or losing, it wasn't about whether you as an individual looked good in the committee; it was about whether it was something you could all agree on, and that's a challenge.

Melrose: When I was an undergrad, I was interested in a career in diplomacy. I went to a Model UN as a student a few decades ago, when there were many fewer and smaller ones. As a professor, I think the big thing is, Model UN makes the textbook more alive. You can sit and read about what it does, but when you're trying to put yourself in that position, you get to experience some of the same thoughts and experiences. We in the United States particularly have a very superficial understanding of the UN, its complexities and many activities that go beyond the General Assembly and the Security Council. Doing Model UN helps certain skills, like public speaking, research, perhaps above all trying to put yourself in someone else's shoes who has maybe a totally different life expectancy and life experience. A good diplomat needs to understand the context of the country he's working in and the population and how that impacts the policy.

Reitano: We're very lucky with our National Model UN in that, for example, this past spring we had about fifty-one hundred delegates from, I believe, forty-four countries. What about the interaction not only with other Americans who are representing Country X or Country Y but also with delegates coming from countries abroad? Was that valuable for you?

Smith: Definitely. It's a really fun way to make friends from a completely different country. Especially in today's world of Facebook, it's pretty easy to keep in contact with people that you met four years ago at a Model UN. That especially helps with the personal relationships. Participants in the Model UN really need to understand that those friendships that they're forming, it's OK to let them show in committee a little bit. You're not a completely different person when you walk through that door. It also helps with cross-cultural communication, not just when you're representing two different countries but also when you're from two different countries and you go out to have dinner in between committees or whatever, and you learn about students your own age and what they deal with, and they learn more about you.

Reitano: Just to follow up on the business of putting yourself in someone else's shoes, could you comment on that in terms of learning and understanding the rest of the world?

Melrose: If you're going to make any progress in this area, you have to understand the views of the person you're dealing with, the background, how they came to be, the historic situation that pertains to that particular country. If you understand where another person is coming from in a negotiation, you're better able to negotiate. It is important to talk to people from overseas, from other member states' schools that are coming. That's probably one of the two most valuable parts of the conference because you create understanding, create relationships, create bonds.

Reitano: What advice do you have in terms of preparation for prospective Model UN students as they begin the process of learning another nation's foreign policy?

Smith: As far as prep goes, definitely start early because there's a lot more that you need to understand other than the basic statements that another country gives. You really need to understand the current situation that country is in domestically, not just where their foreign policy is. Because the Model UN requires not only what your position paper says but also that you're able to think on your feet and to know immediately what your country would or would not agree to. What resources they have, what they have done in the past, and what they would be likely to do in a different situation. So if you're looking for information for your position paper, look on that country's mission web site, their government's web site, and then for more background look at their domestic news forums—anything to learn about their domestic situation and to prepare early.

About preparing for the conference, especially if you've never done this before, the hardest part is to prepare for the protocol of the actual Model UN. What we always did was run a sort of Model UN mini-simulation for the class, so they could practice things like how you ask to speak, what the speakers' list is, the speakers' language, the difference between a speech and making a point of order or something like that. So definitely study the protocol for how you behave in committee. I think that one of the bigger challenges when you're in committee is knowing what's allowed and what's not. Also, to have a little fun with it, you don't have to work all the way through until four in the morning to make sure the resolution is exactly how you wanted. Remember that this is a professional atmosphere when you're in committee, that you should be behaving with protocol, with decorum, even in informal sessions because that is the way the real UN functions.

Melrose: A lot of the diplomatic work of the UN is done outside of the UN, at receptions, dinners, lunches, over coffee or whatever, where I could talk one-on-one or in a small group. In terms of preparation, I would recommend that everybody read the statement made in the general debate by the head of government or whoever because that goes to the domestic issues as well to where they see their priorities. Those two things are almost always in the general debate speech.

In the closing ceremonies we say it's not a winner-take-all competition. It's learning to work together, appreciate each other. If you're going to make progress in the world, it's going to be small steps by people who come together, not one country doing everything.

## The Universal Declaration of Human Rights

PREAMBLE

Whereas recognition of the inherent dignity and of the equal and inalienable rights of all members of the human family is the foundation of freedom, justice and peace in the world,

Whereas disregard and contempt for human rights have resulted in barbarous acts which have outraged the conscience of mankind, and the advent of a world in which human beings shall enjoy freedom of speech and belief and freedom from fear and want has been proclaimed as the highest aspiration of the common people,

Whereas it is essential, if man is not to be compelled to have recourse, as a last resort, to rebellion against tyranny and oppression, that human rights should be protected by the rule of law,

Whereas it is essential to promote the development of friendly relations between nations,

Whereas the peoples of the United Nations have in the Charter reaffirmed their faith in fundamental human rights, in the dignity and worth of the human person and in the equal rights of men and women and have determined to promote social progress and better standards of life in larger freedom,

Whereas Member States have pledged themselves to achieve, in cooperation with the United Nations, the promotion of universal respect for and observance of human rights and fundamental freedoms,

Whereas a common understanding of these rights and freedoms is of the greatest importance for the full realization of this pledge,

Now, Therefore the general assembly proclaims this universal declaration of human rights as a common standard of achievement for all peoples and all nations, to the end that every individual and every organ of society, keeping this Declaration constantly in mind, shall strive by teaching and education to promote respect for these rights and freedoms and by progressive measures, national and international, to secure their universal and effective recognition and observance, both among the peoples of Member States themselves and among the peoples of territories under their jurisdiction.

*Article 1.*
All human beings are born free and equal in dignity and rights. They are endowed with reason and conscience and should act towards one another in a spirit of brotherhood.

*Article 2.*
Everyone is entitled to all the rights and freedoms set forth in this Declaration, without distinction of any kind, such as race, colour, sex, language, religion, political or other opinion, national or social origin, property, birth or other status. Furthermore, no distinction shall be made on the basis of the political, jurisdictional or international status of the country or territory to which a person belongs, whether it be independent, trust, non-self-governing or under any other limitation of sovereignty.

*Article 3.*
Everyone has the right to life, liberty and security of person.

*Article 4.*
No one shall be held in slavery or servitude; slavery and the slave trade shall be prohibited in all their forms.

*Article 5.*
No one shall be subjected to torture or to cruel, inhuman or degrading treatment or punishment.

*Article 6.*
Everyone has the right to recognition everywhere as a person before the law.

*Article 7.*
All are equal before the law and are entitled without any discrimination to equal protection of the law. All are entitled to equal protection against any discrimination in violation of this Declaration and against any incitement to such discrimination.

*Article 8.*
Everyone has the right to an effective remedy by the competent national tribunals for acts violating the fundamental rights granted him by the constitution or by law.

*Article 9.*
No one shall be subjected to arbitrary arrest, detention or exile.

*Article 10.*
Everyone is entitled in full equality to a fair and public hearing by an independent and impartial tribunal, in the determination of his rights and obligations and of any criminal charge against him.

*Article 11.*
(1) Everyone charged with a penal offence has the right to be presumed innocent until proved guilty according to law in a public trial at which he has had all the guarantees necessary for his defence.

(2) No one shall be held guilty of any penal offence on account of any act or omission which did not constitute a penal offence, under national or international law, at the time when it was committed. Nor shall a heavier penalty be imposed than the one that was applicable at the time the penal offence was committed.

*Article 12.*

No one shall be subjected to arbitrary interference with his privacy, family, home or correspondence, nor to attacks upon his honour and reputation. Everyone has the right to the protection of the law against such interference or attacks.

*Article 13.*

(1) Everyone has the right to freedom of movement and residence within the borders of each state.

(2) Everyone has the right to leave any country, including his own, and to return to his country.

*Article 14.*

(1) Everyone has the right to seek and to enjoy in other countries asylum from persecution.

(2) This right may not be invoked in the case of prosecutions genuinely arising from non-political crimes or from acts contrary to the purposes and principles of the United Nations.

*Article 15.*

(1) Everyone has the right to a nationality.

(2) No one shall be arbitrarily deprived of his nationality nor denied the right to change his nationality.

*Article 16.*

(1) Men and women of full age, without any limitation due to race, nationality or religion, have the right to marry and to found a family. They are entitled to equal rights as to marriage, during marriage and at its dissolution.

(2) Marriage shall be entered into only with the free and full consent of the intending spouses.

(3) The family is the natural and fundamental group unit of society and is entitled to protection by society and the State.

*Article 17.*

(1) Everyone has the right to own property alone as well as in association with others.

(2) No one shall be arbitrarily deprived of his property.

*Article 18.*

Everyone has the right to freedom of thought, conscience and religion; this right includes freedom to change his religion or belief, and freedom, either alone or in community with others and in public or private, to manifest his religion or belief in teaching, practice, worship and observance.

*Article 19.*

Everyone has the right to freedom of opinion and expression; this right includes freedom to hold opinions without interference and to seek, receive and impart information and ideas through any media and regardless of frontiers.

*Article 20.*

(1) Everyone has the right to freedom of peaceful assembly and association.

(2) No one may be compelled to belong to an association.

*Article 21.*

(1) Everyone has the right to take part in the government of his country, directly or through freely chosen representatives.

(2) Everyone has the right of equal access to public service in his country.

(3) The will of the people shall be the basis of the authority of government; this will shall be expressed in periodic and genuine

elections which shall be by universal and equal suffrage and shall be held by secret vote or by equivalent free voting procedures.

*Article 22.*

Everyone, as a member of society, has the right to social security and is entitled to realization, through national effort and international cooperation and in accordance with the organization and resources of each State, of the economic, social and cultural rights indispensable for his dignity and the free development of his personality.

*Article 23.*

(1) Everyone has the right to work, to free choice of employment, to just and favourable conditions of work and to protection against unemployment.

(2) Everyone, without any discrimination, has the right to equal pay for equal work.

(3) Everyone who works has the right to just and favourable remuneration ensuring for himself and his family an existence worthy of human dignity, and supplemented, if necessary, by other means of social protection.

(4) Everyone has the right to form and to join trade unions for the protection of his interests.

*Article 24.*

Everyone has the right to rest and leisure, including reasonable limitation of working hours and periodic holidays with pay.

*Article 25.*

(1) Everyone has the right to a standard of living adequate for the health and well-being of himself and of his family, including food, clothing, housing and medical care and necessary social services, and the right to security in the event of unemployment, sickness, disability, widowhood, old age or other lack of livelihood in circumstances beyond his control.

(2) Motherhood and childhood are entitled to special care and assistance. All children, whether born in or out of wedlock, shall enjoy the same social protection.

### Article 26.

(1) Everyone has the right to education. Education shall be free, at least in the elementary and fundamental stages. Elementary education shall be compulsory. Technical and professional education shall be made generally available and higher education shall be equally accessible to all on the basis of merit.

(2) Education shall be directed to the full development of the human personality and to the strengthening of respect for human rights and fundamental freedoms. It shall promote understanding, tolerance and friendship among all nations, racial or religious groups, and shall further the activities of the United Nations for the maintenance of peace.

(3) Parents have a prior right to choose the kind of education that shall be given to their children.

### Article 27.

(1) Everyone has the right freely to participate in the cultural life of the community, to enjoy the arts and to share in scientific advancement and its benefits.

(2) Everyone has the right to the protection of the moral and material interests resulting from any scientific, literary or artistic production of which he is the author.

### Article 28.

Everyone is entitled to a social and international order in which the rights and freedoms set forth in this Declaration can be fully realized.

### Article 29.

(1) Everyone has duties to the community in which alone the free and full development of his personality is possible.

(2) In the exercise of his rights and freedoms, everyone shall be subject only to such limitations as are determined by law solely for the purpose of securing due recognition and respect for the rights and freedoms of others and of meeting the just requirements of morality, public order and the general welfare in a democratic society.

(3) These rights and freedoms may in no case be exercised contrary to the purposes and principles of the United Nations.

*Article 30.*
Nothing in this Declaration may be interpreted as implying for any State, group or person any right to engage in any activity or to perform any act aimed at the destruction of any of the rights and freedoms set forth herein.

## UN Member States

Here are the 193 member states, with the date on which each joined the United Nations. Some joined UNESCO or another UN organization before they were full-fledged members of the UN and eligible to vote in the General Assembly.

Afghanistan, November 19, 1946
Albania, December 14, 1955
Algeria, October 8, 1962
Andorra, July 28, 1993
Angola, December 1, 1976
Antigua and Barbuda, November 11, 1981
Argentina, October 24, 1945
Armenia, March 2, 1992
Australia, November 1, 1945
Austria, December 14, 1955
Azerbaijan, March 2, 1992
Bahamas, September 18, 1973
Bahrain, September 21, 1971
Bangladesh, September 17, 1974
Barbados, December 9, 1966

Belarus, October 24, 1945
Belgium, December 27, 1945
Belize, September 25, 1981
Benin, September 20, 1960
Bhutan, September 21, 1971
Bolivia, November 14, 1945
Bosnia and Herzegovina, May 22, 1992
Botswana, October 17, 1966
Brazil, October 24, 1945
Brunei Darussalam, September 21, 1984
Bulgaria, December 14, 1955
Burkina Faso, September 20, 1960
Burundi, September 18, 1962
Cambodia, December 14, 1955
Cameroon, September 20, 1960
Canada, November 9, 1945
Cape Verde, September 16, 1975
Central African Republic, September 20, 1960
Chad, September 20, 1960
Chile, October 24, 1945
China, October 24, 1945
Colombia, November 5, 1945
Comoros, November 12, 1975
Congo, Democratic Republic of the, September 20, 1960
Congo, Republic of the, September 20, 1960
Costa Rica, November 2, 1945
Côte d'Ivoire, September 20, 1960
Croatia, May 22, 1992
Cuba, October 24, 1945
Cyprus, September 20, 1960
Czech Republic, January 19, 1993
Denmark, October 24, 1945
Djibouti, September 20, 1977
Dominica, December 18, 1978
Dominican Republic, October 24, 1945
Ecuador, December 21, 1945
Egypt, October 24, 1945
El Salvador, October 24, 1945
Equatorial Guinea, November 12, 1968

Eritrea, May 28, 1993
Estonia, September 17, 1991
Ethiopia, November 13, 1945
Fiji, October 13, 1970
Finland, December 14, 1955
France, October 24, 1945
Gabon, September 20, 1960
Gambia, September 21, 1965
Georgia, July 31, 1992
Germany, September 18, 1973
Ghana, March 8, 1957
Greece, October 25, 1945
Grenada, September 17, 1974
Guatemala, November 21, 1945
Guinea, December 12, 1958
Guinea-Bissau, September 17, 1974
Guyana, September 20, 1966
Haiti, October 24, 1945
Honduras, December 17, 1945
Hungary, December 14, 1955
Iceland, November 19, 1946
India, October 30, 1945
Indonesia, September 28, 1950
Iran, Islamic Republic of, October 24, 1945
Iraq, December 21, 1945
Ireland, December 14, 1955
Israel, May 11, 1949
Italy, December 14, 1955
Jamaica, September 18, 1962
Japan, December 18, 1956
Jordan, December 14, 1955
Kazakhstan, March 2, 1992
Kenya, December 16, 1963
Kiribati, September 14, 1999
Korea, Democratic People's Republic of, September 17, 1991
Korea, Republic of, September 17, 1991
Kuwait, May 14, 1963
Kyrgyzstan, March 2, 1992
Lao People's Democratic Republic, December 14, 1955

Latvia, September 17, 1991
Lebanon, October 24, 1945
Lesotho, October 17, 1966
Liberia, November 2, 1945
Libyan Arab Jamahiriya, December 14, 1955
Liechtenstein, September 18, 1990
Lithuania, September 17, 1991
Luxembourg, October 24, 1945
Macedonia, Republic of, April 8, 1993
Madagascar, September 20, 1960
Malawi, December 1, 1964
Malaysia, September 17, 1957
Maldives, September 21, 1965
Mali, September 28, 1960
Malta, December 1, 1964
Marshall Islands, September 17, 1991
Mauritania, October 27, 1961
Mauritius, April 24, 1968
Mexico, November 7, 1945
Micronesia, Federated States of, September 17, 1991
Moldova, Republic of, March 2, 1992
Monaco, May 28, 1993
Mongolia, October 27, 1961
Montenegro, June 28, 2006
Morocco, November 12, 1956
Mozambique, September 16, 1975
Myanmar, April 19, 1948
Namibia, April 23, 1990
Nauru, September 14, 1999
Nepal, December 14, 1955
Netherlands, December 10, 1945
New Zealand, October 24, 1945
Nicaragua, October 24, 1945
Niger, September 20, 1960
Nigeria, October 7, 1960
Norway, November 27, 1945
Oman, October 7, 1971
Pakistan, September 30, 1947
Palau, December 15, 1994

Panama, November 13, 1945
Papua New Guinea, October 10, 1975
Paraguay, October 24, 1945
Peru, October 31, 1945
Philippines, October 24, 1945
Poland, October 24, 1945
Portugal, December 14, 1955
Qatar, September 21, 1971
Romania, December 14, 1955
Russian Federation, October 24, 1945
Rwanda, September 18, 1962
Saint Kitts and Nevis, September 23, 1983
Saint Lucia, September 18, 1979
Saint Vincent and the Grenadines, September 16, 1980
Samoa, December 15, 1976
San Marino, March 2, 1992
São Tomé and Príncipe, September 16, 1975
Saudi Arabia, October 24, 1945
Senegal, September 28, 1960
Serbia, November 1, 2000
Seychelles, September 21, 1976
Sierra Leone, September 27, 1961
Singapore, September 21, 1965
Slovakia, January 19, 1993
Slovenia, May 22, 1992
Solomon Islands, September 19, 1978
Somalia, September 20, 1960
South Africa, November 7, 1945
South Sudan, July 14, 2011
Spain, December 14, 1955
Sri Lanka, December 14, 1955
Sudan, November 12, 1956
Suriname, December 4, 1975
Swaziland, September 24, 1968
Sweden, November 19, 1946
Switzerland, September 10, 2002
Syrian Arab Republic, October 24, 1945
Tajikistan, March 2, 1992
Tanzania, United Republic of, December 14, 1961

Thailand, December 16, 1946
Timor-Leste, September 27, 2002
Togo, September 20, 1960
Tonga, September 14, 1999
Trinidad and Tobago, September 18, 1962
Tunisia, November 12, 1956
Turkey, October 24, 1945
Turkmenistan, March 2, 1992
Tuvalu, September 5, 2000
Uganda, October 24, 1962
Ukraine, October 24, 1945
United Arab Emirates, December 9, 1971
United Kingdom of Great Britain and Northern Ireland, October 24, 1945
United States of America, October 24, 1945
Uruguay, December 18, 1945
Uzbekistan, March 2, 1992
Vanuatu, September 15, 1981
Venezuela, Bolivarian Republic of, November 15, 1945
Viet Nam, September 20, 1977
Yemen, September 30, 1947
Zambia, December 1, 1964
Zimbabwe, August 25, 1980

## SELECTED ABBREVIATIONS

ACABQ—Advisory Committee on Administrative and Budgetary Questions
CND—Commission on Narcotic Drugs
CONGO—Conference on Non-Governmental Organizations in
    Consultative Status
CTBTO—Preparatory Commission for the Comprehensive Nuclear
    Test-Ban Treaty Organization
DPA—Department of Political Affairs
DPKO—Department of Peacekeeping Operations
E10—Elected ten members of the Security Council
ECOSOC—Economic and Social Council
FAO—Food and Agriculture Organization
G-77—Group of 77, a coalition of developing countries
GA—General Assembly
GAO—US Government Accountability Office
HCHR—High Commissioner for Human Rights
HRC—Human Rights Council
IAEA—International Atomic Energy Agency
ICAO—International Civil Aviation Organization
IMO—International Maritime Organization
IPCC—Intergovernmental Panel on Climate Change
ITU—International Telecommunication Union

MINUSTAH—United Nations Stabilization Mission in Haiti
NAM—Nonaligned Movement
NATO—North Atlantic Treaty Organization
NGO—nongovernmental organization
OIOS—Office of Internal Oversight Services
OPCW—Organization for the Prohibition of Chemical Weapons
P5—Permanent Five members of the Security Council
UNAIDS—Joint United Nations Program on HIV/AIDS
UNAMID—African Union–United Nations Hybrid Operation in Darfur
UNDP—United Nations Development Program
UNEP—United Nations Environment Program
UNESCO—United Nations Educational, Scientific, and
    Cultural Organization
UNFICYP—United Nations Peacekeeping Force in Cyprus
UNHCR—Office of the United Nations High Commissioner for Refugees
UNICEF—United Nations Children's Fund
UNIDO—United Nations Industrial Development Organization
UNMEE—United Nations Mission in Ethiopia and Eritrea
UNMIT—United Nations Integrated Mission in Timor-Leste
UNODC—United Nations Office on Drugs and Crime
UNPOL—United Nations Police
UNTSO—United Nations Truce Supervision Organization
UPU—Universal Postal Union
WEOG—Western Europe and Others Regional Group
WFP—World Food Program
WHO—World Health Organization
WIPO—World Intellectual Property Organization

I drew upon many and varied sources in preparing this book. I interviewed or held informal discussions with "UN insiders"—past and present diplomats and UN officials, experts, and analysts. I attended UN briefings, news conferences, seminars, and other forums, as well as speeches and public statements by UN staff, representatives of member states, and members of the US government. In addition, I reviewed UN, government, NGO, and academic reports and studies

Most quotations in the book come from the interviews and public statements. Quotations from books, articles, and reports are noted below by chapter.

Chapter 2.   Eleanor Roosevelt's role in writing the Universal Declaration appears in Joseph Lash, *Eleanor: The Years Alone* (New York: Konecky and Konecky, 1972). Brian Urquhart's statement on the declaration's importance is from his interviews at the University of California, Berkeley.

Chapter 3.   The secretary-general's comments on his Darfur trip are taken from Ban Ki-moon, "What I Saw in Darfur," *Washington Post*, September 14, 2007.

Chapter 4.   The remarks of Joseph S. Nye Jr. are quoted from his book *The Future of Power* (New York: BBS Publications, 2011), 116, 216.

Chapter 6.   The discussion of the Saudi refusal to serve on the Security Council benefited from the analysis of Richard Gowan, in "Diplomatic Fallout: Saudi Arabia's Security Council Move More than Just a Stunt," *World Politics Review* (October 21, 2013). The quotation about the US government's favorable view of sanctions comes from the US Department of State's *US Participation in the UN* (2006), 54. The survey of General Assembly factions supporting various plans for Security Council restructuring is based on Center for UN Reform Education, "A New Low Point in the Security Council Reform Process" (2013), http://www.centerforunreform.org /node/23.

Chapter 8.   The discussion of Kofi Annan's social life in New York City draws on Frederic Eckhard, *Kofi Annan: A Spokesperson's Memoir* ([New York:] Ruder Finn Press, 2012), p. 61.

Chapter 9.   The DRC intervention brigade is discussed in Jamie Hagen, "Congo Intervention Brigade Will See UN Forces Go on the Offense," *PolicyMic,* March 31, 2013. The NGO reporting on the incidence of sexual abuse among peacekeepers is the Women Under Siege Project. Khalilzad's statement that peacekeeping should not be a substitute for finding a solution appears in Merle D. Kellerhals, "UN Looking for Ways to Enhance African Peacekeeping," *Peace and Security,* April 22, 2008. For the two US government reports on peacekeeping, see www.gao.gov/new.items/d06331.pdf; and www .betterworldcampaign.org.

Chapter 10.   The complaint about the CTC's privacy policy on reviews is discussed in Human Rights Voices, "UN 101: UN Non-Action to Combat Terrorism" (2013), http://www.humanrightsvoices .org/EYEontheUN/un_101/facts/?p=63. Iran's nuclear program is discussed in Hayes Brown, "New U.N. Report Finds Growth of Iran's Nuclear Program Is Slowing," *ThinkProgress,* August 28, 2013. The comments about the UN as a terrorist target come in part from Colum Lynch, "UN Insignia Emerges as a Global Target for Al-Qaeda Attacks," *Washington Post,* December 25, 2007; and a Reuters story,

"UN 'Has Become an Enemy,'" News24 Archives, February 29, 2008,
http://www.news24.com/Africa/News/UN-has-become-an-enemy
-20080228.

Chapter 11.    The discussion about R2P draws on material compiled by the UN and also by the International Coalition for the Responsibility to Protect.

Chapter 18.    Discussion of the Procurement Task Force and
Christopher Burnham comes from Robert W. Hsu's "American UN
Official Steps Down; Post Allocation May Threaten UN Reform" and
Lydia Swart's "UN Will Continue to Fight Corruption in 2008,"
*UNA-USA Publications,* December 5, 2007, and January 8, 2008.
The US government assessments are in Government Accountabil-
ity Office, *United Nations: Progress on Management Reform Efforts Has
Varied,* GAO-08–84, November 14, 2007; and GAO, *UN Internal
Oversight: Progress Made on Independence and Staffing Issues, but Fur-
ther Actions Are Needed,* GAO 11–871, September 20, 2011.

Chapter 19.    For the Obama administration's push to pay the arrears see Louis Charbonneau, "U.S. Pays Off Much of U.N. Arrears,
Now Owes $736 Million," Reuters, January 25, 2011.

Photographs and illustrations are indicated by page numbers in *italic*. Tables are indicated by a "t" following the page number.